Education and Globalization in Southeast Asia

The **ISEAS – Yusof Ishak Institute** (formerly Institute of Southeast Asian Studies) is an autonomous organization established in 1968. It is a regional centre dedicated to the study of socio-political, security, and economic trends and developments in Southeast Asia and its wider geostrategic and economic environment. The Institute's research programmes are grouped under Regional Economic Studies (RES), Regional Strategic and Political Studies (RSPS), and Regional Social and Cultural Studies (RSCS). The Institute is also home to the ASEAN Studies Centre (ASC), the Nalanda-Sriwijaya Centre (NSC) and the Singapore APEC Study Centre.

ISEAS Publishing, an established academic press, has issued more than 2,000 books and journals. It is the largest scholarly publisher of research about Southeast Asia from within the region. ISEAS Publishing works with many other academic and trade publishers and distributors to disseminate important research and analyses from and about Southeast Asia to the rest of the world.

Education and Globalization in Southeast Asia

ISSUES AND CHALLENGES

EDITED BY

LEE HOCK GUAN

ISEAS YUSOF ISHAK
INSTITUTE

First published in Singapore in 2017 by
ISEAS Publishing
30 Heng Mui Keng Terrace
Singapore 119614

E-mail: publish@iseas.edu.sg
Website: <http://bookshop.iseas.edu.sg>

The responsibility for facts and opinions in this publication rests exclusively with the author and his interpretations do not necessarily reflect the views or the policy of the publisher or its supporters.

ISEAS Library Cataloguing-in-Publication Data

Education and Globalization in Southeast Asia : Issues and Challenges.
    1. Education and state—Southeast Asia.
    I. Lee, Hock Guan.
LC94 A9E21   2017

ISBN 978-981-4762-90-8 (soft cover)
ISBN 978-981-4762-91-5 (e-book PDF)

Typeset by Superskill Graphics Pte Ltd
Printed in Singapore by Markono Print Media Pte Ltd

CONTENTS

ACKNOWLEDGEMENTS

This volume had its origins in the workshop on "Education, Globalization and the Nation State in Southeast Asia" held on 16–17 October 2014. We would like to thank the participants who contributed to the workshop and for devoting their time and energy to prepare the papers for the workshop. The two-day workshop went smoothly with constructive exchanges and discussions all round.

We have selected seven papers from the workshop to be revised for publication in this edited volume. Due to unexpected circumstances, I had to defer for a period of time the process to revise and prepare the papers for publication. I would like to offer my apologies to the authors included in this belated publication.

We would to thank Mr Tan Chin Tiong, Director of the ISEAS – Yusof Ishak Institute, for his support for the workshop and the Konrad-Adenauer-Stiftung for their generous financial support for both the workshop and publication of this book. Finally, many thanks to the ISEAS Administration staff for their efforts in helping to organize the workshop, and to ISEAS Publishing for facilitating the publication with efficiency and professionalism.

CONTRIBUTORS

Lubna Alsagoff is Associate Professor, English Language and Literature Academic Group, National Institute of Education, Nanyang Technological University, Singapore.

Mohamad Fahmi is Lecturer, Department of Economics, and Researcher, Center for Economics and Development Studies, Padjadjaran University, Bandung, Indonesia.

Rozilini Fernandez-Chung is currently Vice-President, HELP University College (Malaysia), and was formerly with the Malaysian Qualifications Agency.

Rattana A. Lao is Lecturer, Thai Studies, Pridi Banomyong International College, Thammasat University, Bangkok, Thailand.

Pad Lavankura is Lecturer, Faculty of Political Science, Ramkhamhaeng University, Bangkok, Thailand.

Lee Hock Guan is Senior Fellow, Regional Social and Cultural Studies, ISEAS – Yusof Ishak Institute, Singapore.

T. Marimuthu is Adjunct Professor, School of Education and Cognitive Sciences, Asia e University, Kuala Lumpur, Malaysia, and formerly was Professor, Faculty of Education, University of Malaya, Kuala Lumpur, Malaysia.

Patrick McCormick is Head, Yangon Branch Office, École française d'Extrême-Orient (EFEO), Yangon, Myanmar.

Hena Mukherjee is an education consultant and was previously Lead Education Specialist with the World Bank.

R. Santhiram is Dean and Professor, School of Education, Languages and Communications, Wawasan Open University (WOU), Penang, Malaysia.

Jasbir Singh is former Professor, Faculty of Education, University of Malaya, Kuala Lumpur, Malaysia.

Lorraine Pe Symaco is Senior Lecturer, Department of Curriculum and Instructional Technology, Faculty of Education, University Malaya, Kuala Lumpur, Malaysia.

Tan Yao Sua is Senior Lecturer and Research Fellow, Centre for Policy Research and International Studies (CenPRIS), Universiti Sains Malaysia, Penang, Malaysia.

Brooke Zobrist is an education consultant in Myanmar and the founder of the non-government organization Girl Determined.

INTRODUCTION

Lee Hock Guan

Since Southeast Asian countries attained political independence,[1] they have created "national education systems ... as part of the state forming process which established the modern nation state" (Green 1997, p. 170). Framed in the context of the nation-state, education was tasked with the overlapping objectives of state and nation-building and national economic development. All states in the region nationalized and monopolized education and founded largely public-funded centralized education systems to teach literacy through the medium of a national language — in the case of Singapore, an official language — and to create a shared national culture by using a common syllabus. In recent decades, however, globalization, which has profoundly transformed the economic, social, cultural and technological processes and structures throughout the world, has also impacted in varying ways and degrees the national education systems across the region. How Southeast Asian countries should reformulate and restructure their education systems and which strategy they ought to adopt to prepare to adapt and deal with globalization clearly depended on each country's societal make-up and economic situation and level of economic development.

How has globalization impacted and shaped the development of national education systems in Southeast Asia? In brief, globalization has brought about four interrelated changes to the education systems: (i) increasing demand for highly skilled and qualified labour; (ii) shifts in governance; (iii) privatization or commodification of education; and (iv) internationalization of education (Altbach and Knight 2007; Carnoy 2005; Robertson 2007). The emergent neo-liberal ideological paradigm accompanying globalization also dramatically altered the prevailing post-independent centralized governance and provision of education. In Southeast Asian states, in recent times the education sector has been subjected to varying degrees of decentralization and privatization or commodification. Moreover, the privatization of the region's education sector is occurring in the context of the growing internationalization of education, especially of higher education. Increasing global economic competitiveness and the emergence of the knowledge economy have raised the national, especially for more developed Southeast Asian economies, and international demand for tertiary-educated skilled and qualified personnel. While the scope, timing and pace of these transformations to the education systems differed in each Southeast Asian state, the main observable trend is the downscaling of state role in the governance and provision of education.

Education systems in Southeast Asia are critical sites for building national identity and societal cohesion. In the centralized education systems, national languages and literatures and national histories are codified and memorialized, national customs and values are taught and disseminated, and, more generally, national identities and consciousness are created to "bind each to the state and reconcile each to the other" (Green 1997, p. 174). However, as states in Southeast Asian countries embarked on using education to construct linguistically and culturally homogeneous nations, they deprived the minority citizens of their language and cultural rights. The consolidation of a national education system which is monolingual and centralized thus had dreadful consequences for ethnic minorities' languages and cultures.

In the worst-case scenario, the smaller, weaker ethnic minority languages and cultures became or are becoming extinct when official language[2] and education policies aggressively assimilated their members into the language, culture and values of the dominant group. The pursuant of assimilationist cultural, language and educational policies instead of facilitating social cohesion and national integration frequently triggered ethnic conflicts in the region (Sercombe and Tupas 2014). Moreover, with the advent of globalization countries are becoming more and more diverse as globalization has generated the largest wave of worldwide migration in history. Multiculturalism has become a global trend such that there has emerged a growing demands from minority groups, including the new migrant groups, for access to education and their languages and cultures be taught in schools.

Importantly, minority groups' education, cultural and language rights are articulated in the influential United Nations Educational, Scientific and Cultural Organization's (UNESCO) "2001 Universal Declaration on Cultural Diversity". In varying degrees, some Southeast Asian states have introduced the teaching of minority languages and cultures in schools and also implemented policies to enhance the minority groups' access to education. Symaco's chapter shows that the Malaysian government has helped to raise the enrolment rates among the Orang Asli in peninsula Malaysia and *bumiputra* groups in Sarawak and Sabah. Nevertheless, their enrolment rates are still much lower than that of the Malays, Chinese and Indians due to the fact that they reside in the more remote, rural areas of the country. Symaco also singled out the existing poor access to primary school education for the children of lower income foreign workers and the "undocumented children" of refugees and illegal immigrants, especially in the state of Sabah.

The emergence of English as the global language has made English as "a form of cultural capital". That the English language has become something of a commodity is demonstrated by the proliferation of programmes and schools, usually provided by the private sector, offering the teaching of English as a second language in Southeast Asia. The teaching of English as a subject has also been introduced in public schools in a number of Southeast Asian countries. A widely held opinion is that proficiency in English can help to expedite the acquisition of knowledge, especially scientific and technological knowledge, and enhance economic and business competiveness. As English is the lingua franca of the business world, it meant that competence in the language could enhance competiveness and employment opportunities in the global marketplace.

Therefore Singapore's decision to retain English as the medium of instruction helped to better prepare its citizens in the globalized world, while Malaysia's decision to switch to the Malay language as the main medium of instruction may have contributed to limiting the country's economic competitiveness (Alsagoff in this volume). The downside for Singapore, however, is that Singaporeans' have increasingly adopted English as their "native step tongue" such that "fewer and fewer Singaporeans [are speaking] mother tongues outside of second language classes in school". In contrast, the Malay language has expanded its role as Malaysia's integrative language and national identity marker, but, nevertheless, inconsistent educational policies and ineffective teaching of

English as a subject has led to students failing to master communicative competence in that language.

Unsurprisingly, English is the medium of instruction usually adopted by private and international education programmes and institutions in the region (Lavankura and Lao; Tan and Santhiram; and Mukherjee, Singh, Fern-Chung and Marimuthu in this volume). The growth of private English medium private education programmes and institutions may result in reinforcing (and creating new) inequalities based on English proficiency and accentuate ethnic and class segmentation in education (Lavankura and Lao; Tan and Santhiram; and Mukherjee et al.). Valorization of the English language can lead to a downgrading of the status of national and minority languages where English becomes the preferred language of communication for the cosmopolitan national elite and the language of choice for those who aspire to that status. More broadly, the widespread presence and adoption of the English language can have undesirable impact on the local linguistic and cultural diversity. This is because "languages are not merely tools for communication ... [but] are also the carriers of entire worldviews, the 'repositories of culture and identity' ... [which] means that decreasing lingual diversity can lead to the loss of irreplaceable bodies of knowledge and tradition" (Johnson 2009, p. 137).

Since globalization has raised the global demand for highly skilled and qualified individuals,[3] the demand for university education has grown substantially. The increase in demand for university education in turn pushed states to expand their higher education systems, and, correspondingly, to increase the number of secondary school graduates ready to attend post-secondary. Multilateral organizations (MOs) played an important role in shaping the policies to enhance the provision and quality of education in the developing world. Globalization empowered the role of MOs such as the World Bank, International Monetary Fund (IMF), the United Nations Children's Fund (UNICEF), and the United Nations Development Programs (UNDP) especially in influencing and shaping educational policies in developing countries. Being largely influenced by neo-liberalism, MOs viewed centralized education systems as inefficient and providing poor access to and delivering inferior quality education. As such, they proposed decentralizing education systems as a means to enhance efficiency, improve quality and access, and better serve the local needs.

In Southeast Asia, countries in the region have embarked on different forms and varying degrees of decentralizing their education systems to improve efficiency, transparency, accountability and quality (London 2011; Suryadarma and Jones 2013; Welch 2011). But the concept of decentralization is rather vague and moreover definitions of decentralization have rapidly changed overtime. Zobrist and McCormick's chapter shows that decentralization can be taken to mean "devolution", "delegation", "deconcentration", "divestment/privatization", "administrative de-centralization", and "financial management decentralization". In their Myanmarese case study, they argue that the decentralization of the education system in Myanmar is limited by the institutional culture of the Ministry of Education, the societal attitudes towards education and the roles of students, teachers, and Ministry staff. Also, the Myanmarese state tries to retain control over the decision-making process while off-loading some of the fiscal burden of education service provision to the local government.

The privatization or commodification of education has been the main approach adopted by most Southeast Asian countries to increase student enrolment especially in higher education. Undoubtedly, the privatization of higher education has helped to raise dramatically the total higher education student enrolment in Southeast Asia especially in Malaysia (Mukherjee et al. this volume; Welch 2011). Malaysian private higher education indeed has expanded greatly because the number of students wanting a degree far exceeded the places offered by the public universities. In terms of quality, the picture in Malaysia is rather mix in that there are first-rate and mediocre universities in both the public and private education sectors. Foreign universities and twinning programmes, usually with Australian, British and American universities, provide quality higher education while several local private universities provide lower quality education.

More generally, the privatization and marketization of higher education in Southeast Asia reinforced the existing ethnic and class educational inequalities. In Malaysia, race-based preferential admission policies into public universities resulted in an ethnically divided higher education system; a largely Malay public sector and non-Malay private sector (Tan and Santhiram). In addition, the majority of students enrolled in the first-rate private universities are usually from higher income groups and, conversely, majority of students in the mediocre private universities are from the lower income groups (Mukherjee et al. and Fahmi this volume).

Internationalization of education varies across the countries in Southeast Asia with Malaysia probably having the most extensive and varieties of internationalized education from the primary schools to universities.

The concept of internationalization, similar to that of privatization, is also rather vague and has changed rapidly (Altbach and Knight 2007). In Lavankura and Lao's chapter on the internationalization of higher education in Thailand, they define internationalization to mean "the process of integrating an international, intercultural, or global dimension into the purpose, functions or delivery of post-secondary education". The rationale for implementing the internationalization of higher education is that it can "improve the effectiveness and efficiency of what is currently done" and "alter the fundamental ways in which organizations are put together, including new goals, structures and roles". However, because of ambiguities in government policies and regulations, the internationalization of education in Thailand only brought about creation of new programmes, new offices and new campuses", there is, however, little changes "in terms of the effectiveness and efficiency of the existing programmes".

CHAPTER SUMMARIES

Malaysia and Singapore shared the common experience where an imported foreign language (English) was adopted as the de facto language of administration and main medium of education from primary to tertiary level during the colonial period. The two former colonies' multilingual landscapes were made more complex by the influx of immigrants — Chinese and Indians in particular — who brought with them their own foreign languages. Both countries inherited multilingual school systems consisting of English, Malay, Chinese, and Tamil medium schools from the British colonial state. While English was spread through the educational process, still an English education was limited to a few such that both their populations came to be divided into an elite that could speak English and the masses that were either illiterate or literate only in their mother tongue.

Alsagoff's chapter examines the "different pathways" Singapore and Malaysia had taken in their language planning since political independence. While both countries adopted a bilingual educational policy, different ideologies influenced their choice of medium of education and language planning in general. Singapore strived to manage its "linguistic and cultural diversity through a narrative of cultural pluralism, [and] equality for all 'races' and languages was achieved through an ideology of instrumentalism in language management in which both the economic as well as symbolic value of the official languages were recognized". English, Malay, Chinese

(Mandarin) and Tamil are all recognized as official languages, but only English is anointed as the medium of education and primary working language. The other official languages are treated as heritage languages and taught as second languages to enable the maintenance of ethnic identities and values. In contrast, Malaysian language planning is influenced by a conflicting admixture of "ethnic chauvinism and strong nationalistic fervour", minorities, principally Chinese and Indians, language rights and pragmatic recognition of mastering English for knowledge acquisition and economic development. Inter-ethnic bargain in Malaysia led to the establishment of a multilingual primary school system consisting of Malay, English (until 1976), Chinese and Tamil schools, and from secondary level onwards all instruction are in Malay — the sole national and official language — medium since 1982. Although Malaysia recognized the advantages of mastering English, the "government put far more focus on the way language rights were managed and were circumspect about the value of English in nation-building".

With English attaining the status as the language of globalization, Singapore benefited from the advantages of adopting English as the medium of education and primary working language. However, Singapore also encountered the dilemma of increasingly more Singaporeans adopting English as their native "step-tongue" and as part of their cultural identity. As such, "it seems unclear how the formulaic functional division of English as a working language versus the mother tongues as languages of cultural heritage can be sustained, especially when fewer and fewer Singaporeans even speak these mother tongues outside of second language classes in school". In contrast, in Malaysia inconsistent educational policies and the switch to Malay as the main medium of education appear to have contributed to eroding the quality standards of education, while the ineffective teaching of English as a subject has led to students failing to master communicative competence in that language. Nevertheless, Malay has expanded its role as the country's integrative language and national identity marker, and the multilingual character of Malaysian society is maintained with a majority of Chinese and Indians, majority Tamils, remaining fluent in their mother tongues.

In Chapter 2, Tan and Santhiram observe that "globalization has further raised the global presence of English ... [and] had a profound impact on the development of education worldwide". Two key agents helped in the global spread of English; the "transnational corporations that use English as the in-house working language and the advent of ICT that relies on English as its operational language". In Malaysia, the same two key agents have further enhanced English as the primary working language in the business world despite the status of Malay as the official language and main medium of education. Moreover, the government, convinced by the advantages of raising Malaysians' linguistic competence in English, introduced various measures to expand the usage of English in the education system. Especially since the 1990s, the government elected to permit private sector provision of primary to tertiary education in English medium. At the tertiary level, effectively today there is a dual education system consisting of a Malay-medium public sector and an English-medium private sector in the country.

Malaysia's language planning policy towards augmenting the role of English in education aims to develop a stable diglossic relationship between Malay and English that will help to strengthen the nation-building process, as well as make its economy more competitive. However, Tan and Santhiram assert that "a stable diglossia should be underpinned by equal emphasis given to both languages by their users to ensure that they are not mutually displacive". In Malaysia that means it "should ideally result in balanced bilinguals, who are equally competent in both" Malay and English. A stable diglossia may not materialize in Malaysia because among the non-Malays, for a number of reasons, they tend to favour English over Malay. This linguistic preference contributed to an ethnic divide in the educational system where the majority of students enrolled in the private tertiary institutions are non-Malays, while Malays made up the majority of students enrolled in the public tertiary institutions. This ethnic divide could "result in the widening of linguistic divide" where the non-Malays' greater mastery of English would advantage their economic opportunities in the private sector. That non-Malays would prefer English over the Malay language is "inevitable given the limited role of the Malay language within their socio-cultural domains and the strong instrumental value of English in the (globalized) private sector". The resulting ethnic divide in the educational system and widening linguistic divide between Malays and non-Malays can have "serious repercussion to the nation-building process".

Lavankura and Lao's chapter examines the internationalization of higher education in Thailand. Broadly speaking, internationalization of higher education is usually taken to mean "the process of integrating an international, intercultural, or global dimension into the purpose, functions or delivery of post-secondary education". If properly implemented, the internationalization of higher education could bring about changes "that improve the effectiveness and efficiency of what is currently done" (first-order changes) as well as also "alter the fundamental ways in which organizations are put together, including new goals, structures and roles" (second-order changes).

In Thailand, the internationalization of higher education involves three key actors namely; "the state, the market and the academic oligarchs (members of private and public universities)". Initially, the state played the key role in introducing the internationalization of higher education, but, since the late 1980s, the market has become the dominant actor in shaping Thai higher education both at the institutional and national levels. Consequently, increasingly the internationalization of Thai higher education has been implemented largely to meet market demands that will help boost tertiary institutions' revenues. This has led to the introduction of market-friendly international programmes which are in high demand. The authors argue that ambiguities in government policies and regulations of the internationalization of education enabled tertiary institutions to offer international programmes which brought about second-order changes — but without first-order changes. In particular, the government policy which allows "a programme using any foreign language as a medium of instruction" to be defined as an international programme has resulted in the proliferation of international programmes which are simply Thai curricula conducted in a foreign language, usually English, but without any particular international elements introduced into the curricula and teaching methods. While there are second-order changes in such programmes in terms of the "creation of new programmes, new offices and new campuses", there is, however, little changes "in terms of the effectiveness and efficiency of the existing programmes" (first-order changes).

Mukherjee et al.'s chapter examines the access, equity and quality issues involving the higher education sector in Malaysia. The Malaysian higher education was elitist until the 1990s when the government initiated a comprehensive strategy to raise the proportion of tertiary-educated individuals in the country's labour force. Between 1995 and 1997, the parliament approved a series of legislative acts covering "accreditation and quality assurance, regulations regarding HEIs and international branch campuses, use of English as medium of instruction, corporatization and the Higher Education Student Loan Fund". Perhaps the most important change in the government policy was to allow the private sector to play a bigger role in the provision of higher education. Consequently, the end result was the democratization and massification of Malaysian higher education.

Access to higher education was greatly enhanced with the massification of higher education; the higher education enrolment rates increased from 2.9 per cent in 1990 to 8.1 per cent in 2000 and an impressive 37.8 per cent in 2012. While access to higher education has improved significantly for all ethnic groups over the last four decades, inequity in educational opportunities remains very contentious, and there is also rising concern over the quality of education. Ethnic preferential educational policies continue to create inequities especially in terms of unfair access "to publicly funded higher education; how inputs are allocated; and how benefits are distributed". More worrying, the existing higher educational policies and practices have resulted in producing a limited talent pool and failure to develop a meritocratic academic culture. Also, students are graduating with poor linguistic competency in English and thus are not competitive in the global economy. The authors propose a number of fundamental systemic reforms to the "Malaysian higher education, and indeed the education system as a whole", in order to redress the higher education sector's various maladies.

In the chapter on higher education participation in Indonesia, Fahmi uses a non-linear decomposition method to appraise the effect of upper secondary school quality on participation in higher education. The Indonesian secondary school level has four different types of schools, namely: public secondary school, private non-religious school, private Christian school, and private Islamic school. In 2010, the lower and upper public secondary schools enrolled 63.7 per cent and 50.2 per cent of the lower and upper secondary students, respectively. For admission into higher education, students must attain a certain passing grade in the National Examination. Institutions offering higher education in Indonesia include academies, polytechnics, colleges, institutes and universities.

Fahmi's findings show that students enrolled in private Christian schools have the highest rate for higher education participation followed by, in descending order, students from public schools, private non-religious schools and lastly private Islamic schools. Unsurprisingly, the private Christian schools have the best inputs which include superior funding, better qualified teaching staff, students come from higher socio-economic background, and so on. Conversely, on the other end of the spectrum the private schools are poorly funded, teachers have lower qualification, students are from lower socio-economic status, and so on. The quality differences and "unobservable variables" contributed to the differential rate of higher education participation among students from the private Christian, public secondary, private non-religious and private Islamic schools. As such, the government policies of the further privatization of education would widen the educational inequalities between the upper and lower stratum of Indonesian society.

In the chapter on primary schooling in Malaysia, Symaco examines the patterns of and policies affecting access and retention in the primary school sector as well as address the question of quality and equity. In Malaysia, strong political commitment and consistent substantial government spending on primary and secondary school education enabled the country to significantly raise its "youth literacy rate from 88 per cent in 1980 to near-universal literacy of 99 per cent today". Since the mid-1990s, primary school net enrolment has remained in the high 90 per cent, and the survival rate to year 6 in primary school has also stayed relatively high, averaging 96 per cent from 2005 to 2010. Importantly, "there is no significant gender disparity in enrolment and completion of primary schooling". While there has been "improvements in the quality of education", at the international level Malaysia still lag behind in terms of its students' performance in the Programme for International Student Assessment (PISA) and Trends in International Mathematics and Science Study (TIMSS).

Malaysia has successfully eliminated the historical ethnic disparity in primary school access and retention among the Malay, Chinese and Indian communities. However, while there has been progress made in raising the enrolment rates among the Orang Asli and *bumiputra* groups in Sarawak and Sabah, those rates are still much lower than the enrolment rates for the Malays, Chinese and Indians. As the smaller minority groups such as the Orang Asli and the *bumiputras* in Sabah and Sarawak reside in the more remote, rural areas of the country, to further increase their access to primary school present great challenges. Two other groups of children who have poor access to primary schooling are the children of lower income foreign workers and the "undocumented children" of refugees and illegal immigrants, especially in the state of Sabah.

Since the political changes in Myanmar starting in 2011, the government has announced a number of reforms to the education sector. The chapter by Zobrist and McCormick examines the various government reforms, especially the decentralization policy, to address the various deep-seated problems in the education sector. Among the reforms, the government has raised the education expenditure, decentralized the provision of education, increased the numbers of schools and teachers, expanded the number of years of compulsory education, reformed the curriculum, and drafted an education law. Nevertheless, the authors argue that in reality these reforms have limited impact. For example, "state resources to provide more schools and teachers are constrained, and the possibility of preparing enough teachers, with the proper qualifications, in a short amount of time, is also limited".

The government is cognizant of the need to get "the right kind of legislation, funding, and advice to improve education", and has "placed an emphasis on reorganizing and rationalizing administration and administrative practices". However, besides reorganizing and rationalizing administration and administrative practices, policy reforms must also take into consideration the institutional culture factor. In their case study of the decentralization policy, the authors' findings show that "the institutional culture of organizations like the Ministry of Education, together with societal attitudes towards education and the roles of students, teachers, and Ministry staff, all limit the possibility of decentralization".

Notes

1. Except for Thailand which was never under direct European colonial rule.
2. Most countries do not make the distinction between national and official language.
3. See Carnoy (2005).

References

Altbach, Philip G. and Jane Knight. "The Internationalization of Higher Education: Motivations and Realities". *Journal of Studies in International Education* 11, nos. 3-4 (2007): 290–304.

Carnoy, Martin. "Globalization, Educational Trends and the Open Society". Paper presented at OSI Education Conference 2005: "Education and Open Society: A Critical Look at New Perspectives and Demands", 2005 <https://www.opensocietyfoundations.org/sites/default/files/carnoy_english.pdf>.

Green, Andy. *Education, Globalization and the Nation State*. London: Palgrave Macmillan, 1997.

Johnson, Anne. "The Rise of English: The Language of Globalization in China and the European Union". *Macalester International*, vol. 22 (2009): article 12.

London, Jonathan, ed. *Education in Vietnam*. Singapore: Institute of Southeast Asian Studies, 2011.

Robertson, Susan L. "Globalisation, Rescaling and Citizenship Regimes". In *Changing Notions of Citizenship Education in Contemporary Nation-states*, edited by K. Roth and N. Burbules. Rotterdam: Sense Publishers, 2007 <http://www.bris.ac.uk/education/people/academicStaff/edslr/publications/06slr/>.

Rosnani, Hashim. *Educational Dualism in Malaysia: Implications for Theory and Practice*, 2nd ed. Kuala Lumpur: The Other Press, 1996.

Sercombe, Peter and Ruanni Tupas, eds. *Language, Education and Nation-building: Assimilation and Shift in Southeast Asia*. London: Palgrave Macmillan, 2014.

Suryadarma, D. and Gavin Jones, eds. *Education in Indonesia*. Singapore: Institute of Southeast Asian Studies, 2013.

Welch, Anthony. *Higher Education in Southeast Asia: Blurring borders, changing balance*. London and New York: Routledge, 2011.

1

ENGLISH IN SINGAPORE AND MALAYSIA
Common Roots, Different Fruits

Lubna Alsagoff

INTRODUCTION

Singapore and Malaysia share a common history as colonial territories of the British. Each gained their independence from the British at around the same time, with the two countries even bound together as a single nation for a short period of time. Yet, if we examine the language policies of the two nations, we see a distinct difference in the paths that Singapore and Malaysia have taken in their approaches to managing linguistic diversity, and in their stances towards English. While Singapore has unambiguously embraced the utilitarian value of English and placed it as central to its language in education policies, Malaysia has, in many ways, been more ambivalent and circumspect about the value and place of English especially in relation to Malay.

In this chapter, we examine how their language policies have also sprung from very different sets of ideologies about language, which has meant that despite their common roots, Singapore and Malaysia have taken significantly divergent paths, resulting in very different outcomes or "fruits". The chapter is organized in three sections. In the first section, we trace the historical development of English in Singapore; in the second, we examine that of Malaysia, followed by a discussion which compares and contrasts the language in education policies of these two countries.

SINGAPORE

The Republic of Singapore is a relatively young nation, which celebrated only its fiftieth year of independence in 2015. Despite this, and the fact that it is a small island with no natural resources apart from its geographical position, Singapore has grown to become a thriving metropolitan country with a Gross Domestic Product (GDP) (adjusted for Purchasing Power Parity) per capita that remarkably ranks it as the third richest nation in the world (International Monetary Fund 2014). This outstanding achievement is no mean feat for a country less than half the size of London and which less than fifty years ago had a GDP that placed it as a struggling Third World nation. Among the many factors credited for Singapore's phenomenal economic success are its language policies, seen by the Singapore government as instrumental to its economic competitiveness (Ng 2008). Singapore's language policies have primarily focused on two essential issues. The first has been to manage the diversity of Singapore's linguistic and cultural landscape that comprises 74.1 per cent ethnic Chinese, 13.4 per cent Malays, 9.2 per cent Indians, with the other races including Eurasians making up the remaining 3.3 per cent of the 5.08 million population (Singapore Department of Statistics 2010a, p. 3). The second issue is the careful positioning of English in relation to the three mother tongues of Mandarin, Malay and Tamil, which represent the nation's primary ethnic groups, ensuring that its ascendance as Singapore's working language does not compromise linguistic and cultural plurality. Although the rise of English in Singapore is clearly attributable to British colonization, its continued centrality to Singapore's sociolinguistic landscape, as we shall see, extends well beyond these roots.

The first set of language-in-education policies in independent Singapore came in 1956 in the form of the All-Party Report, formulated by an all-Singaporean committee (All-Party Committee on Chinese Education 1956) at the end of British rule. Several key recommendations were made; critically, the All-Party Report gives official recognition to four languages

— English as well as the three languages seen as representing the largest ethnic groups, namely, Malay for the Malays, Mandarin for the Chinese, and Tamil for the Indians. The All-Party Report echoed the earlier Fenn-Wu Report, commissioned under British rule that was to pave the way for Singapore's independent rule, in promoting cultural pluralism through the principle of equal treatment of all four streams of education. This meant that government funding would be available to schools whatever their medium of instruction. Like the Fenn-Wu Report, the All-Party Report also advocated a nationally oriented curriculum that would use a common set of textbooks, written in the four official languages, to aid in the development of a curriculum that would help foster national identity. Most importantly, the All-Party Report recommended a bilingual education policy, which would continue to be a cornerstone of Singapore's education policies. The policy recommended that all school children be schooled in two languages — English and an ethnic mother tongue — in primary school, and three languages — English, Malay and their ethnic mother tongue — in secondary school. From the very start, English obviously had a special place, despite the end of British colonization. In independent Singapore, it remained an official language despite the lack of affiliation to any ethnic group, and it was a key medium of instruction, either as the primary medium of instruction, or a secondary one.

The recommendations of the All-Party Report in support of cultural pluralism and the equal treatment of all languages were endorsed and adopted by the first governing body during self-rule. Malay, however, was given a special place over the other languages in its Constitution as Singapore's national language. Lee Kuan Yew, Singapore's first prime minister, argued that Malay was the most apt lingua franca for moral, political and practical reasons. However, it was clear that the move to adopt Malay as Singapore's national language was in preparation for its intended merger with the Federation of Malaya, which was the premise upon which Singapore sought to gain full independence from British rule. As Singapore aspired to be part of a united Malaysia, Malay far exceeded English in political importance (Alsagoff 2008). However, even though the Singapore government sought to gain favour with the Malayan government, it stood firm on its language policy that recognized four official languages, rather than just Malay, which was a likely contributor to the eventual collapse of the merger with Malaya after only two short years. With the eventual dissolution of the merger with Malaysia, the role of Malay, not surprisingly was much reduced and primarily ceremonial, even though it continued to be recognized officially as Singapore's national language. Upon gaining independence, Singapore set its sight on ensuring its economic survival through rapid industrialization. Not surprisingly, the importance of English continued to be emphasized, despite the fact that British colonial rule was over. English was seen as an essential means of opening access to the large wealthy markets of the West — both in terms of gaining market access as well as being able to develop a workforce that could avail itself of the advances in Western science and technology necessary for the industrialization of its economy. Complementing the instrumental role of English, the representative mother tongues of the three main ethnic groups — the Chinese, Malay and Indians — were contrastively constructed in the political discourse as cultural ballasts needed to ground Singaporeans in tradition and culture, to stave off "deculturalization" (Goh et al. 1979, pp. 1–5), and thus fend off the corrupting influences of the West (Hill and Lian 1995). English, in contrast, was constructed essentially as abstracted from culture, i.e., in a manner, "cultureless", effected through a representation of English as a working language, purposefully delinked from any association with any of the ethnic groups. English was also reconstructed and re-presented as an "international" language of trade, science and commerce which enabled the government to justify the adoption of English for pragmatic reasons without the attendant association of English with its colonial past (Ho and Alsagoff 1998). Interestingly, the decoupling of English from any ethnic group also meant that English was seen as the ideal language for nation-building in yet another important aspect: its "neutrality" and established role as an inter-ethnic lingua franca (Kuo 1980) made it the perfect language to adopt for government administration because it ensured equal employment and educational opportunities for all ethnic groups. This conveniently aligned with the government's ideological stand of equality among races and among languages — English thus became the key to an economically oriented language-in-education policy that would also ensure cultural pluralism and ethnic equality.

Such narratives that justified the centrality of English in nation-building aligned well with Singapore's English-knowing though bilingual education policy (Kachru 1983; Pakir 1997) that clearly privileged English over the other languages. In Singapore, then and now, bilingual education is understood not simply as education in any two official languages, but as the knowledge and use of English plus one other official language. In English-medium schools, students took a second language that corresponded to their ethnic group membership, while in the Asian-language medium schools, English was the mandatory second language. In addition, as a clear signal of the importance of English, science and mathematics were also taught in English in all schools, whatever the language medium of the school. The Goh Report, commissioned in 1979 to examine the issues regarding the bilingual policy, echoed such a position, arguing that "as Singapore industrializes, the English language becomes more important relative to the other languages" (Goh et al. 1979, p. 4). The value of English was also apparent to Singaporean parents who, as the "invisible language planners" chose overwhelmingly to enrol their children in English-medium schools (Pakir 1997, p. 61). Clearly, English afforded an advantage in relation to social mobility and success as it did in the past (MacDougall and Chew 1976).

In addition, English-medium schools also offered a healthy compromise in mother tongue education through a generous 40 per cent of school curriculum time. Not surprisingly, despite a concerted effort by the Chinese-educated elites to reinvigorate the enrolment of students in the Chinese-medium schools through a "Promote Mother Tongue Education" month, the number of enrolments in such schools continued to fall (Suarez 2005; Tay 1983). Whereas around 50 per cent of children were registered for English stream schools in 1959, the figure rose to 99 per cent in 1983. The attrition in the number of students in the Chinese, Malay and Tamil streams saw the Ministry of Education announce, in December 1983, that the education system would be a single national stream where English was taught as a first language.[1] By 1987, English became the sole medium of instruction in all schools. At the tertiary level, English had also gained ground. Nanyang University, founded in 1956, and a stronghold of Chinese-medium education, began offering subjects in English in addition to Mandarin in 1975 amid fears that it would close because of falling student enrolments. Three years later, in 1978, courses common to Nanyang University and the University of Singapore were combined and offered at the Bukit Timah campus of the University of Singapore. Shortly after that, in 1980, the two universities merged to form the English-medium National University of Singapore.

Interestingly, as new generations of Singaporeans benefited from successes of the bilingual education policy, there grew to be a distinct change in the way English was spoken and used among the population. Increasingly, with the "democratization of English", a vernacular known as Singlish became the lingua franca of the nation, with even Lee Kuan Yew, chief architect of Singapore's language policies, speaking at that point of time as Minister Mentor, conceding this:

> Up to the 1970s in our markets and hawker centres, Bazaar Malay was the lingua franca. Everybody could understand and speak some Malay. Because of our bilingual policy, today the lingua franca is English, or Singlish. (Lee 2005)

Concerns that this form of English would undermine Singapore's position in the global economy arose as early as the late 1990s. In his National Day Rally speech in 1999, Prime Minister Goh Chok Tong pointed to the detriment that the unchecked use of Singlish could have on the economic success of Singapore. In the following year, Goh launched the Speak Good English Movement — his message to Singaporeans at the launch of the Speak Good English was clearly economically driven, consistent with the government's characterization of English in instrumental terms:

> The ability to speak good English is a distinct advantage in terms of doing business and communicating with the world. This is especially important for a hub city and an open economy like ours. If we speak a corrupted form of English that is not understood by others, we will lose a key competitive advantage. My concern is that if we continue to speak Singlish, it will over time become Singapore's common language.
>
> Poor English reflects badly on us and makes us seem less intelligent or competent ... all this will affect our aim to be a First World economy. (Goh 2000)

Notably, Goh warns against valorizing the local English vernacular, Singlish, urging Singapore's citizens to speak an "internationally intelligible English" to ensure continued economic survival and growth. In keeping with the status and economic value of English as a working language and consequently sans culture, the government was not sympathetic to the idea that Singlish was part of the cultural identity of Singaporeans:

> They [younger Singaporeans] should not take the attitude that Singlish is cool or that speaking Singlish makes them more "Singaporean". ... If they speak Singlish when they can speak good English, they are doing a disservice to Singapore. (Goh 2000)

This pragmatic and economically driven attitude towards English in Singapore clearly constructs it in terms of its value as an international language, and thus sees no part in Singlish, even though it has come to be the home language of half of the school-going population (Alsagoff 2012), becoming a marker of Singaporean identity, especially when it becomes a stumbling block for international commerce.

MALAYSIA

Malaysia, which comprises peninsular West Malaysia and East Malaysia, made up of the states of Sabah and Sarawak on the island of Borneo, is a country much larger than Singapore with a population of 30 million. Demographically, Malaysia is very similar to Singapore, with its population comprising primarily of Malays (about 60 per cent), Chinese (about 25 per cent), and Indians (about 7 per cent). With the colonization of Malaysia by the British, English was introduced, and soon grew into prominence, with the Roman script even being added to the Jawi script for the written form of Malay. The arrival of the British also heralded large numbers of Chinese and Indian immigrants at the end of the nineteenth century who sought work in the thriving new economy. These immigrants specialized in specific industries, giving rise to a clear pattern in the geographical spread of the different ethnic groups — the Malays concentrated in the rural areas focusing on agriculture, the Chinese focused on tin mining with many also running businesses in the urban areas, and the Indians working in the rubber estates and railways as labourers (Azirah 2009).

When Malaysia gained its independence from the British in 1957, it faced similar problems as Singapore. As a highly diverse multiethnic and multilingual country where an estimated eighty languages were spoken, Malaysia needed to be able to develop language policies that would allow it to manage this diversity. One key difference between Singapore and Malaysia, however, lay in the fact that, in Malaysia, the Malays were the dominant ethnic group comprising over half of the total population. In addition, their status as the indigenous race — as the *bumiputra* or "sons of the soil" — gave them clear symbolic and political power over the Chinese and Indians who were of immigrant ancestry. And it also allowed the Malays to claim their language, notably named Bahasa Melayu (literally, the language of the Malays), as the language of the nation.

Under British colonial rule, whether by divisive decree or laissez faire rule, Malay, Chinese and Tamil vernacular schools were allowed to flourish, while education in English was restricted to the elite minority. However, in preparation for independence, the British commissioned the Barnes Report (1951) which proposed Malay-English bilingualism, where only Malay and English would be taught in the National schools and be established as Malaysia's official languages. The Barnes Report recommended that Malay, as the mother tongue of the dominant ethnic group, play a central role in education in the country — priority in funding for elementary education, for example, was to be given to the National Schools which used Malay as the medium of instruction. The report deemed mother tongue education not to be worth public expense, and in effect advocated that the Chinese and Indians should be encouraged to give up their vernacular schools and opt for schools which had Malay as the only local language taught. However, in keeping with British interests, the report also advocated that Malay should give way to the English language as a medium of instruction at the secondary and tertiary levels (Gill 2005).

The Barnes Report was of course met with opposition from both the Indians and the Chinese who, while willing to accept Malay as the sole national language on the basis of its status as Malaysia's indigenous language, did not agree to Malay and English as the only official languages (Lee 2007). The Fenn-Wu Report (1951) was commissioned, ostensibly to review Chinese education in the country, but which offered an opposing proposal. It recommended the establishment of a multilingual national education system with four official languages — English, Malay, Chinese and Tamil — a proposal that we saw being taken up by the Singapore government. In 1952, the Education Ordinance in its evaluation of the two reports favoured the Barnes Report, which led to the establishment of the bilingual national school system where either Malay or English was used with the view of establishing a Malay-medium system in the long run. However, the Razak Report in 1956, chaired by the then Minister for Education Abdul Razak bin Hussain, overturned these decisions and supported the development of mother tongue education and vernacular schools. It recommended the establishment of:

> a national system of education acceptable to the people of the federation as a whole which will satisfy the need to promote their cultural, social, economic and political development as a nation, having regard to the

intention of making Bahasa Malaysia the national language of the country while preserving and sustaining the growth of the language and culture of other communities living in the country. (cited in Gill 2005, p. 245)

The Razak Report proposed the establishment of two types of primary schools: the "national school" using Malay as the medium; and the "national-type" school which could use either English, Chinese or Tamil as the medium. Refinements to these policies were made in 1960 — the Rahman Talib Report, named after its chair, the then Education Minister, led to the legislation of a new Education Act, which allowed Chinese and Tamil primary schools to co-exist with national schools. To safeguard the status of Malay, however, the government now made it mandatory that all secondary schools use Malay as the medium of instruction. All schools were also required to adopt a common set of subject syllabi and examinations. At the tertiary level, Malay was also gaining ground. The University of Malaya began converting its courses into Malay — as an interim measure, English was used for science and technology while Malay was used for the arts and humanities. This transformation was completed in 1983, after eighteen years, when all subjects including the sciences, were taught in Malay.

In grappling with its multicultural and multilingual population, the Malaysian government emphasized the need for a single national language — Malay — that would serve to unite the multiethnic nation and form the basis of a national identity. Gill (2005), however, argues that a more compelling reason might have been to reduce the inequities between those who received their education in English and those who did not. Gill suggests that the Malay nationalist group were unhappy about the economic power of the English-speaking, who were, by and large, the Chinese who lived in the urban areas, along with a small number of Indians and Malays who also attended the English-medium schools. The Malaysian government clearly believed that instituting Malay as the national language and the sole official language of Malaysia would elevate its linguistic capital, which in turn would provide the Malays with the capital and economic opportunities they desired. The Chinese and Indian groups were also in favour of the use of their own languages rather than English (Lee 2007). However, this pace of reform that would ensure Malay of its premier linguistic status proved to be slow. In Sabah, for example, English continued to be an official language alongside Malay until 1973, and in Sarawak, English retained its status as an official language until 1985. In 1969, riots broke out, testament to the high level of emotion among the Malay community, especially among Malay nationalists, about the issue of language.

In promoting Malay, Malaysia's language policies clearly relegated the English language to a secondary position compared to Malay — it was to be a second language, lower in status and importance to the Malay language (Asmah 1985). In fact, it had no official status, given that unlike Mandarin and Tamil, which could serve as mediums of instructions in national-type schools, it no longer had any capital within the institutional education framework. Yet this rise in status of the Malay language was curtailed in some measure by the continued reliance of the business community on English, given its clearly dominant role in the global marketplace (Gill 2005). Gill also suggests that demand for scientific and technological knowledge could not be met even though much effort was expended in translation work, which meant that students had no alternative but to learn English. The linguistic capital that English commanded might be seen to have culminated in 2002, when Malaysia instituted a dramatic change in its language policy, known as PPSMI (Pengajaran dan Pembelajaran Sains dan Matematik dalam Bahasa Inggeris) that reversed the government's Malay-dominant language policy and switched the medium of instruction from Malay back to English for the subjects of science and mathematics. The new policy mandated that all fully aided government schools should roll out teaching these two subjects in English from January 2003 to new cohorts of primary and secondary school students.

This change in language policy, although often portrayed as sudden, was in fact already presaged by the continuing trickle of policies that saw English being acknowledged as central to not only science and technology, but to education in general. In 1993, Malaysia's Prime Minister, Mahathir Mohamad, announced that English would be allowed as a medium of instruction in universities and colleges for the teaching of science. Then in 1995, the centrality of English re-emerged in the Malaysian education system in a guideline issued by the Ministry of Education that allowed the use of English in tutorials, seminars, assignments, foreign language classes and other similar activities (Zaaba et al. 2013). These policies were legislated as the Education Act 1996, which allowed the use of English as the medium of instruction for technical areas and post-secondary courses. In conjunction with this was the 1996 Private Higher Education

Institution Act which allowed the use of English in dual university programmes affiliated with overseas institutions. To safeguard the special position of the Malay language, the Education Act 1996 required that Malay be included in the curriculum as a compulsory subject, where the medium of instruction in private education institutions was other than the national language.

The liberalization of higher education in private institutions, which essentially meant the possible use of English as a medium of instruction in such educational settings, created a divide between these institutions and the public universities where the medium of instruction was Malay (except for science and technology courses). The former were attended by the privileged middle-class and upper-class Malays, Indians and Chinese who could afford the high fees, while the latter largely benefitted the working-class *bumiputra* who received subsidies on school fees and were guaranteed places because of the special provision in the "racial quota" policy. Although such policies were clearly meant to ensure the rise in economic power of the *bumiputra* Malays, they had the reverse effect — the Asian economic crisis in the late 1990s gave rise to large numbers of unemployed public university graduates who were clearly at a disadvantage in seeking employment in the private sector because they lacked competence in English (Zaaba et al. 2013).

PPSMI lasted only a decade. With a lack of qualified teachers to carry out lessons in English, especially in the rural schools, and mounting social pressure to ensure greater economic and social opportunities for the ethnic Malays, the Malaysian government announced that PPSMI would be discontinued, and in its place, would be a new policy called MBMMBI (Memartabatkan Bahasa Malaysia Memperkukuh Bahasa Inggeris), literally translated as "to uphold Bahasa Malaysia and to strengthen the English language". The new policy was designed to be a compromise, switching the medium of instruction for science and mathematics back to Malay, but at the same time increasing curriculum time for the teaching of English up to 40 per cent. Critically, MBMMBI would see the re-establishment of Malay as the medium of instruction in schools, in alignment with its position as the national language, would again endow Malay with the educational and administrative capital that would ensure its position as a language of higher status than English. By association, this would then provide the Malays with linguistic capital and economic opportunities which would afford them greater social and professional mobility.

The switch back to Malay raised fresh concerns, within the business community as well as among parents, about Malaysia's competitive position in the global marketplace, given that an increasing number of Malaysians would have limited proficiency in English (Gooch 2009) and that reverting to Malay to teach science and mathematics would also prove detrimental for the advancement of these subjects. Policies regarding Malaysia's medium of instruction, seen as closely related to the quality of Malaysia's education, has in recent years come under criticism. PISA (Programme for International Student Assessment), an internationally benchmarked test, ranked Malaysia's fifteen-year-olds in the bottom third of seventy-four participating countries in 2009, with almost 60 per cent of the Malaysian student participants not proficient in mathematics, 44 per cent not proficient in reading and 43 per cent not proficient in science (Straits Times Asia Report 2013). While it may not be entirely just to put the sole blame of these poor standings on Malaysia's language in education policies, many believe that this is the root of the problem. In particular, the vacillation between Malay and English as mediums of instruction as well as the suppression of English in order to promote Malay have, in the opinion of many, ostensibly led to a lack of stability that has stunted the progress of Malaysia's education system.

SAME ROOTS, DIFFERENT FRUITS

In the accounts of the language policies of Singapore and Malaysia, it is evident that the way English is perceived and valued (or not) is quite different in these two countries. In Malaysia, the attitude towards English is clearly ambivalent: in many respects, the Malaysian government saw the need to acknowledge and exploit the linguistic capital of English, and yet, as the language of the British colonizers, English had no place in independent Malaysia and was even seen as a threat to the status of Malay. The strong sense of nationalism felt by the *bumiputras* led to Malay being accorded status as the first language of the nation — both as the sole official language that gave Malay its administrative and educational roles, and as the national language, which accorded Malay its role in nation-building. The designation of a common language is an essential part of nation-building especially in multiethnic contexts where the presence of multiple languages can give rise to linguistic complexity, often seen to be a challenge to the development of a unified national identity. The designation of Malay as this unifying language, argued on the basis of its historical roots as the true indigenous language of the region speaks of policy that views language as a right (Ruiz 1984). However, unlike other linguistic contexts where issues regarding language planning involves minority ethnic groups that fight for the right to be educated in their own language rather than the majority tongue; in the context of Malaysia, it was the majority ethnic group, the Malays, who asserted their rights as the indigenous population to establish their language, Malay, as the national language.

The Chinese and Indian communities were also accorded the right to use their mother tongues as mediums of instruction, albeit in a limited way. Firstly, these languages were replaced by Malay at the secondary school level, signalling the latter's importance to Malaysia's nationhood. Secondly, despite being the medium of instruction of vernacular primary schools, the national-type schools, neither of these languages was recognized as official languages in Malaysia. This lack of official recognition extended most particularly to English, which had no recognized institutional role in the country — it was not recognized as having a role in the government, nor was it a medium of instruction. As the language of the former British colonial masters, English was perhaps seen as anathema to nation-building. What problems there were in terms of social and economic inequities between the Malays and the other races were also seen as rooted in English hegemony because of its former status as the language of Malaysia's colonial masters. Yet, Malaysia's linguistic history evidently presents evidence that not having English as a central part of the education system has disadvantaged the *bumiputras* who were not able to compete for jobs in an increasingly global marketplace.

Singapore, on the other hand, has openly embraced English, transforming it from the language of its colonial masters to an international language of science, technology, business and finance needed that it has used to achieve economic success. The primary thread in the language policies of post-independence Singapore is one characterized by a pragmatic and economically driven approach to the management of languages in which languages are seen as a means to desired ends (Gopinathan 1998, p. 20). The fine balance between advocating English as the working language of the nation and the valuing of the other three languages as heritage languages was struck through a careful delineation of the functions of these languages (Wee 2003). Managing linguistic and cultural diversity through a narrative of cultural pluralism, equality for all "races" and languages was achieved through an ideology of instrumentalism in language management in which both the economic as well as symbolic value of the official languages were recognized. Thus, although the different languages were regarded as equal, and protected by law to be so, they were not equally valued. The languages were instead measured in terms of their usefulness in ensuring Singapore's social and economic well-being. Clearly, its choice of English as the primary working language was motivated by the economic advantages that English offered. However, the government was always careful to show that equity among the languages was at all times maintained.

Singapore has also not had cause to alter its language policy — it has slowly and carefully created a coherent narrative about the place and value of each of the official languages. It has nurtured English as necessary to Singapore's future, but played down its importance in the building of cultural identity. Ostensibly, Singapore's language policies have, as can be seen, served Singapore well economically — enabling the country to enjoy phenomenal economic growth as well as social stability. Singapore seems to have fared much better than Malaysia, which has had seemingly less stability in its language policies. Singapore has ranked consistently among the top-performing countries in a range of internationally benchmarked tests such as TIMSS (Trends in International Mathematics and Science Study), PIRLS (Progress in International Reading Literacy Study) and PISA; Malaysia, on the other hand, ranks in the bottom third, and appears to have suffered from the flip-flopping of its language policies, first in 1967 to have moved from English to Malay, and then back to English in 2003 only to have this reversed in 2012 to having the medium of instruction back as Malay.

Yet, I would argue, Malaysia's language policies in its orientation to the notion of language as right (Ruiz 1984) has more aptly acknowledged the close link between language and identity. The argument made by Malay nationalist leaders, for example, that Malay should be established as the sole medium of instruction was one motivated by the need to build a national identity. Argued to be a lingua franca that would promote unity amongst the ethnic groups, Malay was constructed as a marker of identity shared by all Malaysians; hence it was deemed necessary to learn it in order to be considered Malaysian. The renaming, in 1969, of Malay from Bahasa Melayu, literally, the language of the Malays to Bahasa Malaysia, the language of Malaysia, signalled the way in which Malaysia's language policies completed the argument, in a sense, of this link between language and identity. But as would be expected, when policies take into account identity and the rights that people have to be educated in the language of their cultural groups, language planning becomes messy and far more organic in nature. Thus, in the advent of the Asian economic crisis, Malaysia began to realize the unemployability of its Malay youth because they lacked competency in English, which precipitated a change in policy where English was again "let in" as a medium of instruction for science and technology, only to be "banned" from such classrooms barely a decade later from what was essentially nationalistic pressure to uphold the status of the national language.

Malaysia's linguistic history certainly demonstrates this messiness, especially when it stands in contrast to the neat reductionist approach taken in Singapore. Facilitated by an instrumental view of language (Wee 2003), Singapore has effectively argued for the place of languages in relation to a rubric based on economic and social value. The discourse around language planning focused much less on what rights people had to speak or use their own languages. For the government, the important issue facing the nation at the time of independence was its economic survival. For this, the government saw English as the most expedient and most logical means of obtaining access to Western markets, although, clearly, racial harmony was as essential in ensuring that the nation could progress without obstacles. Thus, as a counterpoint, the government's recognition of three languages as mother tongues, representative of each ethnic group — Mandarin for all of the Chinese, Malay for the Malays, and Tamil for all of the Indian community — as the cultural ballasts that allowed Singaporeans to remain rooted in their culture. Wee (2003) in fact intimates that this relation of language to culture is highly formulaic and does not represent reality, given that the mother tongue languages are in fact post-hoc constructions to justify the neat classification of the ethnic groups, with an increasing number of Singaporeans more comfortable in English than their assigned mother tongues.

Although economic concerns were also relevant in the Malaysian context, they did not appear to be the drive for the Malaysian government; unlike Singapore which clearly privileged discussions of economic survival in its decision to give English such a central role, the Malaysian government put far more focus on the way language rights were managed and were circumspect about the value of English in nation-building. However, as

Gill (2005) writes, the unplanned aspects of Malaysia's language policy mean that English still continues to dominate in the key and unlegislated area of business, which relies centrally on English to maintain a foothold in the global economy. Even while Malay interests are protected through according special privileges to *bumiputra* citizens, the reliance on English is clear.

These and other issues provide insight into the far more nuanced and complex path that language planning has taken in Malaysia, often buffeted by the winds of ethnic chauvinism and strong nationalistic fervour. In contrast, while seeming to acknowledge the relation between language and identity in its recognition of the three mother tongue languages, Singapore's neat packaging of languages shows a more formulaic and instrumentally driven ideology. After all, Mandarin was clearly not the native language of most of Singapore's Chinese population, and Tamil was clearly not the only Indian language spoken by the Indian community. More telling was the labelling of Malay as the national language of Singapore, but which did little but to serve as the language of the national anthem and to give marching commands to the armed forces. Malaysia's use of Malay as its national language, on the other hand, signalled a real recognition of the role of the language in nation-building. Additionally, while bilingualism has often said to be the cornerstone of Singapore's education system, the Singapore education system does not in fact practise bilingualism in the sense of the use of two languages as mediums of instruction "to teach subject matter content rather than just the language itself" (Cummins 2003, p. 3). Rather, mother tongue languages are simply subjects in Singapore schools. In contrast, Malaysia has an education system that can be considered bilingual — students who attend national-type schools, for example, study in Mandarin or Tamil at the primary school level, and then in Malay at the secondary school level. When PPSMI was introduced into classrooms in 2003, students were taught science and mathematics in English, and other subjects in Malay. During the transition period in the 1970s, when English was being phased out, Tan (2005) notes that a mixed English and Malay medium bilingual education was in fact enacted.

The lack of engagement with the idea that language and identity are inextricably linked has come to be a problem for Singapore because of the rise of its local vernacular, Singlish. Unlike countries like Australia and the Philippines which have embraced the development of a national variety of English, the Singapore government has continued to maintain a position where the standard of English advocated continues to be an exonormative one. In the current incarnation of the English Language Syllabus, released in 2010, the Ministry of Education has continued to stress the need for students to develop an "internationally acceptable" English, and has placed added emphasis on the standards of English, clearly embracing a more structural approach to language, along with a renewed concern for accuracy in grammar and pronunciation. The term "Singapore English" continues to be absent from official policy documents, and there continues to be little or grudging official recognition of Singlish as Singapore's "badge of identity", this despite the fact that English in Singapore has come a long way — from a "foreign" language of the British colonizers, it has evolved into a variety with a growing population of native speakers. English has clearly become the de facto lingua franca. Literacy in English has risen significantly, from a low 21.0 per cent in pre-independent Singapore of 1957 to 33.7 per cent in 1970 (Kuo 1980, p. 55), and to 70.9 per cent in 2000 (Singapore Department of Statistics 2000, p. 2). In 2010, this figure has risen yet again, and stood at 79.9 per cent (Singapore Department of Statistics 2010b, p. 9). Even more interestingly, the census data also show more children using English as their most frequently spoken language at home than youths and adults. In 2000, for example, 36 per cent of Chinese children aged 5–14 years spoke English most frequently at home compared with 22 per cent of youths aged 15–24 years and 25 per cent of those aged 25–54 years. In just ten years, this figure has again risen, with now 52 per cent of Chinese children aged 5–14 years speaking English as a home language (Singapore Department of Statistics 2010b, p. 11).

Without a doubt, English will continue to flourish in Singapore. However, potential problems lie ahead if Singapore refuses to embrace and manage the development of its own brand of English. As more and more speakers of English as their native "step-tongue" (Gupta 1994) enter adulthood and claim English as part of their cultural identity, it seems unclear how the formulaic functional division of English as a working language versus the mother tongues as languages of cultural heritage can be sustained, especially when fewer and fewer Singaporeans even speak these mother tongues outside of second language classes in school. Furthermore, Singapore faces a considerable challenge in culturally integrating the large numbers and diverse range of migrants and migrant workers who now make up an overwhelming 36 per cent of Singapore's population (Singapore Department of Statistics 2010c, p. 1,[2] Alsagoff 2012). Without a real national language to unify this melting pot, can Singapore really build a cohesive nation with a clear national identity?

In contrast, Malaysia's future will hold a different set of challenges, the foremost of which will be to build a credible and strong education system around its new language policy. Malaysia's poor showings in PISA points to the challenge it faces in ensuring that it can develop a workforce that can realize its economic potential — it is a country rich in natural resources, and is well placed geographically to become a hub for Asia. While carving its own path in terms of the insistence of Malay as the medium of instruction, Malaysia has to ensure that its education system equips students with the skills and knowledge required for the twenty-first century workplace. Although the Malaysian education system has made significant progress in ensuring the accessibility of education to especially the rural areas, it must now move towards an improvement in the quality of its education, especially when it is clear how weakly the Malaysian students perform relative to the other nations, even those far less economically wealthy (Ministry of Education, Malaysia 2012). To address these challenges, Malaysia has proposed an ambitious plan of reform as outlined in the Malaysia Education Blueprint 2013–2025. However, its quest to meet universal standards in areas of reading, mathematics and science will be tested in the implementation and enactment as Malaysia continues to grapple with keeping up with the pace of development that requires an enormous effort in translating information that is primarily in English. Its relationship with English will also be an area that will be constantly tested as globalization continues its rise. How it will continue to ensure that its ideological stance of language as right can be balanced with the increasing needs of the nation to ensure a high level of communicative competence in English will be a challenge. While it is clear that Malay — Bahasa Malaysia — will continue to be the main language of communication and the language for nation-building as is Malaysia's intent, it remains to be seen whether moving forward, that Malay can be its main language of knowledge. And while Phan, Kho and Chng (2013) make a worthy case that MBMMBI is "a necessary, firm, strategic and timely response by the Malaysian government to globalization, nation-building, the increasing international role of English, and the pressure to maintain national cultural identity in today's world" (p. 68), it remains to be seen whether in its enactment such intractable challenges can be addressed in a globalized world of intensely compressed time and place.

CONCLUDING REMARKS

Although sprung from common roots, the nations of Singapore and Malaysia have taken vastly different pathways in their language planning. In this chapter, our primary thesis has been to demonstrate the different ideologies in language planning that have been adopted by the two nations. In its quest to ensure linguistic harmony and economic success, Singapore has chosen an instrumental model, heavily laced with pragmatism. Malaysia, in contrast, has chosen to place a stronger emphasis on linguistic rights. Both countries will face challenges, albeit different ones, based on their pathways. The common roots have thus borne different fruits, both present and future.

Notes

1. The term "first language" in Singapore education policy does not refer to the status of the individual's native tongue, but rather reflects the primacy of the English language as the medium of education in which all subjects, except for the Mother Tongue and Civics and Moral education, are taught in.
2. This statistic is derived from the 0.54 million permanent residents and the 1.31 million foreign workers who make up the immigrant population residing in Singapore (Singapore Department of Statistics 2010c, p. 1).

References

All-Party Committee on Chinese Education. *Report of the All-Party Committee of the Singapore legislative Assembly on Chinese education*. Singapore: Government Printing Office, 1956.

Alsagoff, L. "The commodification of Malay: Trading in futures". In *Language as commodity: Global structures, local marketplaces*, edited by Tan P.K.W. and R. Rubdy, pp. 44–56. London and New York: Continuum, 2008.

———. "The development of English in Singapore: Language policy and planning in nation building". In *English in Southeast Asia: Features, policy and language in use*, edited by Low E.L. and A. Hashim, pp. 137–54. Amsterdam: John Benjamins, 2012.

Asmah, H.O. "The language policy of Malaysia: A formula for balanced pluralism".

In *Papers in South-East Asian linguistics No. 9: Language policy, language planning and sociolinguistics in South East Asia*, edited by D. Bradley, pp. 39–49. Pacific Linguistics, 1985.

Azirah, H. "Not plain sailing: Malaysia's language choice in policy and education". *AILA Review* 22 (2009): 36–51.

Bokhorst-Heng, W. "Language planning and management in Singapore". In *English in new cultural contexts: Reflections from Singapore*, edited by J.A. Foley, T. Kandiah, Z. Bao, A.F. Gupta, L. Alsagoff, C.L. Ho, L. Wee, I. Talib and W.D. Bokhorst-Heng, pp. 287–319. Singapore: Oxford University Press, 1998.

Cummins, J. "Bilingual education". In *World yearbook of education: Language education*, edited by J. Bourne and E. Reid, pp. 3–20. London: Kogan Page, 2003.

Gill, S.K. "Language policy in Malaysia: Reversing direction". *Language Policy* 4 (2005): 241–60.

Goh, C.T. Speech by Prime Minister Goh Chok Tong at the launch of the Speak Good English Movement on 29 April 2000, at the Institute of Technical Education (ITE) Headquarters Auditorium, Singapore. Ministry of Information, Communication and the Arts <http://stars.nhb.gov.sg/stars/public/> (accessed 12 December 2009).

Goh, K.S. and the Education Study Team. *Report on the Ministry of Education 1978*. Singapore: Singapore National Printers, 1979.

Gooch, L. "In Malaysia, English Ban Raises Fears for Future". *New York Times*, 9 July 2009 <http://www.nytimes.com/2009/07/10/world/asia/10iht-malay.html?_r=0> (accessed 2 November 2014).

Gopinathan, S. "Language policy changes 1979–1997: Politics and pedagogy". In *Language, society and education in Singapore: Issues and trends*, edited by S. Gopinathan, A. Pakir, W.K. Ho and V. Saravanan, pp. 19–44. Singapore: Times Academic Press, 1998.

Gupta, A.F. *The step tongue: Children's English in Singapore*. Clevedon: Multilingual Matters Ltd, 1994.

Hill, M. and Lian K.F. *The Politics of nation building and citizenship in Singapore*. London: Routledge, 1995.

Ho, C.L. and L. Alsagoff. "English as the common language in multicultural Singapore". In *English in new cultural contexts: Reflections from Singapore*, edited by J.A. Foley, T. Kandiah, Z. Bao, A.F. Gupta, L. Alsagoff, C.L. Ho, L. Wee, I. Talib and W.D. Bokhorst-Heng, pp. 201–17. Singapore: Oxford University Press, 1998.

International Monetary Fund. (2014). *World economic outlook database October 2014*. <http://imf.org/external/pubs> (accessed 2 December 2014).

Kachru, B.B. "Models for non-native Englishes". In *The other tongue: English across cultures*, edited by B.B. Kachru, pp. 31–57. Oxford: Pergamon Press, 1983.

Kuo, E.C.Y. "The sociolinguistic situation in Singapore". In *Language and society in Singapore*, edited by E. Afendras and E.C.Y. Kuo, pp. 39–62. Singapore: Singapore University Press, 1980.

Lee, H.G. "Ethnic politics, national development and language policy in Malaysia". In *Language, Nation and Development in Southeast Asia*, edited by Lee H.G. and L. Suryadinata, pp. 118–49. Singapore: Institute of Southeast Asian Studies, 2007.

Lee, K.Y. Speech by Minister Mentor Lee Kuan Yew at the Tanjong Pagar Chinese New Year Dinner at Radin Mas Community Club, Singapore on 17 February 2005. Ministry of Information, Communication and the Arts <http://stars.nhb.gov.sg/stars/public/> (accessed 12 July 2009).

MacDougall, J.A. and Chew S.F. "English language competence and occupational mobility in Singapore". *Pacific Affairs* 49, no. 2 (1976): 294–312.

Ministry of Education, Malaysia. *Malaysia Education Blueprint 2013–2025: Preliminary Report*. 2012 http://www.moe.gov.my/userfiles/file/PPP/Preliminary-Blueprint-Eng.pdf (accessed 9 August 2014).

Pakir, A. "Education and invisible language planning: The case of the English language in Singapore". In *Education in Singapore: A book of readings*, edited by Tan J.T., S. Gopinathan and W.K. Ho, pp. 57–74. Singapore: Prentice Hall, 1997.

Phan, L.H., J. Kho and B. Chng. "Nation building, English as an international language, medium of instruction, and language debate: Malaysia and possible ways forward". *Journal of International and Comparative Education* 2, no. 2 (2013): 58–71.

Ruiz, R. "Orientations in language planning". *NABE Journal of Research and Practice* 8, no. 2 (1984): 15–34.

Singapore Department of Statistics. *Singapore census of population 2000: Advance data release No. 3 Language and literacy*. Singapore: Department of Statistics, Ministry of Trade and Industry, 2000 <www.singstat.gov.sg> (accessed 5 April 2010).

———. *Singapore census of population 2010: Advance census release*. Singapore: Department of Statistics, Ministry of Trade and Industry, 2010*a* <www.singstat.gov.sg> (accessed 30 May 2011).

———. *Singapore census of population 2010: Statistical release 1: Demographic characteristics, education, language and religion*. Singapore: Department of Statistics, Ministry of Trade and Industry, 2010*b* <www.singstat.gov.sg> (accessed 30 May 2011).

———. *Population trends 2010*. Singapore: Department of Statistics, Ministry of Trade and Industry, 2010*c* <www.singstat.gov.sg> (accessed 30 May 2011).

Straits Times Asia Report, The. "Malaysia moves to raise English standards". 2013. <http://www.stasiareport.com/the-big-story/asia-report/malaysia/

story/malaysia-moves-raise-english-standards-20130907#sthash.2caN6BSn. dpufMBMMBI> (accessed 2 November 2014).

Suarez, S.L. "Does English rule? Language instruction and economic strategies in Singapore, Ireland, and Puerto Rico". *Comparative Politics* 37, no. 4 (2005): 459–78.

Tan, P.K.W. "The medium-of-instruction debate in Malaysia: English as a Malaysian language?". *Language Problems & Language Planning* 29, no . 1 (2005): 47–66.

Tay, M.W.J. *Trends in language, literacy and education in Singapore.* Singapore: Department of Statistics, 1983.

Wee, L. "Linguistic instrumentalism in Singapore". *Journal of Multilingual and Multicultural Development* 24, no. 3 (2003): 211–24.

Zaaba, Z., M. Mooradian, H. Gunggut, I.N.A. Aning, F.I.M. Ramadan and A. Arapa. "Teaching Science and Technology in English: Language-in-Education Policy in Malaysia". In *Recent technological advances in education: Proceedings of the 9th International Conference on Educational Technologies (EDUTE '13) & Proceedings of the 1st International Conference on engineering and technology education (ETE '13).* edited by E. Pop, C. Barbu, A. Zaharim and K. Sopian, pp. 131–35. Kuala Lumpur, Malaysia, 2–4 April 2013.

2

GLOBALIZATION, EDUCATIONAL LANGUAGE POLICY AND NATION-BUILDING IN MALAYSIA

Tan Yao Sua and R. Santhiram

INTRODUCTION

Globalization is a complex and multifaceted phenomenon. It is best understood as a modern process as well as one with historical antecedents and continuities with past eras (Tazreiter and Tham 2013). From the contemporary perspective, it involves the intensified flows of capital, goods, people, images and discourses around the globe, driven by technological innovations mainly in the field of media and information and communications technology (ICT) and resulting in new patterns of global activity, community and culture (Blommaert 2010).

Globalization has had a profound impact on the development of education worldwide. One of its impacts is in the area of educational language policy, which has a lot to do with the global spread of English brought about by globalization. Within the contemporary context of globalization, the global spread of English has been accentuated by agents of globalization, especially the neo-liberal ideology embraced by transnational corporations (TNCs) that use English as the in-house working language and the advent of ICT that relies on English as its operational language (Tan and Santhiram 2014). Both agents of globalization have increased the instrumental value of English in periphery-English countries, leading to the spread of English to these countries. For instance, in Russia alone, 50 million people are learning English. Meanwhile, English is the main foreign language in China (Watson 2000), and proficiency in this language is a key university entry requirement (Stanley and Lee 2011). What is worthy of note here is that the number of speakers of English as a second language (350 million according to one estimate) has exceeded the number of native English speakers (Nettle and Romaine 2000). Among other things, this spread of English is facilitated by increased emphasis given to English via educational policy intervention. In fact, a United Nations Educational, Scientific and Cultural Organization report (2002) notes that as the result of challenges arising from globalization, educational systems around the world are paying "special attention to foreign languages, first and foremost it is English" (cf. Rizvi and Lingard 2010, p. 176). Consequently, educational institutions become the sites where "the hegemony of the English language is spread, reproduced, but also contested" (Coulby 2005, p. 279).

In the case of Malaysia, there was a radical change of educational language policy from the early 1990s in response to the global spread of English. This radical change of educational language policy began with the decision of the government to allow selective courses at the public institutions of higher learning to be taught in English. Such a radical change of educational language policy had largely compromised the common language policy upheld by the state since independence in 1957. This common language policy was underpinned by the Malay language, the national language of Malaysia as well as the language of the dominant group, as the main medium of instruction in the national educational system. It was meant to facilitate inter-ethnic interactions and to develop a shared identity given that Malaysia is a plural society comprising three main ethnic groups with diverse languages and cultures, namely, Malays, Chinese and Indians.

This radical change of educational language policy was deemed necessary following declining standard of English among Malaysian students that stemmed from the phasing out of the English-medium school system beginning in the 1970s. This decline in the standard of English threatened, it was argued, the economic development of the country on the global stage. The decision by the government to allow for the establishment of more private institutions of higher learning that used English as the main medium of instruction beginning in 1996 had also helped to improve the proficiency of English among Malaysian students, though such a decision was also influenced by other intervening factors.

Efforts by the government to improve the proficiency of English among Malaysian students reached new heights with the implementation of the policy of teaching science and mathematics in English in 2003 at the school level. But the implementation of this policy was hotly contested by the opposition political parties, the Malay nationalists as well as the Chinese and Indian educationists. In the end, the government was forced to terminate the policy. However, it was the strong stand of the Malay nationalists over the threat posed by the policy to the national language that had played a crucial role in influencing the decision of the government to terminate the policy. But the termination of the policy did not deter efforts by the government to address declining standard of English among Malaysian students.

Nevertheless, these efforts were undertaken together with efforts to safeguard the national language. It culminated in the introduction of the bilingual policy of "upholding the Malay language alongside the strengthening of English" (Memartabatkan Bahasa Malaysia Memperkukuh Bahasa Inggeris, or MBMMBI). This Malay-English bilingual policy was subsequently incorporated into the recently launched Malaysia Education Blueprint (2013–15) and implemented in stages beginning from the most fundamental level of education, i.e., the primary schools. A host of intervening measures were put in place by the Blueprint to achieve this bilingual policy (Ministry of Education Malaysia 2013).

Clearly, the government has resorted to the strategy of glocalization or "vernacular globalization" (Lingard 2000) in dealing with the contrasting linguistic needs of the country, which have resulted in "tension between global and local concerns" (Tollefson and Tsui 2004, p. 290). By glocalization is meant "the simultaneity — the co-presence — of both universalizing and particularizing tendencies" (Liu and Guo 2009, p. 153) or "the interplay of local and global forces" (Anderson-Levitt 2003, p. 28). For one thing, the MBMMBI policy has engaged the Malay language in a diglossic relationship with English. In fact, diglossic relationship between languages has now become a global phenomenon arising from the accelerated pace of globalization. Daniel Nettle and Suzanne Romaine note that "globalization has increasingly led to layers of diglossia on an international scale" (2000, p. 31).

In the case of Malaysia, the key question one should ask is: Will this diglossic relationship lead to a stable diglossia that will help to strengthen the nation-building process? By stable diglossia is meant that "each language has its own set of functions and space without threatening the other" (Nettle and Romaine 2000, p. 191). However, given the fact that most studies on diglossia tend to focus on "the functional dependency and complementarity between participating languages, arguing that where one language is used the other is not and vice versa" (Kamwangamalu 2010, p. 120), it is, therefore, the contention of this chapter that a stable diglossia should be underpinned by equal emphasis given to both languages by their users to ensure that they are not mutually displacive. In other words, the outcome of this diglossic relationship should be the principal concern. Thus, a stable diglossia should ideally result in balanced bilinguals, who are equally competent in both languages. Such a diglossic relationship is crucial to the nation-building process in Malaysia, especially in relation to the respective roles of the Malay language and English. Asmah Hj. Omar, a Malaysian linguist, posits that:

> Nation building has to have as its basic ideology which is both economic and political in nature. This means that the process of building a nation needs a sound policy which ensures economic prosperity and political strength for the nation as a whole" (1993, p. 18).

As far as the MBMMBI policy is concerned, the upholding of the Malay language is to fulfil the political needs of the country, while the strengthening of English is to fulfil the economic needs of the country on the global stage. Thus, Malaysian students should embrace both languages on equal terms to bring about a stable diglossic relationship between the two languages.

There is a high possibility that the MBMMBI policy may not bring about a stable diglossia, especially among the non-Malay students. For some reason, the non-Malays in Malaysia, more so the Chinese, tend to favour English over Malay. This linguistic preference has existed before the implementation of the MBMMBI policy. It goes without saying that this linguistic preference will be further consolidated by the MBMMBI policy. The main concern here is that this linguistic preference will widen the existing ethnic divide within the Malaysian educational system via the pursuance of different educational pathways among the non-Malays. This widening of ethnic divide will affect the tertiary level where a dual system of higher education has been instituted in Malaysia since 1996. It will also affect other levels of education following the phenomenal growth of international schools in Malaysia in recent years. Given that this widening of ethnic divide will also lead to the widening of linguistic divide, its impact on the nation-building process should not be taken lightly, more so when it involves a dominant global language.

This chapter begins with a discussion on the common language policy adopted by Malaysia prior to the early 1990s. It then goes on to examine policy inventions to improve the proficiency of English among Malaysian students. Finally, it explains the reasons for the introduction of the MBMMBI policy and explores the educational outcome of the diglossic relationship between the Malay language and English in relation to the nation-building process.

COMMON LANGUAGE POLICY

Up until the early 1990s, the main thrust of the Malaysian educational language policy was to ensure that the Malay language serve as a common denominator to unify the three main ethnic groups in the country. This common language policy is mainly driven by Malay linguistic nationalism as the underlying "ideological construct" (Tollefson and Tsui 2004, p. 284). By linguistic nationalism is meant "the association of one language variety with the membership in one national community" (Kramsch 1998, p. 72). It was hoped that such an educational language policy would be able to foster both "sentimental and instrumental attachments" (Kelman 1971) to the nation state to uphold the supremacy of Malay linguistic nationalism.

This common language could be traced to the Razak Report promulgated in 1956. Among other things, this report stipulated the ultimate objective to elevate the Malay language as the main medium of instruction in the national educational system (Federation of Malaya 1956). This common language policy was aimed at the post-primary levels. At the primary level, the Razak Report allowed the vernacular primary schools, namely Chinese and Tamil primary schools, to co-exist with the Malay-medium and English-medium primary schools. But these schools were subjected to a common content curriculum that was intended to serve as the overarching link between the multilingual primary schools. It was hoped that this common content curriculum would help to bring about a common process of enculturation among the students regardless of medium of instruction (Federation of Malaya 1956).

The common language policy espoused by the Razak Report was subsequently adopted by the 1960 Rahman Talib Report and enforced through the 1961 Education Act (see Federation of Malaya 1960, 1961). The immediate casualty of this common language policy was the Chinese secondary schools managed by the Chinese educationists affiliated to the United Chinese School Committees' Association (UCSCA, or Dong Zong) and the United Chinese School Teachers' Association (UCSTA, or Jiao Zong). These schools were required to switch to the national medium of instruction in exchange for state funding (grants-in-aid) or else they would have to exist as Independent Chinese Secondary Schools (ICSSs) or Duli Zhongxue (Duzhong) outside the ambit of the national educational system. In the end, out of the dire need for state funding, fifty-five of the existing seventy-one Chinese secondary schools acted against the advice of the Chinese educationists and decided to conform to state policy and became the National-Type Chinese Secondary Schools (NTCSSs) or commonly known as the conforming schools (Gaizhi Zhongxue) (Tay 2003; Tan 1988, 1997; Tan and Santhiram 2010).

The NTCSSs initially used English as the medium of instruction but when a new educational policy was promulgated in the early 1970s, their medium of instruction was switched to the Malay language in stages. This switch of medium of instruction was supposed to come much earlier, i.e. in 1967, when the status of English as an official language of the country was reviewed ten years after independence as stipulated by the Federal Constitution. This constitutional review was meant to elevate the Malay language as the sole official language of the country to further consolidate the common language policy advocated by the state. However, for some reason, the Malaysian government had decided to retain the use of English for official purposes in the enactment of the National Language Act, though it had elevated the Malay language as the sole official language of the country (Roff 1967; Haris 1983; Ibrahim 1986; von Vorys 1976).

The new educational policy promulgated by the government in the early 1970s also enforced the conversion of other types of English-medium schools (primary and secondary), namely the missionary English schools and the government English schools, to Malay-medium schools to uphold the common language policy advocated by the state. With this conversion, only the vernacular primary schools were allowed to teach in a medium of instruction other than the Malay language. This common language policy made further inroads into the Malaysian educational system when all first year courses in the public institutions of higher learning were conducted in the Malay language beginning in 1983 (Asmah 1976). However, this common language policy, which served the internal needs of the country since independence, finally succumbed to external pressure beginning in the early 1990s that stemmed from the global spread of English following the accelerated pace of globalization spearheaded by neo-liberal ideology and the advent of ICT.

ENGLISH AS A MEDIUM OF INSTRUCTION

Since the phasing out of English-medium education from the 1970s and with English being relegated to the status of a second language within the school curriculum, there was a sharp decline in the standard of English among Malaysian students. In fact, the passing rate of English in public examinations was among the lowest in any subject. Despite a host of intervening measures, there was no marked improvement in the proficiency of English among Malaysian students. The global spread of English following the accelerated pace of globalization beginning in the 1990s placed the Malaysian government at "a linguistic crossroads" (Gill 2002, p. 103) with regard to its future educational language policy.

Clearly, the Malaysian government could no longer ignore the adverse impact of this poor proficiency in English on its global competitiveness as a workforce proficient in English is a key requirement to spur its economic growth within the global context. This is particularly important to sustain its reliance on foreign direct investments (FDIs) from the TNCs for economic growth. This reliance on FDIs from the TNCs actually began in the 1970s when the Malaysian economy shifted from import substitution to export promotions through the development of labour-intensive industries by the TNCs (Ghosh 1999). Meanwhile, the aspirations of the Malaysian government to transform the Malaysian economy into a knowledge-based economy (KBE) following the construction of the Multimedia Super Corridor in 1996 (Tan 2002) also required a workforce proficient in English to capitalize on the advent of ICT that had become a key component of the KBE. Admittedly, the KBE has emerged as a main feature of the global economy following the advent of ICT that has accelerated the pace of globalization. Alarmingly, because of poor proficiency in English among students, the Malaysian government is unable to optimize its human capital development to enhance its global competitiveness, especially in the expanding (globalized) private sector that relies on English as the working language. This is indicated by the high rate of graduate unemployment in this particular sector. The poor quality of graduates produced by the public institutions of higher learning is also a major stumbling block to the optimizing of human capital development. One of the contributing factors is their poor proficiency of English following the switch from English-medium education to Malay-medium education beginning in the 1970s. The fact is that despite this switch of medium of instruction, Malaysian students continue to rely on English academic texts because of the lack of Malay translated academic texts and this is where their proficiency of English is found to be most wanting (Gill 2002; Khoo 2008). In fact, students spend more time translating these texts than actually studying the subject (Sato 2007).

It is against the above backdrop that increased emphasis has been given to English in the Malaysian educational system beginning in the early 1990s. However, this change of educational language policy was also facilitated by the pragmatic attitude of the political elites within the Malaysian coalition government, in particular the Malay political elites affiliated to the United Malays National Organisation (UMNO) — the dominant political party in the Malaysian ruling coalition. Since independence, UMNO has been the main driving force in the upholding of the Malay language as the main thrust of the country's educational language policy. The question then is: Why did the UMNO political elites choose to change an educational language policy that has favoured the Malays all this while? The answer lies in the implementation of the New Economic Policy (NEP) (1971–90), a social engineering policy that was originally implemented to redress the socioeconomic disparity between the Malays and non-Malays in the country but eventually favoured the socioeconomic mobility of the Malays. It is generally accepted that the NEP had led to the emergence of Malay professionals who formed a new Malay middle class (Abdul Rahman Embong 2001; Maznah 2005; Rahimah 2012). These professionals were subsequently co-opted into the UMNO power structure and replaced the Malay teachers as the mainstay of UMNO politics. It is this group of

Malay elites who are pragmatic enough not to be overwhelmed by Malay linguistic nationalism that has underpinned the educational language policy of the country since independence. Instead, they recognized the need for the Malays to strengthen their proficiency in English to enhance their global competitiveness. More importantly, they felt that such a move would not jeopardize the well-entrenched position of the Malay language within the country. Apart from this newfound pragmatism, their advocacy of a wider use of English was also influenced by their ethos as elites of the society. As Halim Salleh puts it, "English is regarded as the language of the successful, modern, urban and educated wealthy class" (2000, p. 159). The UMNO political elites certainly come under this category of social class.

The radical change of educational language policy in Malaysia began in 1993 following the announcement by Dr Mahathir Mohamad, then Prime Minister of Malaysia, that public institutions of higher learning that used Malay as the main medium of instruction would be allowed to use English to teach courses related to science and technology (Ambigapathy 2001). Subsequently, some public institutions of higher learning took the decision to allow more courses to be taught in the English medium of instruction. Even Universiti Kebangsaan Malaysia (UKM) or the National University of Malaysia, which was established in the 1970s to promote a greater use of Malay at the tertiary level, opted for this decision. Its Vice-Chancellor was reported to have said that UKM aspired to conduct 50 per cent of its courses in English (*New Straits Times*, 28 March 2002, cited in Gill 2002, p. 120). It was also reported that Universiti Pendidikan Sultan Idris (UPSI) or the Sultan Idris Teaching University intended to conduct 30–40 per cent of its courses in English (*New Sunday Times*, 16 September 2007). Apparently, all these measures were aimed at improving the English proficiency of Malaysian students.

The position of English in the Malaysian educational system was further consolidated when the government enacted several Acts in 1996 to spur the development of private higher education that used English as the main medium of instruction. First, the 1996 Education Bill, which recognized private education as an integral part of the national educational system. Section 143 of the Bill empowers the Minster of Education to approve the establishment of educational institutions that use other languages as media of instruction (MDC Legal Advisers 2005). Second, the 1996 National Council on Higher Education Bill, which put in place a single governing body to oversee both the public and private institutions of higher learning to ensure better coordination of the country's higher educational system. Third, the Private Higher Education Bill, which defined the government's regulatory control powers over all private institutions of higher learning (Lee 1999). Fourth, the 1996 National Accreditation Board Bill, which provided for the setting up of an accreditation board to formulate policies on the standard and quality control of courses of study and certificates, diplomas and degrees awarded by private institutions of higher learning (Lembaga Penyelidikan Undang-Undang 2002).

Such widespread legislation to a system of education that had otherwise virtually remained unchanged for more than thirty years has since allowed private higher education to grow at a phenomenally rapid pace and emerged as a parallel system of tertiary education to the public institutions of higher learning (Santhiram and Tan 2009). Prior to this, private higher education played a peripheral role in the tertiary education sector in Malaysia. Its enrolment rates were 9.1 per cent in 1985, 15.4 per cent in 1990 and 34.7 per cent in 1995. These enrolment rates were far below that of the public institutions of higher learning, which were at 52.5 per cent, 53.0 per cent and 51.5 per cent for the corresponding years (Lee 1999). But by 2005, the enrolment of private institutions of higher learning had exceeded that of the public institutions of higher learning. They managed to enrol 113,105 students as compared to 80,885 students enrolled by the public institutions of higher learning (Kementerian Pengajian Tinggi Malaysia 2006). Meanwhile, the number of private institutions of higher learning (16 private universities, 11 private university colleges and 532 private colleges) had also exceeded the number of public institutions of higher learning (11 public universities, six public university colleges, 20 polytechnics and 34 community colleges) (Malaysia 2006). Although the establishment of private institutions of higher learning were underpinned by several reasons, such as the lack of capacity of the public institutions of higher learning to cope with the surging demand for higher education and the aspirations of the government to make Malaysia the regional educational hub, they had helped to strengthen the proficiency of English among Malaysian students.

Efforts by the Malaysian government to strengthen the proficiency of English among Malaysian students reached new heights with the implementation of the policy of teaching science and mathematics in English in 2003 at the school level. This policy was implemented in stages and was expected to fully cover all levels of schooling by 2008. It began with three groups of students, namely Primary Year One, Secondary Year One and first year pre-university (Lower Six) students (Jiao Zong Tiaocha Yanjiu ji Zixunzu 2007). Clearly, the selection of science and mathematics as the subjects to improve the proficiency of English among Malaysian students is driven by the fact that English is the de facto international language of science and technology (Baker 1995) — it is the universal medium of scientific communication (Wright 2004), displacing major world languages such as French and German as the language of science and academia (May 2008). It is perhaps for this reason that Tony Pua notes that "the attempt to use English to teach the 2 subjects were certainly noble as the vast majority of science and mathematics literature is written in the language and the frequent use of the English language will also indirectly improve the declining competence of Malaysian students in the language" (2010, p. 256).

Despite the dire need to improve the proficiency of English among Malaysian students, the policy of teaching science and mathematics in English invoked strong reactions in many quarters for various reasons. For instance, Lim Kit Siang of the Democratic Action Party, the main Chinese-based opposition political party in the country, urged the government to resort to other means to strengthen the proficiency of English among Malaysian students. Lim called on the government to make English a compulsory pass subject in the public examinations as a means to improve the proficiency of English among Malaysian students (Lim 2009). The strongest challenge to the policy of teaching science and mathematics in English came from the Malay nationalists and the Chinese educationists but for different reasons. The Malay nationalists were worried that this policy would pose a threat to the supremacy of the Malay language as the national language and the official language of the country, while the Chinese educationists feared that this policy would erode the character of Chinese primary schools, which is associated with the use of Chinese as the language of classroom instruction, school administration and wider communication. But the government was determined to see through the policy.

The opposition to the policy of teaching science and mathematics in English continued unabated despite its implementation and intensified upon the completion of a full cycle of implementation in 2008. It was the opposition from the Malay nationalists that had been most instrumental in influencing the decision by the government to terminate the policy in

July 2009. This opposition reached new heights in early 2009 when the Malay nationalists, headed by A. Samad Said, a national laureate, staged a mass rally in the Federal Capital to protest against the policy and succeeded in submitting a memorandum to the Yang di-Pertuan Agong (His Majesty, the King). Soon after that, the government announced the termination of the policy. Despite the strong contestation from advocates of the policy, mostly parents from urban areas within the vicinity of the Federal Capital, the government stood firm on its decision on the policy (Tan and Santhiram 2014). However, the termination of the policy did not deter efforts by the government to improve the proficiency of English among Malaysian students. Immediately after the termination of the policy, the government introduced the MBMMBI policy. Clearly, this new educational language policy had resorted to the strategy of glocalization to address the contrasting linguistic needs of the country by taking into account the stand of the Malay nationalists vis-à-vis efforts by the government to improve the proficiency of English among Malaysian students. It hoped to ensure that the Malay language would not be marginalized by the increased emphasis given to English to cope with new challenges arising from the accelerated pace of globalization.

MBMMBI POLICY

The incorporation of the MBMMBI policy into the recently released Malaysia Education Blueprint marked a new conjuncture in the development of educational language policy in Malaysia. The incorporation of this policy indicates the strong commitment of the government to ensure that Malaysian students are equipped with Malay-English bilingual proficiency to meet the contrasting linguistic needs of the country. The government hoped that Malaysian students would be, at minimum, operationally proficient in these two languages (Ministry of Education Malaysia 2013). Going by the definition of operational proficiency provided by the Blueprint, i.e. "the linguistic fluency required to participate fully in professional and academic life" (Ministry of Education Malaysia 2013, pp. 4–10), it is clear that "cognitive-academic language proficiency" (Cummins 1984, 2000), which is closely related to literary skill (Romaine 1995), is the ultimate target of the Blueprint. As far as the Malay language is concerned, the Blueprint is no longer contented with the basic communicative role of the national language to foster national integration. It has moved on to ensure that the national language could become a working language as well as a language of knowledge production and dissemination to promote a higher level of sentimental and instrumental attachments to the language.

A host of intervening measures are put in place by the Blueprint to achieve the MBMMBI policy. The upholding of the Malay language is mainly targeted at the vernacular primary school students as their proficiency in the Malay language is found to be most wanting. It involves the adoption of a new curriculum, i.e. the Primary School Standard Curriculum or Kurikulum Standard Sekolah Rendah, specifically designed for teaching students whose mother tongue is not the Malay language and who do not experience immersion in the Malay language as in the Malay-medium primary schools. This new curriculum defines fewer learning requirements in the early years of primary education but converging to similar acquisition standards in the Malay-medium primary schools by the end of primary education through the introduction of more Malay teaching periods starting from Primary Year Four to Year Six. In addition to early intervention measures such as Literacy and Numeracy Screening (LINUS), teachers delivering the new curriculum will be upskilled to effectively teach the language to the vernacular primary school students. Intensive remedial classes will also be conducted for students who face problems in acquiring the language (Ministry of Education Malaysia 2013).

In the case of the strengthening of English, the Blueprint has undertaken several measures such as early intervention programmes (expansion of the LINUS programme and the provision of remedial support), upskilling of teachers (testing and retraining of teachers) as well as the introduction of literature in English and technology-assisted learning pedagogy (blended learning models) to improve the proficiency of English among Malaysian students. Meanwhile, from 2016 onwards, English will be made a compulsory pass subject in the Malaysian Certificate of Education examination or Sijil Pelajaran Malaysia (SPM) examination, a public examination taken at the end of Secondary Year Five (Ministry of Education Malaysia 2013). With this, the Blueprint envisages that after three years of schooling, every child will achieve 100 per cent basic literacy in Malay and English and by the end of Secondary Year Five, 90 per cent of the students will score a minimum of a Credit in both languages in the SPM examination (Ministry of Education Malaysia 2013).

The MBMMBI policy has clearly engaged the Malay language in a diglossic relationship with English. The question then is: Will this relationship bring about a stable diglossia that is underpinned by equal emphasis given to both languages by Malaysian students? The most likely scenario is that it may not lead to such an ideal diglossic relationship, more so among the non-Malay students who are not known to acquire the Malay language for its integrative value apart from the mere requirement to pass public examinations, largely because of the limited role of the language to serve as a tool for inter-ethnic interactions for the non-Malay students. Among other things, this could be attributed to residential segregation and mono-ethnic schooling (especially at the primary level where most non-Malays attend the vernacular primary schools) that result in the role of the Malay language as a language of inter-ethnic communication becoming largely dysfunctional for the non-Malay students. As is always the case, when a language is acquired for the purposes of examinations, this may not bring about the desired outcome of language acquisition, primarily because language acquisition needs a strong element of practical usage.

Above all, the eventual outcome of the diglossic relationship between the Malay language and English will be strongly dictated by the status of the two languages. It is generally recognized by scholars of bilingualism that when a weaker language is pitted against a stronger language in a diglossic relationship, the result will be subtractive rather than additive bilingualism. In other words, the weaker language will be marginalized or even displaced by the stronger language, more so when the stronger language is deliberately promoted at the early stages of schooling (Lambert 1980; d'Anglejan 1982). Thus, as far as the MBMMBI policy is concerned, there will be a strong tendency for Malaysian students to favour English over Malay given the dominant status of English as the global lingua franca.

While both the Malay and non-Malay students will be affected by this language learning orientation, the impact on the non-Malay students will be greater, primarily because English has always been popular among the non-Malays. This popularity could be seen from their adoption of the language as a home language or as a supplementary home language to their mother tongues. This is particularly true among the middle and upper classes residing in major urban areas. This linguistic preference is mainly driven by the immense instrumental value of English among the non-Malays given their predominance in the private sector that relies on English as a working language, though it could also be influenced by the ethos of the upper and middle classes who generally regard English as a superior language. All in all, the strengthening of English by the MBMMBI policy may not bring about a stable diglossic relationship between the Malay language and English among the non-Malays. Instead, it will further consolidate the favoured position of English among the non-Malays.

There is a high possibility that the strengthening of English by the MBMMBI policy will result in more non-Malays opting for educational institutions that teach in English, especially at the tertiary level where private institutions of higher learning exist in large numbers. The problem is that these private institutions of higher learning are predominantly attended by the non-Malays, especially the Chinese, for a host of different reasons (including preference for English medium of instruction), and since the public institutions of higher learning are predominantly attended by the Malays (non-Malays are found in substantial numbers only in critical courses), this has resulted in an ethnic divide at the tertiary level. This ethnic divide will be widened if more non-Malays are to opt for the private institutions of higher learning as a result of current measures by the government to strengthen the proficiency of English among Malaysian students. This is because prior to these measures, many non-Malay parents, especially those from smaller urban areas where English is not pervasively used, were quite reluctant to send their children to the private institutions of higher learning for the simple reason that their children may not be able to cope with the English medium of instruction. However, this linguistic barrier will be reduced following the implementation of the MBMMBI policy and these parents will now have the confidence to send their children to the private institutions of higher learning.

There is also a high possibility that current efforts by the government to strengthen the proficiency of English among Malaysian students will lead to more parents sending their children to international schools that offer the International General Certificate of Secondary Education or the Cambridge 'O' Level. Such a possibility is not entirely unfounded given the impressive growth of international schools in the country in recent years. International schools have long existed in Malaysia. They were originally established for the expatriate population but subsequently opened their doors to local students with a stipulated quota (initially 10 per cent and subsequently 40 per cent). The strong development of international schools actually began in 1996 when the government allowed the establishment of private educational institutions that used English as a medium of instruction. By 2008, there were 40 international schools in the country with a total enrolment of 13,811 students (Ministry of Education Malaysia 2008).

The development of international schools was given a big boost in 2010 when the government put in place a host of measures to scale up these schools to capitalize on the immense economic gains generated by these schools. For instance, the government provided international school operators with support on the issues of land acquisition and soft loans. It is expected that by 2020, international schools will generate gross national income amounting to RM2.6 billion and create approximately 10,000 jobs in the country. The scaling up of international schools was one of the entry point projects of the Economic Transformation Programme launched by the Performance Management and Delivery Unit (PEMANDU) of the Prime Minister's Department (PEMANDU 2010). Subsequent developments showed that there was a marked increase in the number of international schools, i.e. from sixty-three schools in 2010 to around ninety-seven schools in little more than three years (Hamilton 2014), surpassing the government's target of eighty-seven international schools by 2020. This impressive growth of international schools was also spurred by the decision of the government to abolish enrolment quota imposed on local students (Chi 2014). Alarmingly, non-Malays from the middle and upper strata of the society, in particular the Chinese, form the bulk of local students attending these international schools. Admittedly, such an enrolment trend has resulted in an ethnic divide within the Malaysian educational system. This ethnic divide will be widened if more non-Malays are to opt for these international schools. While the high fees charged by international schools used to deter many parents, especially those from the middle class, to enrol their children in these schools, they are now in an affordable position to enrol their children in these schools with the establishment of more mid- and lower-range international schools in recent years (Chi 2014).

From the foregoing, it is clear that efforts by the government to strengthen the proficiency of English among Malaysian students may be to the advantage of the non-Malays with serious repercussions to the nation-building process. The widening of ethnic divide within the Malaysian educational system is certainly a threat to the nation building process. What is more threatening is that this widening of ethnic divide will also lead to the widening of linguistic divide, which is straddled between a high-status (H) language (English) and a low-status (L) language (Malay). From the perspective of sociolinguistics, the H language is often associated with power and those who cannot master it are usually socially marginalized (Spolsky 1998; Shin 2013). In contrast, the L language is only useful in maintaining value as a marker of membership of a peer or ethnic group (Spolsky 1998). Undoubtedly, such a demarcation of linguistic boundaries that offers two different identities will not augur well for the nation-building process as far as "language socialization" (Bayley and Schecter 2003) in a plural society is concerned, more so when the local language is pitted against a global language as in the case of Malaysia. This widening of ethnic and linguistic divide may be at the expense of rural students who are deprived of a congenial environment to acquire English. Since Malay students constitute the bulk of rural students in Malaysia, this will heighten the ethnic dimension of this divide.

It is most unfortunate that the MBMMBI policy may not bring about a stable diglossic relationship between the Malay language and English, and with English gaining increased popularity among the non-Malays, this will create other problems that threaten the nation-building process of Malaysia. The most obvious problem will be in terms of job disparity along ethnic and linguistic lines between graduates from the public and private institutions of higher learning, especially in the private sector. Since graduates of the private institutions of higher learning use English as a medium of instruction, their proficiency in English is, therefore, generally better than graduates from the public institutions of higher learning. This linguistic advantage will no doubt give them better job opportunities and career advancement in the private sector. A report in the December 1991 issue of the *Far Eastern Economic Review* notes that especially in the private sector, the best jobs go to those who are fluent in English and compared to those who are less proficient in English, the former face less difficulties where promotions are concerned (Hafriza 2006). In other words, employers in the private sector tend to regard "language as a professional skill" (Sonntag 2009, p. 20) and more often than not, this justifies their differential treatment based on linguistic skills. This is clearly a case whereby "English opens doors for some, it closes them for others" (Phillipson 2009, pp. 97–98) — a form of structural inequality that favours those who have the required English proficiency. All in all, this job disparity along ethnic and linguistic lines can lead to serious political and socioeconomic consequences, which can destabilize a country (Gill 2002).

CONCLUSION

Bernard Spolsky notes that the spread of English is producing a new sociolinguistic reality by threatening to take over important functions from other major languages and by furthering the language shift. He also notes that the association of English with modern technology, with economic progress and with internationalization (one aspect of globalization) has encouraged people all over the world to learn English and to have their children learn it as early as possible (1998, p. 77). As far as Malaysia is concerned, the emergence of such a new sociolinguistic reality is particularly evident when English was introduced to teach science and mathematics in 2003 at the expense of the Malay language. It was precisely because of this threat that the government was forced to terminate the policy and replace it with the MBMMBI policy following intense opposition from the Malay nationalists who were determined to uphold the Malay language as the main thrust of the nation-building process. Clearly, the MBMMBI policy has engaged the Malay language in a diglossic relationship with English. However, this educational language policy, which is guided by the strategy of glocalization, may not be able to fend off the threat posed by English to the nation-building process. While the position of the Malay language within the official domain is secure, it is the strengthening of English that will pose a different kind of threat to the nation-building process.

As this chapter has argued, this strengthening of English may lead to more non-Malay students attending educational institutions that teach in English, especially the private institutions of higher learning and the international schools. Given that these educational institutions have already created an ethnic divide within the Malaysian educational system due to their predominantly non-Malay enrolments, it follows that increased non-Malay enrolments in these educational institutions will further widen the ethnic divide. Critically, this widening of ethnic divide will also result in the widening of linguistic divide. This widening of linguistic divide is most worrying as it is straddled between a high-status language and a low-status language with serious repercussions to the nation-building process. It is most unfortunate that the dualistic system of education within the Malaysian educational system has allowed the non-Malays to capitalize on their preference for English medium of instruction. Such an educational pathway benefits their career advancement in the private sector where employment requires a high degree of competence in English as compared to those who have gone through Malay medium of instruction.

In the final analysis, globalization and the global spread of English have a profound impact on the educational language policy in Malaysia with serious repercussion to the nation-building process. The favouring of English over the Malay language by the non-Malays in Malaysia is inevitable given the limited role of the Malay language within their socio-cultural domains and the strong instrumental value of English in the (globalized) private sector.

References

Abdul Rahman Embong. "Beyond the Crisis: The Paradox of the Malaysian Middle Class". In *Southeast Asian Middle Class: Prospects for Social Change and Democratisation*, edited by Abdul Rahman Embong, pp. 80–102. Bangi: Penerbit Universiti Kebangsaan Malaysia, 2001.

Ambigapathy, P. "English Language Education in Malaysia: Past, Present and Future". In *Literacy Matters: Issues for New Times*, edited by M. Kalantzis and P. Ambigapathy, pp. 67–80. Common Ground Publishing in association with Universiti Sains Malaysia, 2001.

Anderson-Levitt, K.M. "A World Culture of Schooling". In *Local Meanings, Global Schooling: Anthropology and World Culture Theory*, edited by K. Anderson-Levitt, pp. 1–26. New York: Palgrave Macmillan, 2003.

Asmah Hj. Omar *The Teaching of Bahasa Malaysia in the Context of National Language Planning*. Kuala Lumpur: Dewan Bahasa dan Pustaka, 1976.

――――. *Language and Society in Malaysia*. Kuala Lumpur: Dewan Bahasa dan Pustaka, 1993.

Baker, C. *A Parents' and Teachers' Guide to Bilingualism*. Clevedon: Multilingual Matters, 1995.

Bayley, R. and S.R. Schecter, eds. *Language Socialization in Bilingual and Multilingual Societies*. Clevedon: Multilingual Matters, 2003.

Blommaert, J. *The Sociolinguistics of Globalization*. Cambridge: Cambridge University Press, 2010.

Chi, Melissa. "As Doors to International Schools Open, Race to Snag Malaysian Students is On". *The Malay Mail Online*, 2014 <http://www.themalaymailonline.com> (accessed 15 May 2014).

Coulby, D. "Cultural Relativism and Cultural Imperialism in a Globalized Economy and Monopolar Polity". In *World Yearbook of Education 2005: Globalization and Nationalism in Education*, edited by David Coulby and Evie Zambeta, pp. 272–86. London and New York: RoutledgeFalmer, 2005.

Cummins, J. *Bilingualism and Special Education: Issues in Assessment and Pedagogy*. Clevedon: Multilingual Matters, 1984.

――――. *Language, Power and Pedagogy: Bilingual Children in the Crossfire*. Clevedon: Multilingual Matters, 2000.

d'Anglejan, A. "An Overview of Language-in-education Policy-Making". *Annual Review of Applied Linguistics*, edited by R. Kaplan, pp. 106–11. Rowley: Newbury House, 1982.

Federation of Malaya. *Report of the Education Committee 1956*. Kuala Lumpur: Government Press, 1956.

————. *Report of the Education Review Committee, 1960*. Kuala Lumpur: Government Press, 1960.

————. *Education Act, 1961*. Kuala Lumpur: Acting Government Printer, 1961.

Ghosh, B.N. *Malaysia: The Transformation Within — A Socioeconomic Perspective*. Petaling Jaya: Longman, 1998.

Gill, S.K. *International Communication: English Language Challenges for Malaysia*. Serdang: Universiti Putra Malaysia Press, 2002.

Hafriza Burhanudeen. "Science and Mathematics in English: Revisiting the Road Taken". *Education Quarterly* 38–39 (2006): 24.

Halim Salleh. "Globalization and the Challenges to Malay Nationalism as the Essence of Malaysian Nationalism". In *Nationalism and Globalization: East and West*, edited by Leo Suryadinata, pp. 132–74. Singapore: Institute of Southeast Asian Studies, 2000.

Hamilton, A. "Is it Time we Regulated our International Schools?". *The Edge Malaysia*, 7–13 April 2014 <http://www.fz.com/content/it-time-we-regulated-our-international-schools> (accessed 15 April 2014).

Haris bin Md. Jadi. "Ethnicity, Politics and Education: A Study in the Development of Malayan Education and its Policy Implementation Process". PhD dissertation, University of Keele, 1983.

Ibrahim Saad. *Pendidikan dan Politik di Malaysia* [Education and Politics in Malaysia]. Kuala Lumpur: Dewan Bahasa dan Pustaka, 1986.

Jiao Zong Tiaocha Yanjiu ji Zixunzu [UCSTA Survey, Research and Information Unit], ed. *Yinyu Jiao Shuli Kexing Ma*? [Can English be used to Teach Science and Mathematics?]. Kajang: UCSTA, 2007.

Kamwangamalu, K.K. "Multilingualism and Codeswitching in Education". In *Sociolinguistics and Language Education*, edited by N.H. Hornberger and S.L. McKay, pp. 116–42. Bristol: Multilingual Matters, 2010.

Kelman, H.C. "Language as an Aid and Barrier to Involvement in the National System". In *Can Language be Planned?* edited by J. Rubin and B.H. Jernudd, pp. 21–51. Hawai'i: University Press of Hawai'i, 1971.

Kementerian Pengajian Tinggi Malaysia [Ministry of Higher Education Malaysia]. *Perangkaan Sepintas Lalu Pengajian Tinggi Malaysia 2005* [Brief Statistics on Malaysian Higher Education 2005]. Putrajaya: Bahagian Perancangan dan Penyelidikan, Kementerian Pengajian Tinggi Malaysia, 2006.

Khoo Boo Teik "An Apex of Mediocrity? A Reflection on the State of Our Public Universities". In *Out of the Tempurung: Critical Essays on Malaysian Society*, edited by Fong Chin Wei and Yin Ee Kiong, pp. 148–85. Sydney: East West Publishing, 2008.

Kramsch, C. *Language and Culture*. Oxford: Oxford University Press, 1998.

Lambert, W.E. "Cognitive, Attitudinal and Social Consequences of Bilingualism". In
    Patterns of Bilingualism. Selected Paper from the RELC seminar on "Acquisition
    of Bilingual Ability and Patterns of Bilingualism with Special Reference to
    Southeast Asian Context", edited by E.A. Afendras, pp. 3–24. Singapore:
    Singapore University Press for SEAMEO Regional Language Centre, 1980.
Lee, N.N. Molly. *Private Higher Education in Malaysia*. Monograph Series No. 2/1999.
    Penang: School of Educational Studies, Universiti Sains Malaysia, 1999.
Lembaga Penyelidikan Undang-Undang [Legal Research Board]. *Akta Lembaga
    Akreditasi Negara 1996 (Akta 556) dan Peraturan-Peraturan* [National Accreditation
    Board Act 1996 (Act 556) and Regulations]. Kuala Lumpur: International Law
    Book Services, 2002.
Lim Kit Siang (2009). *Cabinet Decision on ETeMS [PPSMI]: A Raw Deal*. Petaling
    Jaya: Democratic Action Party.
Liu Yan and Guo Yingtao. "Which Way of Life? Chinese College Students'
    Perceptions and Values in China's Englishization". In *Englishization in Asia:
    Language and Cultural Issues*, edited by Kwok-kan Tam, pp. 140–61. Hong Kong:
    Open University of Hong Kong Press, 2013.
Malaysia. *Ninth Malaysia Plan 2006–2010*. Putrajaya: Economic Planning Unit, Prime
    Minister's Department, 2006.
May, S. *Language and Minority Rights: Ethnicity, Nationalism and the Politics of
    Language*. New York and London: Routledge, 2008.
Maznah Mohamad. "Bumiputera, Malays and Islam in the Politicization of the
    New Economic Policy". *Kajian Malaysia* 21, nos. 1 & 2 (2003): 163–76.
MDC Legal Advisers. *Education Act and Regulations* (all amendments up to January
    2005). Kuala Lumpur: MDC Publishers, 2005.
Ministry of Education Malaysia. *Education in Malaysia: A Journey of Excellence*.
    Putrajaya: Ministry of Education Malaysia, 2008.
———. *Malaysia Education Blueprint 2013–2025 (Preschool to Post-Secondary Education)*.
    Putrajaya: Ministry of Education Malaysia, 2013.
Nettle, D. and S. Romaine. *Vanishing Voice: The Extinction of the World's Languages*.
    Oxford: Oxford University Press, 2000.
New Sunday Times, 16 September 2007.
Performance Management and Delivery Unit (PEMANDU). *Economic Transformation
    Programme: A Roadmap for Malaysia*. Putrajaya: Prime Minister's Department,
    2010.
Phillipson, R. "The Tension between Linguistic Diversity and Dominant English".
    In *Social Justice through Multilingual Education*, edited by T. Skutnabb-Kangas,
    R. Phillipson, A.J. Mohanty and M. Panda, pp. 85–124. Bristol: Multilingual
    Matters, 2009.
Pua, Tony. *The Tiger that Lost its Roar: A Tale of Malaysia's Political Economy*. Kuala
    Lumpur: Democratic Action Party, 2010.

Rahimah Abdul Aziz. "New Economic Policy and the Malaysian Multiethnic Middle Class". *Asian Ethnicity* 13, no. 1 (2012): 29–46.

Rizvi, F. and B. Lingard. *Globalizing Education Policy*. London and New York: Routledge, 2010.

Roff, M. "The Politics of Language in Malaya". *Asian Survey* 7, no. 5 (1967): 316–28.

Romaine, S. *Bilingualism*, 2nd ed. Massachusetts: Blackwell, 1995.

Santhiram, R. and Tan Yao Sua. "The Transformation from Elitist to Mass Higher Education in Malaysia: Problems and Challenges". *Journal of Applied Research in Education* 13 (2009): 124–39.

Sato, M. *Dilemmas of Public University Reform in Malaysia*. Clayton: Monash University Press, 2007.

Shin, S.J. *Bilingualism in Schools and Society: Language, Identity and Policy*. New York and London: Routledge, 2013.

Sonntag, S.K. "Linguistic Globalization and the Call Center Industry: Imperialism, Hegemony and Cosmopolitanism?". *Language Policy* 8 (2009): 5–25.

Spolsky, B. *Sociolinguistics*. Oxford: Oxford University Press, 1998.

Stanley, G. and John C.K. Lee. "Future Educational Reform Policies and Measures". In *Changing Schools in an Era of Globalization*, edited by John C.K. Lee and B.J. Caldwell, pp. 181–97. New York and London: Routledge, 2011.

Stromquest, N.P. and K. Monkman. "Defining Globalization and Assessing its Implications on Knowledge and Education". In *Globalization and Education: Integration and Contestation across Culture*, edited by N.P. Stromquest and K. Monkman, pp. 3–25. New York: Rowman and Littlefield Publishers, 2000.

Tan Ai Mei. *Malaysian Private Higher Education: Globalisation, Privatisation, Transformation and Marketplaces*. London: ASEAN Academic Press, 2002.

Tan Liok Ee. "Chinese Independent Schools in West Malaysia: Varying responses to changing demands". In *Changing Identities of the Southeast Asian Chinese since World War II*, edited by J.W. Cushman and Wang Gungwu, pp. 61–74. Hong Kong: Hong Kong University Press, 1988.

———. *The Politics of Chinese Education in Malaya, 1945–1961*. Kuala Lumpur: Oxford University Press, 1997.

Tan Yao Sua and R. Santhiram. *The Education of Ethnic Minorities: The Case of the Malaysian Chinese*. Petaling Jaya: Strategic Information and Research Development Centre, 2010.

———. *Educational Issues in Multiethnic Malaysia*. Petaling Jaya: Strategic Information and Research Development Centre, 2014.

Tay Lian Soo. *Malaixiya Huawen Jiaoyu Fazhanshi* [The Historical Development of Chinese Education in Malaysia]. Vol. IV. Kuala Lumpur: UCSTA, 2003.

Tazreiter, C. and Tham, S.Y. "Globalization as Localized Experience, Adaptation and Resistance: An Introduction". In *Globalization and Social Transformation in the Asia-Pacific: The Australian and Malaysian Experience*, edited by C. Tazreiter and S.Y. Tham, pp. 1–11. Hampshire: Palgrave Macmillan, 2013.

Tollefson, J.W. and Amy B.M. Tsui. "Contexts of Medium-of-Instruction Policy". In *Medium of Instruction Policies: Which Agenda? Whose Agenda?*, edited by J.W. Tollefson and Amy B.M. Tsui, pp. 283–94. New Jersey: Lawrence Erlbaum Associates, 2004.

von Vorys, K. *Democracy without Consensus: Communalism and Political Stability in Malaysia*. Kuala Lumpur: Oxford University Press, 1976.

Watson, K. "Globalisation, Educational Reform and Language Policy in Transitional Society". In *Globalisation, Educational Transformation and Societies in Transition*, edited by T. Mebrahtu, M. Crossley and D. Johnson, pp. 41–67. United Kingdom: Symposium Book, 2000.

Wright, S. *Language Policy and Language Planning: From Nationalism to Globalisation*. New York: Palgrave Macmillan, 2004.

3

SECOND-ORDER CHANGE WITHOUT FIRST-ORDER CHANGE
A Case of Thai Internationalization of Higher Education

Pad Lavankura and Rattana Lao

INTRODUCTION

Internationalization of higher education has become a worldwide phenomenon that impacts education systems across contexts, countries and continents. The expansion of the internationalization process and its complexity is well illustrated in the evolution of academic attention paid to the definitions of internationalization. Arguably, the most acclaimed definition was given by Knight (1994) who defines it as the "process of integrating an international and intercultural dimension into the teaching, research and service functions of the institution" (p. 7). This working definition represents one of the first attempts to situate the internationalization process as a central part of every function of higher education institutions. Ten years on, the definition of internationalization of higher education was equated, to better include internationalization's varying idiosyncratic characteristics; as "the process of integrating an international, intercultural, or global dimension into the purpose, functions or delivery of post-secondary education" (Knight 2003, p. 2). Note the inclusion of the "global dimension" and the changing terminology from "institution" to "post-secondary education". This revised definition was intended to incorporate the growing diversity of the international process, which has indeed expanded in both its breadth and depth.

To understand the internationalization of higher education and its relationship to policy change, Van der Wende's (1996) framework is useful. According to him, the internationalization of higher education could be viewed as a "process of educational change" that comprises of first-order and second-order changes. The first-order changes mean "those [changes] that improve the effectiveness and efficiency of what is currently done", while the second-order changes alter the fundamental ways in which organizations are put together, including new goals, structures and roles. (Van der Wende 1996, p. 26) Internationalization of higher education can bring about both first-order and second order changes simultaneously. Examples of second-order changes include preparing students to join the international labour market, establishing special units to facilitate international cooperation and exchange, becoming partners in international alliances, and having performance assessed in accordance with international comparative perspectives (Van der Wende 1996, pp. 26–27, cited in Nilphan 2005, p. 39). Thus Van der Wende's definition of first-order and second-order change can help researchers assess and analyse the level of policy "success" that internationalization has brought about. Invariably, the definition must assume also the improvement of existing education and the introduction of new ideas to systems, institutions and individuals, and that those changes should bring about both short-term and long-term effects to the system (Van der Wende 1996, pp. 8–9).

Whether the first-order or second-order changes can occur depends fundamentally on the nature, structure and system of higher education in each context. This chapter will use the case of Thailand to analyse the different levels of policy change in relation to the internationalization of higher education. Similar to other Asian countries, the internationalization process has been a significant factor shaping the Thai higher education system. For the past twenty five years, since the term "internationalization" was first mentioned in the First Long-Range Plan of Thailand Higher Education in 1990, the country has undergone enormous transformation in the introduction, interpretation and implementation of this phenomenon. This is evident from the proliferation of international programmes and international students facilitated by the increasing numbers and types of Memorandums of Understanding (MOUs). To analyse and understand the trajectory of internationalization of higher education in Thailand and the different levels of policy changes that have occurred, this chapter will adopt a qualitative methodology using document analysis, semi-structured elite interviews and as well as participant observation in the national conferences on the internationalization of Thai higher education.

There are four parts to this chapter. The first part maps out the different key actors involved in the internationalization of Thai higher education namely; the state, the market and the academy. The second part traces the government policy rationales on this phenomenon while the third discusses the quantitative expansion of internationalization in terms of international programmes, international students and international agreements between Thailand and foreign countries and/or institutions. The last part discusses the levels of policy changes in Thailand.

TRIANGLE OF COORDINATION: ACTORS IN THAI HIGHER EDUCATION SECTOR

Following Clark's idea of the triangle of coordination, Nilphan (2005) and Lao (2012) identified the state, academic oligarchs, and the market as the three most important actors shaping education policy changes in Thailand. The state is represented mainly by the Ministry of University Affairs (MUA), which later became the Office of Higher Education Commission (OHEC) under the National Education Act in 2003. The "academic oligarchs" refer to members of the public and private universities. Due to the growing power of global forces and internal economic demands by the late 1980s, the market also became influential in Thai higher education. When the characteristics of Thai higher education changed over time, there was also a movement in the "triangle of coordination" from "state authority" to first the "academic oligarchs" and then to the "market" (Nilphan 2005). Thus while the state played a dominant role in Thai higher education between the 1900s and the 1970s, there was a shift in power from the state to academic oligarchs in the 1970s. From the late 1980s onwards, gradually the market became critically influential in Thai higher education both at the institutional and national levels.

Lao (2012) argued that in studies of Thai higher education two caveats are worth mentioning. Firstly, there is a close link between the state and academic oligarchs in public policymaking. The so-called "academic oligarchs", who are mostly administrators of higher education institutions, have also actively participated in state-level policymaking. In the case of Quality Assurance (QA), Lao (2012) revealed that the partnership between the state and academic oligarchs is also evident by their mutual views of the problems of and solutions to higher education. Their common policy beliefs come from their management perspectives which are mostly based on their scientific academic backgrounds. Secondly, however, there are different fractions and beliefs within the "academic oligarchs". The two major fractions are those academics who hold administrative positions and those who do not pursue the administrative track. While the former has allied themselves with state priorities and economic-centric preferences, the latter group is often the one who upholds academic interests.

STATE POLICY ON INTERNATIONALIZATION: RATIONALES AND REQUIREMENTS

This section traces the trajectory of internationalization policy as articulated in Thai state documents and analyses the changing rationales in relation to the international literature. There are different goals which internationalization of higher education intends to achieve. While some scholars strongly argued that internationalization can be the goal in itself (Zha 2003), Knight and De Wit (1999) pointed out that the major rationales that drive the internationalization process include social/cultural, political, academic, and economic (p. 174). Knight (2004) further argued that the rationales also differ at the national and institutional level. At the national level, the objectives include human resources development, commercial trade, and social/cultural development. In contrast, at the institutional level, there are more explicit rationales driving the process such as "academic standards, income generation, cultural diversity, and student and staff development", and the branding, profile and reputation of the institutions and knowledge production (ibid., pp. 20–21).

Although the rationales are differentiated at the national and institutional levels, the factors at play are not mutually exclusive. For example, with increasing attention given to international league tables and international organizations on quality assessment, both state and institutions are compelled to improve their international reputation in order to boost their reputations and rankings. At the same time, given the state declining financial support for higher education budgets, institutions are forced, with or without their consent, to generate more incomes by other means in order to survive. These rationales provide useful heuristic devices to analyse and understand the trajectory of internationalization of higher education in Thailand.

As the Thai policy elites became aware of the increasing importance of globalization, the latter has been used as the main rationale to justify the policy need for internationalization. Since the 1980s, Thailand's economic boom has created a fertile ground for the higher education sector to prepare for greater "international" dimensions in its structure and outlook. Phongpaichit and Baker (1998, p. 180) argued that in conjunction with Thai economic prosperity and the ever-expanding middle class, the terms "international" or "internationalization" became equated with the improvement of people's socio-economic status. Undoubtedly, this positive interpretation of economic globalization has shaped Thai education planning. Evidently, from the latter half of the 1980s onwards, "internationalization" was considered to be a "new catchword" and was seen as "a term guiding the future development of Thai higher education" as well as to "help Thailand realize her dreams of becoming a leading industrialized country in the region" (Nakornthap and Srisa-an, 1997, p. 164).

It was in the "Fifteen Years First Long-Range Plan on Higher Education" (hereinafter referred to as "Plan") that the term "internationalization of higher education" was first introduced in Thai policy texts. According to the Plan, the objectives of Thai higher education include "equity", "excellence", "efficiency" and "internationalization". Subsequently, the Plan identified four areas which have to be more "internationalized", that is: teaching, researching, academic services, and preservation of culture. In terms of "teaching", the Plan argued that Thai higher education needs to focus on providing international skills such as computer and information technology, management and communication. There should be more international programmes, more joint degree programmes between Thai and foreign universities, and more collaboration between Thai and foreign academics.

The Plan also encouraged more research collaboration between Thai and foreign academics and the exchange of researchers. It suggested that there should be greater academic services between Thai and foreign universities. Lastly, it recommended the establishment of Thai Studies in foreign universities (Ministry of University Affairs (MUA) 1990). Most importantly, the Plan articulated the need to establish international, regional and local networks amongst different higher education institutions in order to promote and facilitate academic exchanges and ensure that Thai students and academics acquire greater "global perspectives". Nilphan (2005) argued that "the discourse of 'global challenges' has become prevalent in the Thai bureaucracy; the MUA's long-term plan is peppered with such terms such as global awareness, economic competitiveness, international level competence and specific skills" (p. 107).

Since the First Long-Range Plan recognized the importance of "internationalization", the Seventh (1992–96), the Eighth (1997–2000) and the Ninth (2002–06) Higher Education Development Plans have also endorsed this as an important aspect of Thai higher education. Lao (2015) analysed these policy papers and highlighted the Thai state's aspiration to include and integrate "international" dimensions into the system. Particularly, in the Eighth Higher Education National Development Plan two policy objectives were outlined. In the first objective, the Thai state expressed its aspiration to make Thailand the educational hub of the Southeast Asian region. Given its geographical advantage, it was argued that Thailand is in a strategic position to become an educational hub. The Eighth Plan's second objective specified different strategies to upgrade Thai higher education to become more internationalized and regionalized. These strategies include the need to ensure that the quality of International Programmes in Thailand to be on par with international standards, enable credit transfers between Thai higher education and foreign institutions, and encourage collaborations between Thai and foreign academics. Furthermore, the Eighth Plan argued that it is necessary to equip Thai students to become "visionary" in order to survive in the global market place. To achieve this goal, it outlined six policy strategies: (1) establish more international programmes; (2) use foreign languages as medium of instruction; (3) develop more academic exchanges; (4) create the institutional environment conducive to become "international"; (5) create more Area Studies Centre to encourage more international and cultural understanding; and (6) use information technology in teaching (MUA 2003, p. 91).

While the MUA/Office of Higher Education Commission (OHEC) has reiterated the importance of the internationalization process, it has also provided policy requirements on what constitute international programmes. The MUA/OHEC thus imposed four conditions on the public universities as requirements to establish international programmes. These are:

- The proposed curriculum should already be part of the higher education development plan. If it is not, the university must consult the MUA in order to adjust it according to the plan.
- The proposed curriculum's structure and standards must be in accordance with the MUA's regulations.
- The proposed curriculum must be approved by the university council or institution council before taking effect.
- When the curriculum has been approved, the MUA must be informed within thirty days from the first day of approval. All documents related to the curriculum must be sent to the MUA in accordance with the MUA's regulations; the MUA will then process this document and forward it to the Office of Civil Service Commission (OCSC), which will consider and certify the qualifications of graduates from that curriculum accordingly (MUA 1995, p. 2).

Although these guidelines empower the MUA/OHEC to control the approval of international programmes, their implementation have left much flexibility and autonomy to the institution. The following sections will map out the quantitative expansion of international programmes in Thailand.

Twenty Five Years of Expansion: Analysing the Policy Change

This chapter argues that the internationalization of Thai higher education has brought about second-order changes, while bypassing first-order changes. It will illustrate that the expansion of international programmes, international students and international collaborations have proliferated in the past twenty-five years. Meanwhile, little, if at all, has changed in terms of educational effectiveness and efficiency. In fact, one can argue that the emergence of international programmes has hindered the effectiveness and efficiency of the existing Thai programmes because of the scarce supply of qualified professors and lecturers to handle increasing workloads. Due to excessive and increasing demands for international and English programmes, the Thai state and universities looked for changes at the second-order level, while ignoring the first-order changes. Thailand, as a developing country, has to be quick to "catch up with the West" such that Thai higher education pursues "new goals", "structures" and "roles" without concerning themselves with improving the existing content, and thereby creating short-term negative effects to the higher education system. The end result is that Thai higher education would experience only superficial level change without fundamentally altering the system.

QUANTITATIVE EXPANSION OF INTERNATIONALIZATION IN THAILAND

This section illustrates the quantitative expansion of internationalization of Thai higher education. Three types of issues are discussed: the expansion of international programmes, the proliferation of international students, and the increase in the number of Memorandums of Understanding (MOUs) between Thai and foreign institutions.

International Programmes

Over the past twenty-five years, the number of international programmes has increased considerably (see Figure 3.1).

While the first international programme began in the 1960, it was not until the mid-1990s that there has been a significant proliferation in Thai higher education. The MUA (2003) reported that there were approximately 100 international programmes in 1992: fifty-eight Bachelor's degree programmes, fifty-five Master's degree programmes and nineteen Doctoral programmes for public and private universities. Within a span of six years, the number of international programs in Thailand had doubled at all levels. While there were only 465 programmes in 2004, the number of programmes had increased to 1,027 as of 2012. Table 3.1 shows the growth of international programmes differentiated by degree.

The top ten institutions with the highest number of international students are Assumption University, Mahachulalongkorn University, Mahidol University, Ramkhamheang University, Durakijpundit University, Burapa University, Chulalongkorn University, Chiang Rai Rajabhat University, Khon Kean University and Thammasat University (Office of Higher Education Commission [OHEC] 2011b, p. 17). Lao (2015) argued that international programmes in Thailand reflects the institutional aspiration

FIGURE 3.1
Growth of International Programmes in Thailand, 1960–2012

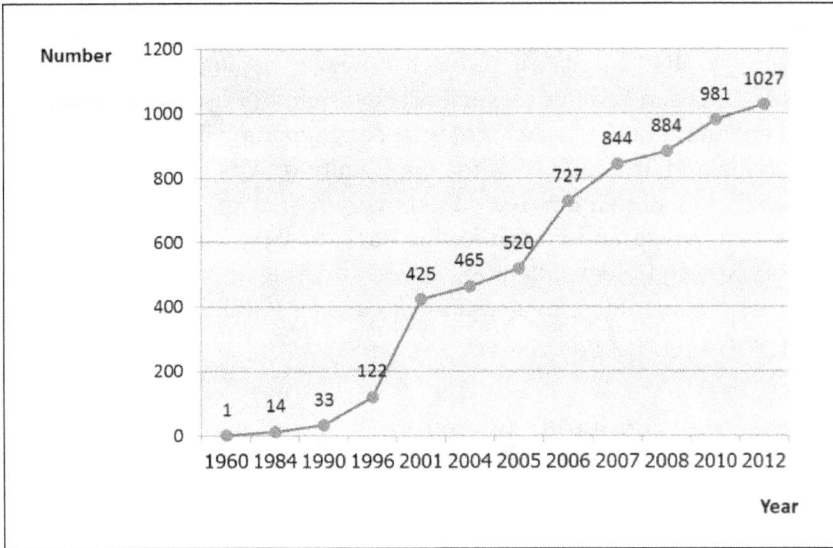

Source: Tong-In et al. (1995), pp. 28–32; Ministry of University Affairs (2003); Office of the Higher Education Commission (2011b); Lavankura (2013), p. 668; Office of Higher Education Commission (2013).

TABLE 3.1
Growth of International Programmes Differentiated by Degree

	2001	2004	2005	2006	2007	2008	2010	2012
Bachelor's	143	153	176	241	277	296	342	344
Master's	205	203	217	290	327	350	389	394
Doctoral	77	109	127	178	220	215	255	249
Others	N/A	0	0	18	20	23	25	30
Total	425	465	520	727	844	884	981	1,027

Source: Office of Higher Education Commission (2013); Office of Higher Education Commission (2014).

to specifically address the market demands, students' demography and Thailand's comparative advantages. As each public university gains greater institutional autonomy, there is a greater emphasis for faculties and universities to open international programmes in order to boost its income. According to Chalapati (2007), international programmes in Thailand mostly focus on the "sell well" programmes such as Business and Engineering. Although Business Administration and International Business remain the most popular international programmes with international students in Thailand, latest research however demonstrates a greater specialization and diversity of subjects. For example, Kasertsart University offers an international Bachelor of Science programme in Agro-Industrial Innovation and Technology, while the Faculty of Arts at Chulalongkorn University has started international courses in Thai Studies, Chinese as a Foreign Language, and French for the Business World. At the same time, there are more students attending courses on Thai language, Buddhism, and Thai Traditional and Alternative Medicines (OHEC 2011a; Sinhaneti 2011a, p. 372).

International Students

Similar trends can also be found in terms of the increase in the number of international students in Thailand. Since 2005, the OHEC has conducted surveys on international students in Thailand in selected public and private higher education institutions. In 2007, 96 institutions participated in the OHEC survey: 62 public institutions and 34 private institutions. In the 2008, 2009 and 2011 surveys, out of the 103 institutions which participated, 64 were public institutions and 39 were private institutions. The most recent data indicate that there is a total of 20,309 international students in Thai higher education.

A recent survey conducted showed that students from more than 130 countries are studying in Thailand; 41 Asian countries, 34 European countries, 10 North American countries, 33 African countries, 4 Australian/ Oceanian countries and 8 South American countries (OHEC 2011b). It is evident that the majority of students are from Asia. In 2011, students from China, Myanmar and Laos, the top three sender countries to international programmes in Thailand, accounted for 41.90 per cent, 7.35 per cent and 6.67 per cent of the total international students respectively (OHEC 2011b). Thailand is a popular destination for Asian students due to its lower educational costs, which are much less than going abroad to study in Europe, North America or Australia (Chalapati 2007). Even though the number of foreign students participating in Thai higher education has more than doubled from 8,543 to 20,309 between 2006 and 2011, the

Thai state aimed to increase the number of foreign students to 100,000 (Sinhaneti 2011).

Memorandums of Understandings (MOUs)

In addition to establishing international programmes, Thai public and private universities have also actively signed MOUs and created joint programmes with universities from various countries. Thai academics from public universities have boosted the institutional enthusiasm to sign MOUs with other foreign institutions:

> At the level of institutions, many universities have been proactive in attending conferences and exhibitions to recruit students and exchange ideas on the internationalization process. There have been extensive efforts to sign MOUs in order to integrate the international aspects into Thai higher education. We are trying to integrate foreign students into Thai higher education so that our classrooms are also comprised of international students. This is to create an international culture and allow our students to interact with other foreign students and also travel to other countries to explore new experiences (Interview, 9 April 2014).

According to a survey conducted by the OHEC (2011), 46 public universities in Thailand have signed a total of 2,171 MOUs, and 18 private universities have signed 363 MOUs. In total, Thai institutions have 2,534 MOUs with other countries. It is worth noting that the majority of MOUs are signed between Thai public and private institutions with other institutions within Asia, which accounted for 52.24 per cent of the total MOUs signed. This indicates that internationalization in Thailand is closely linked to the regionalization process. A closer scrutiny shows that Japan, China, the United States, France and Australia are the countries that Thailand has signed the most MOUs with. In terms of field of studies, official data show that the five top fields of collaboration between Thai and foreign institutions are: (1) Language, Culture, Literature and Linguistics (91 MOUs); (2) Engineering (70 MOUs); (3) Business Administration (58 MOUs); (4) Science (39 MOUs); and (5) Economics (30 MOUs). Public universities which have signed the most MOUs with other countries are Kasetsart University (295 MOUs), Thammasat University (259 MOUs) and Mahidol University (233 MOUs). For private universities, Assumption University (138 MOUs), Bangkok University (68 MOUs) and Payap

University (40 MOUs) are the top three universities which have signed the most MOUs with other countries.

Although Thai public and private universities have signed multiple MOUs with various countries and institutions, there are several problems regarding the implementation and success of the agreements. For example, there are limited financial resources allocated to promote the activities and exchanges agreed on in the MOUs, there is a lack of clear policy strategy to fulfil the agreements, and the discrepancy of academic schedules make it problematic to encourage student exchange. An academic in a Thai public university pointed out the discrepancy between MOU on paper and in practice: "we have multiple international co-operations. The university and the faculty have signed a lot of agreements and MOUs but we do not see the implementation results or the encouragement for faculty members to utilize them" (Interview, 2 July 2014).

SECOND-ORDER CHANGES WITHOUT FIRST-ORDER CHANGES: QUESTIONS ON QUALITY

The previous section offers an insight into the quantitative expansion of the internationalization of Thai higher education in terms of international programmes, international students and the MOUs, which illustrate that the second-order changes have occurred. This section analyses whether there has been first-order changes to Thai higher education. While "special units to facilitate international cooperation and exchange" (Van der Wende 1996, pp. 26–27, cited in Nilphan 2005, p. 39) have been established, deeper integration of the internationalization processes such as the international cadre of lecturers and international curriculums are still lacking in Thai higher education. When considering the international programmes, Van der Wende (1996, p. 18) found that the international content of the curricula and teaching methods need to be taken into consideration. He further proposed that the "content of the curriculum" is more important than the "method of instruction"; a curriculum taught abroad, or by a foreign guest lecturer, or delivered in a foreign language, or whose students have attended some courses abroad are not automatically perceived as being internationalized.

In Thailand, the MUA has attempted to promote international programmes since the seventh higher education plan (1992–96). Such encouragement together with the external and internal socio-economic demands led to the rising number of international programmes in quantitative terms. For a while, the MUA was undecided on what the "international programme" in Thailand should look like. This reflects the classic problem of Thai state's higher education policymakers who want to move the sector towards global trends and meet the growing needs of the business sectors by promoting the establishment of new programmes, but they have no clear mechanism to balance the quantity growth with the quality dimension.

In 1999, the MUA published a guideline booklet for universities on "international and foreign language programmes provision". In that booklet, it divided the term "international programme" into two main categories: the first was the "international studies programme" which focused on the economics, culture and politics of different countries and the second was the "international programme". The second category is the programme that covers all disciplines, not limited only to specific international subjects in the social science area. For the second category, the MUA further defined them to be:

- curricula which are open to both domestic and foreign students;
- curricula with international content;
- curricula in which lecturers have experience in the subject and excellent capability in the language of instruction;
- curricula in which supporting facilities such as textbooks, and information technology should be up to date, allowing students to enjoy maximum benefits;
- curricula incorporating academic activities designed to promote the international dimension such as student and lecturer exchange programmes, cross-cultural activities and international cooperation with foreign institutions;
- curricula which include academic cooperation with foreign institutions (MUA 1999).

The above list shows the objectives of the Thai state regarding international programmes. However, it is difficult to make all international programmes in Thai universities to strictly abide by the above objectives. This is because along with the above objectives, the MUA also defined the term "foreign language programme" as "a programme using any foreign language as a medium of instruction". As such, the latter programme definition is not linked to "curricula with international content" or integration of international dimensions into the "teaching methods". Thus this provided the loophole for institutions to establish either "international programme" or foreign language programme. In most cases, Thai universities chose to employ English as the language of instruction for both programmes.

In principle, "international programme" should denote programmes that pay particular attention to the "international content of the curricula" and "teaching methods", and "foreign language programme", meaning in practice "English programme", to designate programmes that use English, or other foreign language, as the medium of instruction without paying particular attention to the curricula and teaching methods. However, due to MUA's unclear and inefficient position, acting only as a "point of acknowledgement" for universities, Thai universities have opted to define their programmes as "international programme", rather than just "English programme". Based on research with Thai policymakers, it is evident that a majority of the so-called international programmes in Thailand would be better characterized as "English programme". While the Office of Higher Education Commission casted doubt to the extent in which these programmes are "international", little research and evaluation has been done to assess this (Nilphan 2005, pp. 143–44).

Generally then, Thai universities commonly use English language as the language of instruction for their international programmes. In these programmes, the universities have tried to bring in foreign lecturers and students to create the international environment. The universities have also promoted the academic activities by pursuing students' exchange programmes, cross-cultural activities, and signing MOUs to collaborate with foreign institutions. These attempts have been seen as positive changes to further develop international programmes in Thailand. However, driven by market forces, there are certain aspects that have not changed. Many Thai universities are overwhelmed with the quantitative demands and the growing need of the market for "international programmes". As such, international programmes' development and quality have been compromised. With regards to Thai universities' international programmes, each programme has its own system of managing the teaching methods, depending on the way the programmes are administered and the nature of the universities.

Regarding lecturers, some universities tend to employ Thai lecturers who graduated from foreign universities to teach while others chose to employ foreign lecturers. In a university which employs foreign lecturers, its programme administrator explained:

> We use *"farang"* lecturers because although we were offering the same programmes as other universities, they use mostly Thai lecturers. So we wanted to create an image for our programme, and *farang* lecturers could increase the popularity of our programme. If we had used Thai lecturers like the others, there would have been no reason for students to come to us. (Interview)

The interview makes it clear that the university employed Western lecturers as an important part of its marketing strategy to attract Thai students. To many Thai students, it is important to be taught by Western lecturers whose mother tongue is English. This is because the perception among Thai students and society in general is that "international programmes" function as a means to improve the students' mastery of the English language, and secondly to introduce Western culture. Interviews with Thai students who studied in international programmes indicate that they prefer *farang* professors to Thai or other Asian professors as the former can provide better English or Western examples, and allow more open discussions in the classroom. They outwardly equate being *foreigners* with being *Westerners*. Amongst the other factors, American or European accents are preferable compared to the Thai accent. The interviews elucidate that the students' perception of their international programmes depend largely on the presence of *farang* academics in their educational experiences.

Thus there is a strong cultural preference, or bias, in favour of lecturers from Europe and North America whose mother tongue is English for reasons of accent and intonation. That English is valued as the premium language is reiterated by an American lecturer in an international programme from a Thai public university who said: "I think the most important benefit of this programme is the English language. Students speak and write better after they have graduated from us". Students' preference for European and American lecturers are also reflected in the composition of academic staff in the international programmes.

Table 3.2 shows the number of foreign and Thai lecturers in a Bachelor of Business Administration (international programme) in a college during the first semester of the 2014 academic year. The college has thirty-seven lecturers for the semester out of which thirty-one are foreign lecturers. The majority of foreign lecturers are adjunct or invited lecturers who teaches

TABLE 3.2
Number of Foreign and Thai Lecturers in Business Administration

Number of Thai lecturers	Number of foreign lecturers	Total
6	31	37
(5 are adjunct or invited from other faculties, universities; 1 full-time lecturer hired by the college)	(5 are adjunct lecturers and 26 are invited lecturers from Europe (10), USA (8), other Thai universities (3), China (1), and others (4)	

Source: Statistics from an international college, semester 1, 2014 academic year.

on a short-term basis. There is only one full-time Thai lecturer. Most of the lecturers teach one or two courses at the college on a part-time basis, and the quality and commitment of the lecturers fluctuate. This has enormous repercussion in terms of the quality of education as this way of hiring teachers creates deficiencies in the quality of teaching. The problem of part-time teachers in international programmes arises from two factors. On the one hand, international programmes are such that they would not attract full-time lecturers who would commit to teach and research. On the other hand, there is a high demand among Thai lecturers who need to earn extra income through extra teaching. Given such a scenario, it is questionable how one can control the quality of international education in Thailand.

Also, in Thailand the international programmes are largely Western oriented, which essentially followed the long-established value and reliance of Thai education on Western education since the early modernization period (Dhiravegin 1978, p. 120; Osatharom 1990, p. 252; Sivaraksa 1991, p. 51). However, to hire lecturers from the preferred developed countries is costly. This leads to universities choosing not to hire foreign lecturers on a full-time basis. For example, for an undergraduate course the university has to spend about 81,600 baht (1,700 baht × 6 hours × 8 days) per lecturer per one course, plus other supplementary costs such as accommodation (20,000 baht for more than 22 days stay), air ticket, and in-country travel expenses. Because of the policy of hiring mostly part-time foreign lecturers, programmes are organized around a system of "block courses" where every subject is allocated a strict timetable. Instead of learning seven different subjects per semester as in a normal university programme, students in international programme take two subjects per month; each subject is taught for two days per week, and six hours per day. Exams are taken at the end of each month. Under this system, the institute is able to save costs by employing lecturers only for about a one-month period after which they return home (Interview, 10 April 2014).

An analysis of the scheduling of classes shows that some lecturers invited to teach a subject in the BBA programme (for example, Basic Mathematics) are normally also invited to teach another subject (for example, Calculus for Business 1). Thus during the 22 to 30 days of the lecturer's stay in Thailand, he has to teach at least 16 days from 9.00 a.m. to 4.00 p.m. One lecturer interviewed mentions that some lecturers invited for the BBA programme will also teach in the MBA or PhD programmes, mainly to save on the costs of accommodation and airfares (Interview, 10 April 2014). This arrangement means that lecturers have to teach on both weekdays and weekends because the MBA and PhD courses are taught on Saturdays and Sundays for six hours each day. The practice of employing Western lecturers to teach several courses over an intensive working period of one month shows that the methods of managing the programme are largely determined by costs considerations.

In addition to the high costs of hiring foreign academics, there is also the problem of quality control. The programmes' costs considerations prevented the establishment of an effective procedure to select high-quality and committed lecturers. The lack of a proper selection and employment system makes it difficult to find committed lecturers who are willing to stay for an extended period of time. The majority of foreign lecturers only come to Thailand for a short period. As a result, intensive classes are given for a few weekends and compromise the quality of education. The quality also differs substantially amongst foreign academics. While some require extensive reading, others barely cover the essentials. Different strategy is needed to attract foreign lecturers to stay in the country for a longer time frame in order to acclimatize with the academic environment and the need of students.

Since applicants were attracted by the short-term benefits rather than academic benefits, there were many who submit false educational qualifications and teaching experiences. Some foreigners only have working experience in the private sector or with training companies and so they falsify their academic credentials. Meanwhile poor commitment from many lecturers is also an issue. A strong commitment to academic excellence is rare among foreign lecturers because they are not hired based on academic reasons or through exchange programmes, nor are they given full-time positions that would make them feel as part of the university. This marginalized selection and employment process make it difficult to ensure the quality of foreign lecturers (Van der Wende 1996, p. 139).

Indeed, a limited number of full-time lecturers could hinder universities from strengthening their areas of expertise. Adjunct lecturers or guest lecturers have limited rights to access research grants and to proper office spaces. Although a number of MOUs have been signed over the past decade, their actual implementation have been limited to the exchange of students between home and host institutions. The opportunities for Thai universities to exchange academic materials, publications, and faculty members, or to conduct joint research activities and organize symposiums have not been enlarged. Having no adequate full-time lecturers of their own prevented fundamental changes in quality of the programmes. In fact, even though one of the ultimate aims of international programmes is to develop the quality of lecturers in Thailand, there is only ad hoc teaching and learning process since universities are mainly concerned with increasing their incomes.

As far as teaching methods in Thai international programmes are concerned, we have witnessed certain changes, mainly in respond to the market demands and adjustment to international trends. Changes are still at a very superficial level and universities are still struggling to introduce fundamental changes. The system of organizing teaching methods used in universities continues to impede integration and fundamental changes. While students gained limited qualities, they would still adhere to the cultural value of "West is best". What students in international programmes get that their counterparts in normal Thai programmes do not get are foreign lecturers and textbooks, English as the medium of instruction, and some opportunities to spend a semester abroad. However, currently such changes are not enough for the internationalization of higher education in global terms.

The premium being placed on English as the medium of instruction and foreign teachers makes it questionable whether the internationalization process in Thailand is in fact "international". International programmes in Thailand are simply English programmes, which translate the Thai curriculum into English without adding any particular international elements (Chalapati 2007, p. 10). Recently, there was a controversial case involving a Thai public university attempt to create a "bilingual" programme for dentistry. This case brought the question of "international" and "English" programme to the forefront of the debate. While the annual tuition fee for the Thai programme is around 44,000 baht, the fee for the bilingual programme is almost 1.2 million baht. In a meeting between faculty members and student representatives, advocates of the bilingual programme openly admitted that the reason for creating the new bilingual programme is because "the Faculty needs to generate extra income" (Interview, 5 October 2014). Although the administrator has strongly supported the bilingual programme to gain extra income, the plan was controversial and contested by students and academics in the faculty because the curriculum for the two programmes were almost identical. The difference between the two was in the language of instruction such that faculty members had to teach the same subject twice, in English and in Thai. In fact, a student representative argued that the language of instruction should not be used as the selling point of the lucrative bilingual programme:

> because the subjects we are studying are comprised of technical terms, which are mostly in English, it does not make sense to have a bilingual programme. The content of our lecture is in English anyway. Of course you cut out the Thai word at the end of each sentence (Interview, 5 October 2014).

The argument on justice, quality and effectiveness has been put forward by the group resisting the higher costs for the bilingual programme. Firstly, it is unfair for students in the bilingual programme to pay so much more for the title of "bilingual programme", while all the curriculum is similar to that of the Thai programme. Secondly, there are issues of quality education and its effectiveness. Ultimately, lecturers have to teach the same subject twice, which increases their workloads and would affect the existing "Thai programme". Nevertheless, the fact that there are students who are willing to pay so much more reflect the growing market demands for anything "international" and anything "English" without questioning the link between that and the quality of education.

This case is also reflective of the weak state capacity to ensure the quality of international programmes. Currently, although the OHEC has not approved this bilingual dentistry programme, its advocates are using the legal loophole to establish the programme. Given that the state has delegated greater autonomy to each institution, the advocates of this bilingual dentistry programme argued that it is the same curriculum as the already approved Thai programme except that it is taught in a different language. Therefore, they do not see the need to request state approval again.

FUTURE DIRECTION AND POLICY DILEMMA

There are several issues facing the internationalization of Thai higher education, especially with regards to question of the quality of higher education itself. Firstly, there is the issue of *economic vis-à-vis academic* rationales driving the internationalization of Thai higher education. Overtly, it is admitted that the Thai internationalization agenda is driven by market rationale both at the national and institutional levels. At the national level, the Thai state has a strong aspiration to "catch up" with the global economy. Therefore, the rhetoric and rationale to push for internationalization of higher education is to equip Thai students to be ready to join the global workforce and/or to create a qualified Thai workforce that is competitive at the global markets. At the institutional level, interviews with administrators and academics confirm that the lucrative tuition fee generated by international programmes is the most important incentive driving the expansion of international programmes in Thailand. This economic incentive has driven the establishment and expansion of international programmes in Thailand, which has resulted in all the "new" and looking good for all Thais. This illustrates that second-order change has occurred and by-passed the first-order change on effectiveness and efficiency.

Secondly, the issue of *state authority vis-à-vis institutional autonomy* presents another challenge for the internationalization of Thai higher education. The MUA/OHEC official stance is that, given the current circumstances, the best way to support the international programmes is to grant the universities flexibility in accordance with the 1992 deregulation process. An MUA/OHEC officer claimed that the elusiveness of international programmes is a direct result from the state's laissez-faire approach to policymaking. Since the state has delegated most of the responsibility to approve curriculums to the university council, it empowered institutions greater autonomy to decide and design their curriculum:

> The success of both internationalization and the international programmes that we can see now is a result of the MUA's "laissez-faire" policy. It's true that we don't treat them seriously, and don't take strategic action, but what

we can do is to provide support and give universities a certain flexibility in curriculum terms. For example, if a university has a curriculum that is used in its Thai programmes and wants to change it to English, it can do it right away without waiting for approval. More than that, we allow the university council to approve it; the curriculum doesn't need to accord with the plan as long as the demands are clear; and when the university council has approved it, that programme can be taught and the university can inform the MUA later. (Interview, MUA administrator cited in Niphan 2005).

On the other hand, the officer also asserts that the "success" of the policy is due to the laissez-faire approach of the state.

However, the lack of a clear "product control" criteria and procedure would carry a risk in qualitative terms as the MUA/OHEC has provided universities with a loophole where they can simply rebadged their Thai programmes as "international" programmes. Thus when state authority is transferred to institutions, universities may use their institutional autonomy to establish more "international" and "English" programmes. The case of the dentistry programme provides an interesting insight to the new configuration of power between state and academic oligarchs. The academic group resisting against the bilingual programme shows the possibility of quality control if and only if the academic group is strong enough to push academic incentive over economic-driven rationale

There is also another debate regarding the *international vis-à-vis Thai lecturers*. Because students in international programmes prefer foreign, preferably European and American, lecturers, there is a shortage of qualified foreign academics in Thailand. In part this is due to the low salary given by Thai institutions, poor working conditions, and, above all, the lack of academic incentive to build international programmes to attract better-quality foreign academics in the first place. This situation has led to a less than perfect scenario. Should the international programmes in Thailand welcome foreign lecturers despite their lack of academic qualification? Alternatively, should Thailand focus on recruiting qualified Thai academics with international experiences to teach? The debate is not as easy as one between "accent" vis-à-vis "content". The use of Thai academics in international programmes also has a negative repercussion on the quality of existing education in Thai programmes. This debate is succinctly captured by McBride (2012) whose interviews with Thai policy elites highlighted the quality aspect of the international partnerships: "they are talking in terms of quantity more than quality. Definitely to be, to grow a programme, they have some criteria but we haven't really highlighted the quality of students as such as the quality of scholars" (p. 137). This chapter argues that while internationalization of higher education has taken place in Thailand, the quantitative expansion has not resulted in raising the quality of the overall education. Internationalization, in Thailand, has been translated to simply the creation of international programmes. Meanwhile, its quality is narrowly defined by the presence of Western lecturers. To meet the increasing demand for internationalization, the second-order change has materialized in terms of the creation of new programmes, new offices and new campuses. However, little has happened in terms of the effectiveness and efficiency of the existing programmes as the proliferation of international programmes is faced with a dearth of qualified academics willing to take up full-time positions and have significant educational impacts. The problem of quality is coupled with the limited and weak state capacity to ensure quality education to students. Because the market incentive has trumped the academic rationale at the national and institutional levels, the only hope to ensure the quality of international programmes in Thailand is to generate greater awareness amongst the academics of the need to push for quality education.

References

Chalapati, S. "The internationalisation of higher education in Thailand: Case studies of two English-medium business graduate programs". Doctoral dissertation, RMIT University, Australia, 2007.

Dhiravegin, Likhit. *The Bureaucratic Elite of Thailand: A study of their sociological attributes, educational backgrounds and career advancement pattern.* Bangkok: Wacharin Press, 1978.

Knight, J. *Internationalisation: Elements and checkpoints.* Research monograph No. 7. Ottawa: Canadian Bureau for International Education, 1994.

———. "Updated internationalisation definition". *International Higher Education* 33 (2003): 2–3.

———. "Internationalisation remodeled: Definition, approaches, and rationales". *Journal of Studies in International Education* 8, no. 1 (2004): 5–31.

Knight, Jane and Hans De Wit. "Reflections on Using IQRP". In *Quality and Internationalisation in Higher Education: Programme on Institution Management in Higher Education*, edited by Organisation for Economic Co-operation and Development. Paris: Organisation for Economic Co-operation and Development, 1999.

Lao, R. "The Logic of the Thai Higher Education Sector and Quality Assessment". Doctoral dissertation, Columbia University, New York, 2012.

———. *A critical study of Thailand's higher education reforms: The culture of borrowing.* New York: Routledge, 2015.

Lavankura, Pad. "Internationalizing Higher Education in Thailand: Government and University Responses". *Journal of Studies in International Education* 17, no. 5 (2013): 663–76.

Mcbride, K.A. "Thai perspectives on the internationalisation of higher education in Thailand: A mixed methods analysis and three mini-case studies". Doctoral dissertation, University of Minnesota, Minnesota, 2012.

Ministry of University Affairs. *Summary of the Long-Range Higher Education Plan 1990–2004.* Bangkok: Ministry of University Affairs, 1990.

———. *The Evaluation on Curriculum Implementation of Thai Public Universities after the Deregulation of the Ministry of University Affairs.* Bangkok: Bureau of Higher Education Standards, Ministry of University Affairs, 1995.

———. *Principles of International and Foreign Language Programmes Provision for Private Higher Education Institutions.* Bangkok: Ministry of University Affairs, 1999.

———. *International Programs in Thailand.* Bangkok: Parb-Pim Limited Partnership, 2003.

Nakornthap, A. and W. Srisa-an. "Internationalisation of Higher Education in Thailand". In *Internationalisation of Higher Education in Asia Pacific Countries*, edited by J. Knight and H. De Wit, pp. 161–70, Amsterdam: Luna Negra, 1997.

Nilphan, P. "Internationalising Thai higher education: Examining policy implementation". Doctoral dissertation, University of Leeds, United Kingdom, 2005.

Office of the Higher Education Commission. *Study in Thailand 2010.* Bangkok: Bangkok Block Ltd., 2011*a*.

———. *Foreign students in Thai higher education institutions 201.* Bangkok: Office of Higher Education Commission, 2011*b*.

———. *Foreign students in Thai higher education in 2011.* Bangkok: Office of Higher Education Commission, 2013.

———. 2014 <Inter.mua.go.th/main2/files/image/Figures/fig_prog_chart3.png> (access 23 March 2014).

Osatharom, V. *Analytical study of the historical policy development of higher education in Thailand: Its implications for current development and future trends.* Bangkok: Ministry of University Affairs, 1990.

Phongpaichit, P. and C. Baker. *Thailand's Boom and Bust.* Chiang Mai: Silkworm Books, 1998.

Sinhaneti, K. "Emerging trends of Thai higher education and a case study of

Shinawatra University in coping with global challenges". *US-China Education Review* 3 (2011): 370–81.

Sivaraksa, S. "The Crisis of Siamese Identity". In *National Identity and its Defenders: Thailand 1939–1989*, edited by C.J. Reynolds. Chiang Mai: Silkworm Books, 1991.

Tong-In, W. et al. *Internationalisation of Thai Higher Education*. Bangkok: Ministry of University Affairs, 1995.

Van der Wende, M.C. *Internationalising the Curriculum in Dutch Higher Education: An international comparative perspective*. Hague: Nuffic, 1996.

Zha Q. "Internationalisation of Higher Education: towards a conceptual framework". *Policy Futures in Education* 1, no. 2 (2003).

4

HIGHER EDUCATION IN MALAYSIA
Access, Equity and Quality

Hena Mukherjee, Jasbir S. Singh, Rozilini M.
Fernandez-Chung and T. Marimuthu

BACKGROUND

Since independence in 1957, Malaysia has transformed itself from an
agrarian to an increasingly industrial and globalized economy. Malaysia
was formed in 1963 comprising Malaya, Sabah, Sarawak and Singapore,
with the last leaving the group in 1965. In the country of 30-odd million,
62.1 per cent are Malays and other indigenous groups, 21.8 per cent
Chinese, 6.5 per cent Indians and 9.6 per cent Others (includes 8.7 per
cent non-citizens). Malaya and Singapore were served by the University of
Malaya (UM), located in Singapore, until 1957 when a branch campus was
established in Kuala Lumpur. In 1962, it split into two entities, University
of Malaya and University of Singapore, as befits the two sovereign states.

Formal steps were taken post-independence to develop higher education
institutions to provide the high-level skills that the industrializing nation
required. These aspirations took particular shape after the civil disturbances
of 1969. Higher education in Malaysia expanded exponentially over the last
four decades with dramatic improvement in access to public and private

higher education institutions (HEIs). The factors contributing to increased access were primarily high secondary enrolment and completion, building on democratization and universalization of the system; an increasingly diversified institutional pattern of universities, colleges, polytechnics and community colleges catering to various levels of achievement; a burgeoning private higher education sector as a result of liberalization policies; and a combination of public and private sources in the financing of HEIs.

This chapter examines current higher education policies and implementation in Malaysia, understanding their historical antecedents in relation to higher education access, equity and quality issues. The issues are analysed within the overall context of the need for well-qualified and highly skilled graduate participation in an increasingly globalized knowledge-based economy with the goal of reaching high income status as envisioned by Vision 2020 (Mohamad 1991). The key challenge is human capital growth. Underlying the discussion is the question: which policies and actions have worked, and which need to be reviewed and adjusted to ensure that the nation's talent pool will match the demands of a high income, knowledge economy?

METHODOLOGY AND DATA

The study draws heavily on government documentation issued by the Ministry of Education (MOE), the Ministry of Higher Education (MOHE), and the Department of Statistics, particularly its Census Reports and Labour Force Surveys. Data provided by officials and politicians to the press have been included.

Lack of data or incomplete data relevant to the issues investigated by the study dogged the researchers. Data collection processes proved to be complicated by the fact that official data put out in the Malaysia Development Plans or by MOE and MOHE are not presented in a consistent format from year to year, rendering comparisons and analysis over time extremely difficult. Many of these inconsistencies result from the varying definitions of categories used by MOE and MOHE and agencies responsible for collecting data. Data may be presented in different ways, with raw data alternating with percentages. Selection of data to be presented is also not consistent: in 2012, unlike previous years, MOHE published data only on the public HEIs and none on the private HEIs, preventing comparisons over time between the two sectors.

Data disaggregated by ethnicity for intake, enrolment, graduands and award of scholarships are not available in the public domain. Ethnic data, considered sensitive, have not been published since 1985 in the five-year Malaysia Development Plans confounding efforts to analyse the advancement of equity in access to higher education. Data for this area have to be gleaned from sources such as an occasional announcement in Parliament or data from political parties. In many instances researchers are left with using proxy data arising from sources such as the Labour Force Surveys which record employment of graduates and attainment of highest qualifications by ethnicity.

HIGHER EDUCATION POLICY FRAMEWORK

The 1969 civil unrest in Malaysia, partly the result of dissatisfaction among the Malays with their progress in the education and economic sectors, brought about sweeping policy changes. It saw the launch of the New Economic Policy (NEP) which was designed to achieve in twenty years a more equitable society through the eradication of poverty and the restructuring of social divisions thereby eliminating the identification of economic participation with ethnicity (Malaysia 1971). Education was identified as the instrument to reduce the gaps in opportunities and expand access to all levels of education particularly for the Malays and other indigenous people, referred to as *Bumiputras*, who were educationally disadvantaged, compared to other ethnic groups.

Affirmative action policies followed to ensure greater access to education and employment. These included preferential mechanisms such as an ethnic-based university admissions quota, provision of scholarships held in local and foreign universities, Malay-only residential colleges, junior science colleges, training programmes, the establishment of the Yayasan MARA (MARA Foundation) and Universiti Teknologi MARA (UiTM). It should be noted that some government support also had been made available to two community-based HEIs, one Chinese and the other Indian. The National University of Malaysia (Universiti Kebangsaan Malaysia or UKM) was established to promote the use of the national language, and four more universities were established in the 1970s to meet the demand for higher education. Malaysia's affirmative action and redistributive policies were widely seen as successful in reducing poverty and creating a prosperous, multiethnic society in the 1980s and 1990s while building a strong middle class among *Bumiputras*. Implementation of NEP policies has continued after the twenty-year period until the present time under other nomenclature such as the New Development Policy.

In 2010, the New Economic Model (NEM 2010) pledged to revise and transform affirmative action policies, promising to uplift the quality of life of the low-income 40 per cent, regardless of ethnicity, in moving towards a high-income, inclusive and sustainable economy. The document identified Malaysia's economic structural woes with affirmative action policies, which had proved to be inefficient, unjust and too entrenched in the system to be mended. The lack of talented and qualified human resources was highlighted, noting large numbers of well-qualified, non-*Bumiputra* Malaysians leaving for non-discriminatory, more financially and socially attractive environments in developed countries. Major policy initiatives have not followed the presentation of the NEM and in fact the NEM goal of inclusiveness has been diluted. In less than two years, the Prime Minister announced on 14 September 2013, the Bumiputra Economic Empowerment Plan (BEEP), promising a new RM31 billion package of support to *Bumiputras* with human capital growth as one of the focal areas. There was no reference to the nation's need to invest in talent wherever the source, a significant departure from the recommendations in the NEM.

Underlying higher education policymaking is Malaysia's Vision 2020's goal of becoming a developed, high-income economy by 2020 with a per capita gross national income (GNI) of US$15,000, which is above the World Bank's definition of US$12,745 (RM40,800) as high income. The current per capita GNI is US$10,060 and, anticipating investment to reach RM444 billion by 2020, the plan is to create 3.3 million jobs by the target year. The Prime Minister's Department states that investment currently stands at RM219.3 billion and economic growth in Malaysia is on track (*Starbiz* 2014), a statement supported by the World Bank (World Bank 2014).

ACCESS TO HIGHER EDUCATION

Significant improvement in access to all education levels took place in Malaysia between 1985 and 2008, particularly at the higher education level. Higher education participation, especially among ethnic groups, women, and those from less developed geographical regions, had increased in step with the growing economy. While enrolments in primary level education had grown modestly at an annual rate of 1.9 per cent and at secondary level at 3.7 per cent, tertiary education enrolment had increased by 58.2 per cent annually, recording an increase in enrolment from 64,024 in 1985 to 921,548 in 2008 (World Bank 2011).

Developments between 2008 and 2012 have seen a decline in enrolment at the primary (–3.1 per cent annual decrease) and secondary levels (–0.7 per cent annual decrease). This may be due to students moving to private local and international schools and declining birth rates. Tertiary education enrolment remained on an upward trend of 4.4 per cent annually, suggesting that numbers seeking admission locally into tertiary institutions has stabilized (MOHE 2008–12).

Demand for Higher Education

Social demand for higher education has increased rapidly to keep pace with industrialization and the need to enhance productivity levels. Existing public universities were unable to meet the demand: in 1992 the shortfall was about 150,000 places (*New Straits Times*, 25 May 1992, p. 4). The government undertook to liberalize private education as a way of increasing post-secondary places without increasing the demand for public funds. Another consideration was the increasing cost of supporting Malaysian students overseas, spurring the government to look for domestic solutions. Between 1995 and 1997 a raft of legislative acts governing public and private HEIs was tabled in Parliament. The acts covered accreditation and quality assurance, regulations regarding private HEIs and international branch campuses, use of English as medium of instruction, corporatization and the Higher Education Student Loan Fund. These Acts provided the framework for the growth and expansion of private higher education in Malaysia.

In 1985, there were 68,000 Malaysian students studying overseas mainly in the United Kingdom, United States, Canada and New Zealand (Marimuthu 2008, p. 272). By 2000, this number was down to 50,000 with funds outflow estimated at RM2 billion (INPUMA 2000, p. 18). With the insufficient capacity of public HEIs, the private sector came into its own. Despite efforts to reduce the numbers overseas, the number of Malaysian students abroad increased to 81,282 in 2012. There are two main reasons for this: one, the premium parents and society at large place on overseas qualifications and experience and, second, students' inability to enrol locally in study areas of their choice.

Higher Education Provision

The phenomenal increase in the access to higher education bears out Malaysia's aim to increase its higher education participation rate from approximately 40 per cent to 50 per cent by 2020 (Tapsir 2012) and is matched by the increase in higher education providers. Currently Malaysia has 20 public universities, 30 polytechnics, and 80 community colleges. In the private sector, there are 75 private universities and university colleges, 9 branch campuses of international universities and 460 colleges (MOE 2013). Collectively, the diversified structure providing degree, diploma and certificate programmes has contributed immensely to student access and expansion in enrolment as shown in Table 4.1.

Tertiary education enrolment, as a whole, increased by 17.6 per cent between 2008 and 2012. The largest increase was in the public universities with an increase of 24.4 per cent, followed by universities in the private sector (14.2 per cent), the polytechnics (8.1 per cent) and the community colleges (3.1 per cent). The percentage of population aged 19–24 enrolled in tertiary education between 1970 and 2012 increased significantly. With a mere 0.6 per cent enrolled in 1970, the enrolment ratio increased to 2.9 per cent in 1990 and 8.1 per cent in 2000. Thereafter the increase in enrolment of the age group 19–24 has been remarkable, moving up to 24.4 per cent in 2007 and to 37.8 per cent in 2012, a figure very close to the 40 per cent government target (World Bank 2011; Department of Statistics 2012). Against the trend of increasing enrolment is Kolej Tunku Abdul Rahman (KTAR) where enrolments have fallen by 9.8 per cent over the same period.

TABLE 4.1
Enrolment in Tertiary Education, 2008–12

Year	Public	Private	Polytechnic	Community	KTAR*	Total
2008	419,334	399,897	85,280	17,082	26,235	947,828
2009	437,420	484,377	86,471	17,279	25,179	1,050,726
2010	462,780	541,629	87,642	18,200	23,774	1,134,025
2011	508,256	428,973	89,292	6,394	23,632	1,056.547
2012	521,793	456,616	92,148	22,380	23,652	1,114,589
% increase	24.4	14.2	8.1	3.1	–9.8	17.6

Note: *KTAR — Kolej Tunku Abdul Rahman is a Chinese community institution which has some government support.
Source: MOHE, various years.

A possible explanation is the expansion of private HEIs which offers a greater selection of academic programmes to students. The contribution of private HEIs to increasing number of graduates in the country is apparent in Table 4.1. While public universities continue to produce the largest number of graduands, the private sector has grown apace in closing the gap. If this pattern continues, one may expect that private HEIs will continue to play an important role in absorbing undergraduate and college students that cannot be served by public HEIs. "Then, public HEIs would maintain their optimal size of total enrolment, reduce the intake of undergraduates and allow room to enhance their graduate enrolment"(UIS 2014, p. 36).

Postgraduate Education

Apart from producing much-needed qualified academic staff for the burgeoning HE sector, the government also aims to accelerate the production of PhD graduates and develop the country's own indigenous research capability to serve the emerging knowledge economy, thereby reducing dependence on industrial research undertaken by foreign companies (MOE 2006). There are currently about 21,000 PhD holders in Malaysia. The goal is to produce 100,000 PhD holders by 2020. Of these, 60 per cent would be in science, technology and medicine; 20 per cent in humanities and applied social sciences, and 20 per cent in professional courses (MyBrain 15, MOHE 2006). To support that priority, the Malaysian government directed special funds to assist the five research institutions to expand their graduate-level research and teaching facilities.

Increase in output of graduates at the Bachelors and Diploma levels stabilized around 1 and 2 per cent between 2009 and 2012 (Table 4.2). Bachelors courses produce the largest number of graduates with numbers ranging between 65,756 and 66,421. Greatest increase in output was for PhD (194.4 per cent) and Masters (68.8 per cent) graduates. The number of PhD graduates jumped from 701 in 2009 to 2,054 in 2012 and Masters from 8,446 in 2009 to 14,261 in 2012.

While HEIs may meet numerical targets, the implications for the quality of programmes and the employment prospects of graduates are grave. The Strategic Plan does not elaborate on the basis for the numbers stipulated (*The Sun*, 17 July 2014, p. 6). It is also silent on graduates' employment prospects. Concerns include the possible need for expensive retraining,

TABLE 4. 2

Output of Graduates in the Public Universities by Level of Study, 2009–12

Year	PhD	Masters	PG Diploma	Bachelor	Diploma	Matriculation	Professional	Others	Total
2009	701	8,446	1,099	65,756	23,534	4,853	190	291	104,870
2010	1,134	10,959	4,545	66,445	21,112	3,897	86	153	108,331
2010	1,527	11,332	1,267	66,372	19,998	3.356	97	0	104.291
2012	2,064	14,261	887	66,421	23,957	5316	243	90	113,239
% +	194.4	68.8	–19.3	1.0	1.8	9.5	27.9	–69.1	8.0

Source: MOHE, various years.

and potential brain drain emigrants if salaries and productivity in the nation remain relatively low.

EQUITY ISSUES

While access to higher education has increased notably over the last four decades, the thorny question of equity remains very much alive. Key issues are whether the system promotes access for all Malaysian groups to publicly funded higher education; how inputs are allocated; and how benefits are distributed. The participation of the various ethnic groups at tertiary level in both local institutions and overseas improved in absolute numbers. Enrolment data between 1970 and 2008 indicate that the *Bumiputra* enrolment increased at a greater rate than non-*Bumiputra* enrolment in the public higher education system with shares for Chinese and Indian students decreasing significantly over the same period.

Enrolment Patterns

Enrolment of Malay/*Bumiputra* students in the public universities rose from 53.9 per cent in 1970 to 71.3 per cent in 1985 and to 83.1 per cent in 2008. This is naturally followed by declining proportions of students of Chinese and Indian origins. Chinese enrolment decreased from 38.5 per cent in 1970 to 11.2 per cent in 2008, while the Indian share of places in public universities declined from 4.9 per cent in 1970 to 2.7 per cent in 2008 (Figure 4.1). Post-2008 data, disaggregated by ethnic group, is not in the public domain.

Data on the total public sector higher education institutions comprising universities, polytechnics and community colleges (Table 4.3) demonstrate the dominance of *Bumiputra* students in all these institutions. In 2008, total public HEIs enrolment showed that *Bumiputras* took up 84.8 per cent of the places followed by 9.7 per cent Chinese, 2.8 per cent Indian and 2.6 per cent others.

Noteworthy as an explanation for the high proportion of *Bumiputra* share in higher education is the Universiti Technology MARA (UiTM) whose main objective is to train students "in professionally recognized courses of study ... (and to prepare) *Bumiputra* students for the professional scientific and technological fields".[1] In 2012, its 30-odd campuses and 22 affiliated colleges took in 73,625 new students, had an enrolment of

FIGURE 4.1
Enrolment in Public Universities by ethnicity, 1970–2009

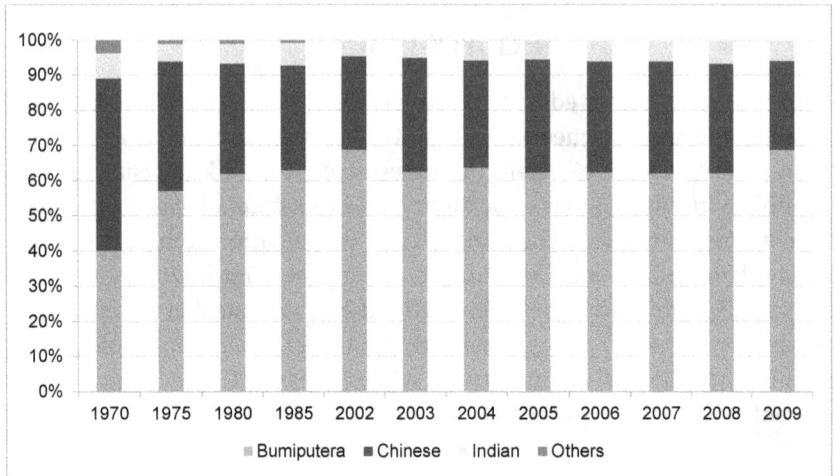

Source: Various Malaysia Development Plans 1971 to 1985; Years 2002–2009 compiled by Yayasan Strategic Sosial Malaysia.

185,635 and an output of 43,946 graduands. UiTM's enrolment constituted 16.7 per cent of the total enrolment of private and public HEIs together. Under the Bumiputra Economic Empowerment Programme (BEEP), UiTM enrolment is to be raised to 250,000 by 2020 with the addition of several new branch campuses.

Student Admissions Based on Meritocracy

In 2002, the student admission policy changed from the ethnic quota system reflecting the population distribution in the country to meritocracy where the minimum entry requirement is 2.0 Cumulative Grade Point Average (CGPA). There are three major pathways to public universities. One, a standardized national examination constituting a two-year programme at the end of eleven years of schooling leading to the Malaysian Higher School Certificate (STPM). Second, a one-year or two-year foundation programme, developed and conducted by some public universities in their Centres for Foundation studies, and the third, a programme run by Matriculation Colleges at the end of eleven years of schooling. Matriculation/Foundation 2-year and 1-year programmes are much sought after compared with the

TABLE 4.3
Enrolment in Public Higher Education Institutions by Ethnicity, 2008

Race	Universities No.	Universities %		Polytechnics No.	Polytechnics %		Community Colleges No.	Community Colleges %		Total No.	Total %	
Bumiputra	333,235	83.1	78.0	78,123	91.6	18.3	15,706	91.9	3.7	427,064	84.8	100.0
Chinese	45,062	11.2	91.9	3,645	4.3	7.4	323	1.9	0.7	49,030	9.7	100.0
Indian	10,901	2.7	76.5	2,678	3.1	18.8	675	4.0	4.7	14,254	2.8	100.0
Other	11,975	3.0	90.8	834	1.0	6.3	378	2.2	2.9	13,187	2.6	100.0
Total	401,173	100.0	79.7	85,280	100.0	16.9	17,082	100.0	3.4	503,535	100.0	100.0

Ministry of Higher Education – information provided in November 2009, World Bank 2011.

STPM programme as the common perception is that the latter examinations are more demanding and the possibility of gaining a university place through a matriculation programme is more likely. Ninety per cent of Matriculation/ Foundation students are *Bumiputras* with non-*Bumiputras* jostling for the remaining 10 per cent of places. It is not clear if assessment requirements are equivalent across the matriculation/foundation/STPM programmes.

Under the meritocracy policy, the intake of ethnic groups into public universities seems to have normalized with ethnic proportions reflecting the population distribution. By 2009, student intake comprised 66.1 per cent *Bumiputras*, 25.2 per cent Chinese, 7.5 per cent Indians and 1.2 per cent Others. Little information is available on how the admission policies based on meritocracy really work, indicating the need for greater transparency in student evaluation and selection processes. For the country as a whole, the system raises serious questions on how talent is identified, nurtured and retained.

A talent pool that falls outside the mainstream public system are the graduates from the private Chinese-medium school system. The school-leaving pre-university examination taken by these students is the UEC (United Examinations Certificate) which does not qualify them for admission to local public universities but is accepted in private HEIs in Malaysia and international HEIs.

Impact on the Labour Force

Ethnic distribution in the labour market reflects student access and enrolment patterns. The increasing *Bumiputra* enrolment and output of graduates over the last forty years has had a marked impact on the ethnic composition of graduates in the labour market. By 1990 *Bumiputra* share in the labour market had exceeded targets set by the government in professional and technical, clerical, service and production categories with some way to go in administration, management and sales (Osman and Shahiri 2014). In 2008 the proportion of *Bumiputra* graduates employed was 60.0 per cent, increasing to 65.4 per cent in 2013. This is naturally accompanied by a lower share of the labour market by the Chinese whose proportion of employed graduates decreased from 31.8 per cent in 2000 to 30.4 in 2008 and to 24.6 per cent in 2013. Indian graduates maintained a share ranging from 7.8 to 6.6 per cent over this period (Department of Statistics 2011, 2013).

It would be correct to conclude that public investments apportioned to public HEIs have succeeded in meeting NEP goals of education and employment opportunities for *Bumiputras*. It would be equally correct to surmise that after having invested with success in the same group for forty-three years, there would be expectations that the returns to government investments would benefit the country as a whole.

Student Financial Assistance

Government financial assistance to students is primarily through scholarships and loans. One of the most coveted sources of scholarship are those offered by the Public Services Department (Jabatan Perkhidmatan Awam or JPA) which is open to all, focusing on priority areas largely in science and technology. Awards, based on academic merit, are tenable in local and foreign universities and are divided according to racial lines. These scholarships play a vital role in the access agenda. For example in 2008, of the 59,107 students studying overseas, 36.4 per cent or 21,517 were sponsored (MOHE 2009). Of these, 2,000 were JPA scholarship holders of which 55 per cent were *Bumiputra* and the balance of 45 per cent were non-*Bumiputra* (see Figure 4.2).

However, Figure 4.2 also shows decreasing numbers of JPA scholarship recipients for foreign study, while maintaining a somewhat similar

FIGURE 4.2
JPA Overseas Scholarships, 2008–12

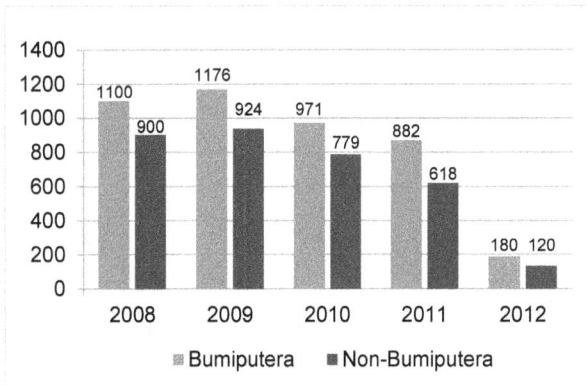

Source: Parliamentary Q&A Session, Minister in Prime Minister's Department, Shahiddan Kassim, October 2013.

ethnic breakdown. In 2012, of the 300 scholarships awarded for foreign studies, 60 per cent were *Bumiputra* and 40 per cent non-*Bumiputra*. The decreasing number in foreign scholarships can be attributed to the higher cost of overseas study and the increase in the local provision of foreign programmes through twinning, three-year foreign university programmes conducted locally and foreign branch campuses. Apart from the JPA scholarships, there are other scholarship schemes provided by state, private and business foundations, international funding agencies and Yayasan Mara. Collectively these "other agencies" sponsor a significant number of students, for example in 2008, to a total of 19,517 (90.7 per cent) of sponsored students studying abroad.

No recent data are available on the number of JPA scholarship for domestic studies; Figure 4.2 however provides the pattern for 2000–08. Firstly, it shows the increasing number of JPA scholarship to study locally. Secondly, while the total number of recipients for the nine years shows a huge disparity between *Bumiputra* and non-*Bumiputra* recipients, yearly data show the narrowing of this gap. For example, in the year 2000, 91.5 per cent or 3,444 scholarships were awarded to *Bumiputra* students and only 319 or 8.5 per cent to non-*Bumiputra* students, but in the year 2008, the percentage of non-*Bumiputra* students rose to 21.5 or 2,174 as opposed to 7,826 *Bumiputra* students or 78.3 per cent. These are indeed

FIGURE 4.3
Public Sector Department Scholarships for Studies at domestic HEIs according to Bumiputera and non-Bumiputera, 2000–08

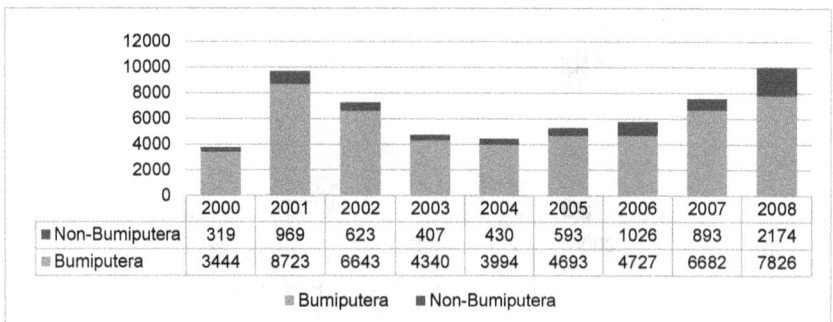

	2000	2001	2002	2003	2004	2005	2006	2007	2008
■ Non-Bumiputera	319	969	623	407	430	593	1026	893	2174
■ Bumiputera	3444	8723	6643	4340	3994	4693	4727	6682	7826

■ Bumiputera   ■ Non-Bumiputera

Source: Public Services Department, November 2009.

small but welcomed measures towards bridging the inherent inequities in the Malaysian HE topography.

The other source of student financing is through government loans. The Higher Education Fund Corporation (Perbadanan Tabung Pendidikan Tinggi Nasional or PTPTN) was established under the National Higher Education Fund Act 1997 (Act 566) with the objective of ensuring efficient management of low-interest loan financing, using public funds, for eligible students (based on monthly family income) in public and private HEIs. Loan holders with a first class honours degree are able to convert their loans retroactively into scholarships, without repayment obligations. Availability of loans has also helped to raise enrolments in the liberalized private sector, now totalling around 50 per cent of all student enrolment in the country.

Accessing loans for study in public and private HEIs has assisted students from needy backgrounds from all ethnic groups to pursue studies at tertiary level. The availability of these loans while providing greater access, particularly to private sector students who would otherwise be left out of higher education, also leaves them to start their careers with a much larger financial burden than those in the highly subsidized public HEIs. This underscores issues of equality of access mechanisms particularly as *Bumiputras* constitute 84.8 per cent (2008) of those enrolled in public HEIs (Table 4.3).

QUALITY AND MALAYSIAN HEIs

Increased access seems to go together with quality deficits: there are more students but not necessarily more learning relevant to individuals and society. Exponential enrolment expansion in public and private HEIs has had a major impact on the quality of teaching and learning, largely through stretching the available pool of academics over multiple institutions, adding new discipline areas, new student configurations, and redirecting resources. Malaysian higher education institutions have been urged to meet enrolment targets to match the government's aspirations for national economic growth. The expectation is that an educated and skilled labour force would attract international students, and foreign business and industry would locate here, with investors finding a high-quality environment attractive. Malaysian government investments in education are among the largest in the region — only China, Hong Kong, Singapore and Japan spend more per student than Malaysia (UIS 2014, Table B5, p. 158). Also at stake is the quality of graduates and their ability to be employed at levels and salaries commensurate with their qualifications. Moreover, the productive capacity of the country to employ graduates needs to be assured if public funds are not to be utilized in supporting a brain drain.

Quality of Secondary Schooling

Countries seek international testimony for their primary and secondary school systems as the quality of secondary graduates seeking university admission is of considerable significance. In recent years, Malaysia has seen a groundswell of private locally and internationally financed schools which contribute to the country's goal of becoming a regional education hub; are increasingly perceived as profitable business investments; and have provided alternatives to Malaysian parents voting with their feet, registering their concerns about the performance of the public school system.

Parents point to recent international performance ratings, Programme for International Student Assessment (PISA)[2] and Trends in International Mathematics and Science Study (TIMSS)[3] which show declining academic achievement compared to ASEAN neighbours such as lower income Vietnam, and much below Korea in the key areas of Mathematics, Science and Reading. In the 2012 PISA data, Malaysia ranked 52nd for Mathematics, 59th for Reading, and 53rd for Science with an overall ranking of 52nd; Vietnam 17th, 20th and 8th with an overall ranking of 17th; and Korea 5th, 5th and 7th with 5th as overall placing. The story is similar for TIMSS ratings. For both Mathematics and Science, scores of Malaysian students declined significantly between 2007 and 2011, from 474 in 2007 to 440 in 2011 in Mathematics and from 471 in 2007 to 426 in 2011 in Science. In 2007 Malaysian students performed better than Thai students in Mathematics but in 2011 Thai students outperformed Malaysian students.

More than achievement scores perhaps, the greater indictment comes from a school-to-work longitudinal study which found that schooling had "in large measure been responsible for a memory-based learning designed for the average student" (Nagaraj et al. 2009). A lawmaker has expressed concern regarding entry into an "extremely competitive job market with insufficient skills…. SPM holders with A or B grades in English remained unable to hold conversations in English, leading to low employability" (*The*

Star, 4 July 2014). Available data on private schools reveal that enrolments have increased in the secondary schools, Chinese private secondary schools, expatriate schools offering their own curricula, international schools, and religious primary and secondary schools. Fees for all categories of school except for Islamic religious are generally high, implying that a move to private schools represents a considered decision (MOE 2009–12).

Academic Staff Qualifications

The key variable in higher education quality is its academic staff. Public universities have better staff qualification profiles than private, particularly in established HEIs. Overall, staff with PhDs increased from 24.4 per cent in 2009 to 33.9 per cent in 2012 in public HEIs but with some of the newer public universities reaching only 15.7 per cent (e.g., Universiti Pertahanan Negara Malaysia). In private HEIs the proportion remained around 10 per cent and below over the same period for better performing universities.[4] The majority of academic staff in both public and private HEIs hold 55 per cent and 43 per cent Masters degrees respectively.

Rapid enrolment expansion has imposed considerable strains on academic staffing, medical schools being a case in point. Malaysia has thirty-two HEIs (eleven public and twenty-two private) offering forty medical programmes, producing 3,500 medical graduates annually. Private HEIs are known to hire part-time academics from public HEIs as a stop-gap measure and to cope with high turnovers in international staff. Comprehensive clinical training for such large numbers of students is a major issue. Exacerbating the situation are the numerous changes in decisions on the number of places available. The total number of qualified candidates applying to the eleven public HEIs was 1,163. Public HEIs have reduced the 690 places available in 2013 to 418 in 2014, moving up to 518, based on appeals. (*The Star*, 16 September 2014). Announcing sudden changes has impacted negatively on institutional planning, academic programme implementation and student choices.

International staff tend to support new programme areas, bringing different perspectives to academic programmes which help institutions to look outwards. Where international branch campuses are concerned, there is the advantage of having education and training in Malaysia under the umbrella of an acknowledged brand. In 2013 out of a total of 29,198 academic staff in public HEIs, 1,765 or 6 per cent were international staff, a large proportion of whom hold PhDs and tend to be in the HEIs with larger enrolments (MOE 2013). Public universities can recruit up to 10 per cent international staff with salary packages restricted by government regulations. Private HEIs have no restrictions regarding the proportion to be recruited or salary packages: clearly, the financially stronger can offer more attractive packages and attract better qualified staff.

Quality of HEIs and Measures of Performance

Quality of institutions may be measured by several proxies: academic staff qualifications, national and international rankings, and publications in top-tier indexed research journals, citations and patents. Probably the acid test of quality is that of graduate employment, bearing witness to the value of acquired learning and work-related skills to society and the economy. Key Performance Indicators have been introduced in public HEIs which provide measures for teaching, research and publications, level of external funding for research, patenting, and community service. These are taken into account for staff appraisal and promotion purposes.

National Rating of HEIs

Annual national mechanisms for rating public and private higher education institutions are found in two instruments developed by the Malaysian Qualifications Agency: Rating System for Higher Education Institutions (or SETARA, its acronym in the national language) for universities and university colleges; and MyQuest (Malaysian Quality Evaluation System for Private Colleges) for colleges. Polytechnics and community colleges have internal quality assurance mechanisms.

SETARA, a quality assurance tool, measures the quality of teaching and learning at the undergraduate level looking at three generic dimensions of: input (talent, resources and governance); process (curriculum matters); and output (quality of graduates as measured by data from tracer studies and employer perception surveys). The resultant six-tier rating system ranges from Tier 6 identified as "Outstanding" and Tier 1 as "Weak" based on institutional scores. By 2012, results showed that out of the fifty-two public and private universities and university colleges rated, thirty-five (67 per cent) of the fifty-four institutions achieved a Tier 5 "excellent" category; sixteen (14 per cent) institutions in Tier 4 as "very good", and the remaining one (2 per cent), in Tier 3 as "good". None were in Tier 6 nor in Tiers 1 and 2.[5] MyQuest was developed by the MOHE as an instrument to evaluate the current performance of private colleges in Malaysia in terms of students, programmes, graduates, resources and governance. It is biennially conducted, based on self-evaluation with external auditors.

The MOHE has shown commendable initiative in implementing the two instruments. However, outcomes indicate that much work still needs to be done. Many in the industry view SETARA results with some reservation as the use of the same indicators for both public and private HEIs across all aspects of quality assurance is questionable. Reviewing the ranking results, conventional wisdom suggests that the instrument needs to be refined and better discriminate between strong and weak performers. Concerns have been expressed also regarding MyQuest's use of measures which tend to be based on arbitrary ratios and percentages, with negligible input from stakeholders and an absence of peer assessment.

International Ranking Exercises

International rankings, however controversial, have played a significant role in Malaysia influencing national and institutional strategic planning, reforms and identification of priorities such as research funding. At the same time they have helped to subject Malaysia's five research universities to more scrutiny and accountability than ever before, increasing inter-university competition for funds and acclaim. The government prizes rankings which can earn international respect, attract and help recruit students and faculty while justifying investments in HEIs. Government also looks for returns to investments usually in terms of higher levels of research productivity which underlies the policy of increasing proportions of postgraduate students. The weak performance of Malaysian institutions in global rankings, despite substantial budgets, has given rise to considerable soul-searching.

Among local public HEIs, UM has fared rather well, gaining 377th place in the 2014 Academic Ranking of World Universities and 151st (up from 167th in 2013) place in the 2014 QS World University Rankings, far ahead of the four other designated research universities in Malaysia. Compared with regional universities, however, such as National University of Singapore (NUS) in 22nd place in the 2014 QS World University Rankings, it is evident that Malaysian universities have a long way to go in the ranking stakes. Information on ranking performance by academic field is useful for institutional planners, where indicators on relative strengths and weaknesses can be used for further analysis within HEIs as well as government and industry. In Engineering and Technology, for example, USM moved up from 222nd in 2012 to 169th in 2013 while UM fell from 165th to 213th place.[6] UM leads the pack with 12,008 papers published between January 2010 and August 2014, 34,652 citations with an average 2.89 citations per paper (Table 4.4). Leading the region are NUS with 6.51 citations per paper and University of Tokyo (6.40), showing a gap in performance between them and Malaysian universities.

A useful proxy measure of an institution's technological inventions which have potential economic value may be derived from levels of patenting, particularly in terms of the number of patents issued by the U.S. Patent and Trademark Office (USPTO). They also indicate technological readiness for moving into a knowledge economy. Between January 2010 and August 2014, USPTO issued five U.S. patents to UM, one each to Universiti Putra Malaysia (UPM) and Universiti Teknologi Malaysia (UTM), and none to UKM and Universiti Sains Malaysia (USM). When compared with NUS's twenty-three patents issued over the same period of

TABLE 4.4
Publication and Citation Statistics of Selected Malaysian Universities and Other Leading Asian Universities, January 2010 – August 2014

University	Country	Number of Papers	Number of Citations	Number of Citations per Paper
Universiti Malaya	Malaysia	12,008	34,652	2.89
Universiti Sains Malaysia	Malaysia	8,984	25,709	2.86
Universiti Kebangsaan Malaysia	Malaysia	7,058	13,546	1.92
Universiti Putra Malaysia	Malaysia	7,927	19,162	2.42
Universiti Teknologi Malaysia	Malaysia	5,245	10,585	2.02
National University of Singapore	Singapore	29,305	190,890	6.51
Hong Kong University	Hong Kong	39,944	204,982	5.13
Seoul National University	South Korea	36,925	172,192	4.66
Tsinghua University	China	29,756	145,440	4.89
University of Tokyo	Japan	43,150	276,153	6.40

Source: Web of Science Core Collections (all available indices) via Thomson Reuters Web of Science.

time, institutional policymakers and researchers would do well to evaluate research quality and the extent to which research outputs are directed to economic activities.

Employability of University Graduates

The quality of higher education institutions may also be judged by the employability of their graduates. In 2012, from a total of 202,328 graduands from both public and private higher educational institutions, 25.6 per cent (51,796) were unemployed. Data from a tracer study conducted by MOHE and thereafter MOE since 2013 show that private HEI graduates have a higher employability rate than graduates from public HEIs. In the same year, 56.7 per cent from private HEIs were employed compared with 47.4 per cent for graduates from the latter. However, the unemployed proportion is higher at 28.8 per cent for private HEIs compared with 24.7 per cent for public HEIs probably due to a larger number of their graduands (20.8 per cent) opting for further studies compared with only 8.7 per cent for private HEIs (MOHE 2012).

A June 2014 report of a survey of Malaysian employers from 200 companies employing 245,000 workers identified skills mismatches between recent graduates and employers' demands (World Bank 2014). Malaysian university graduates lacked soft skills with communication skills as the major deficit, followed by creative/critical thinking, analytical and problem-solving competencies. To boost graduates' employability chances, the government has put in place several training programmes managed by the Graduate Employment Management Scheme which has placed 12,000 graduates in the workforce since 2009. The cumulative costs incurred per trainee on top of highly subsidized undergraduate costs were not available.

A matter of grave concern in efforts to develop an innovative and knowledge economy is the increasing number of professional tertiary-educated Malaysians, aged above 25 years emigrating from the country. It represents high wastage in terms of investment made in their education and training, benefiting the receiving industrialized, higher income economies. A recent study (Lim, Krishnan and Yap 2014) estimated that the total diaspora in 2013 comprises 843,591 individuals, 35 per cent higher than in 2000. Singapore alone attracted 49.2 per cent of the total diaspora, with Australia at 13 per cent, followed by Brunei, United Kingdom and the United States.

The government has established schemes such as TalentCorp to attract qualified overseas Malaysians. A World Bank study (World Bank 2011*b*) on brain drain in Malaysia cited (1) poor career prospects, (2) social injustice, and (3) low wages. Instead of creating market distortions by direct intervention, the government would do well to collaborate with the business sector to increase productivity, allowing market forces to handle career prospects and wage differentials (Lim, Krishnan and Yap 2014, p. 22). More intractable to deal with is emigrants' perception of social injustice.

Quality, Internationalization, and Employability

The internationalization agenda as charted by the MOE is largely propelled today by the concept of education as an export commodity, visible in the growth of transnational education (TNE) enrolment largely within the private HE sector and increasingly the public sector. It includes branch campuses and numerous forms of collaborations usually in the form of franchise, joint degree and twinning arrangements. Currently, the nine international branch campuses together with local private HEIs attract close to a third of foreign students studying for a degree in the country although data tend to be incomplete. The plan is to increase the current 91,000 students to 200,000 by 2020 (MOE announcement, 25 September 2014).

The presence of international programmes and providers contributes to the overall quality of the higher education sector. Foreign HEIs, particularly those of high repute, have introduced effective ways of providing quality higher education in Malaysia with brand status. They provide choices to students and parents, and allow for the market to set acceptable benchmarks on quality. Shorter term quality achievements come through sharing of best practices between foreign and local partners. Policymakers and industry players are aware that the larger and more established private HEIs had built their processes and best practices on the processes and practices of their parent universities.

The presence of TNE providers has influenced graduate employability patterns. A recent study (Fernandez-Chung et al. 2014) of employers shows that next to foreign graduates, TNE graduates from foreign branch campuses are the most sought-after employees. This was followed by graduates from local private universities, private colleges, private university colleges and finally local public universities (see Figure 4.4).

FIGURE 4.4
Distribution of Employer Satisfaction of Graduates According to
Type of Higher Education Providers

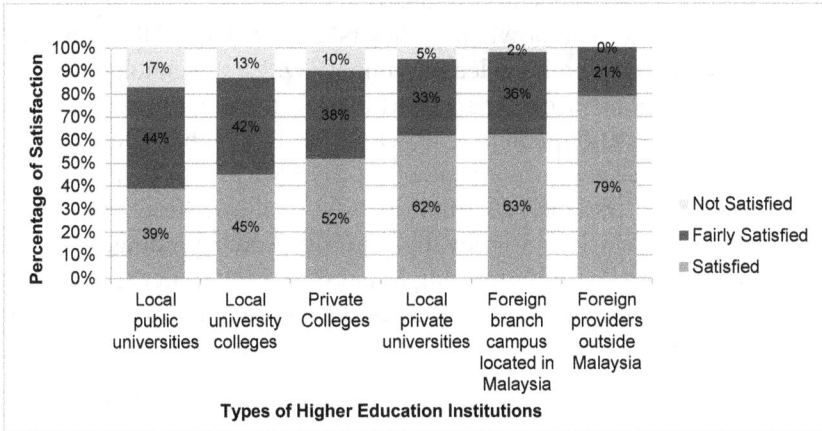

Source: Fernandez-Chung et al. (2014).

MOVING FORWARD

Malaysian higher education, and indeed the education system as a whole, stands at the cusp of vital decision-making which could go in two directions. On the one hand, it could make fundamental systemic reforms taking into serious account, *inter alia*, the need to: identify talent, particularly scientific and technological, irrespective of its source; support overall employability of graduates by strengthening English language (while maintaining Bahasa Malaysia as the national language and main medium of instruction); enhance communication skills as recommended by national and international research studies and surveys; and ensure effective, globally- and future-oriented management who understand how to make policies and decisions work in practical terms.

On the other hand, key decisions could seek to maintain the status quo. Affirmative action policies based on ethnicity could continue maintaining, by policy, a limited talent pool; low levels of English language proficiency might continue hindering Malaysian participation in global research and technology advances; incentives provided to increase and retain high-quality science and technology graduates and academic staff remain insufficient; and high-level management personnel continue to be appointed on a non-competitive basis.

In short, policymakers need to determine if they are to move along a well-trodden linear path or whether they take advantage of the potential exponential growth of a knowledge economy which a technology-based education environment can bring. Fortunately, there are signs that the health of the education system as a whole, and of higher education in particular, has received focused attention from Malaysian policymakers in the last few years. Such attention may be seen in critical areas such as supporting research and innovation through better funding, offering incentives to attract high-performing Malaysians back from their current positions in developed economies, and placing more emphases on planning and evaluation.

Strategic Planning

Malaysia's strategies to increase access to higher education have been successful: every group including ethnic communities, women, and those from rural areas shows positive increases in higher education participation. In some ways the sector has become a victim of its own success which is most visible in the setting of ever-increasing numerical targets. The public announcement of targets, implications for which require thorough study, has enormous consequences for students as well as HEIs, influencing implementation strategies and processes, and above all, quality. Decisions on numbers could benefit from more rigour and caution as seen in the recent case of medical graduates and production of PhD target figures. Additionally, emphasizing improved articulation of inputs at various levels, rather than considering them individually, such as teaching of English in tandem with advances in technology-based studies, would help move the system closer towards its goal of building a globally directed knowledge economy.

Implementing Development Policies

Among recent published declarations of development policy have been the New Economic Model and the Bumiputra Economic Empowerment Plan. The most recent are the Education Blueprints concerned with improving the quality of schooling as well as higher education. Guidelines for implementation emanating from these documents deserve attention but also need to be received with circumspection over the longer term. The learning environment evolves over time and across space thus requiring planning and implementation to take changes on board on an ongoing basis. To keep implementation healthy and relevant in terms of outcomes, more effective systems of programme/policy review and impact evaluation need to be in place so that change processes can function optimally.

Management of Change

For more effective overall planning of enrolment, academic staffing and non-wasteful development of required infrastructure in priority areas, greater transparency and availability of data in the public domain are essential. There is need for more consistent and timely dissemination of government policy changes with prior stakeholder consultation in order to increase efficiency and benefit users, namely students and HEIs. Greater transparency in the form of annual reports in the public domain on the utilization of public funds such as the Higher Education Loan Fund would respond effectively to the need for better public information as well as increased trust in the system.

Human Capital Growth

The shortfall in appropriately qualified and skilled personnel for national development and economic growth calls for a better match between priority development areas and funding at undergraduate, postgraduate and research levels. It is expected that the available additional funding for the five research universities will help provide a larger pool of relevant expertise for the knowledge economy through better concentration of resources. While attention needs to be paid to student choice of disciplines so that more graduates qualify in relevant priority areas such as engineering and science, they also need to be better inducted into inter-disciplinary learning and research approaches as well as those that use modern technology. Above all, opportunities for access to higher education need to be maintained and increased, particularly in science and technology, to expand the talent pool as widely as possible.

Critical Mass of Researchers

While financing for research and research facilities has seen a healthy injection of funds over the last few years, there would be merit in developing a critical mass of individuals and institutions which include HEIs, industry, technoparks and other institutes, local and international, working together on common objectives. High-level scholars and researchers are limited in number. To propel research and innovation forward, awareness of others working in similar areas and the resultant knowledge would increase the potential for innovation and societal change.

Prizing Autonomy

Well-performing private HEIs owe much of their success to institutional autonomy which allows for nimble and innovative responses to the market. A number of HEIs has been established by government-linked companies or where a significant share of ownership belongs to national investment arms. There is concern that these HEIs could become multi-layered bureaucratic organizations. Such organizations contrast with those led by private sector "edu-preneurs" (a distinct characteristic of the Malaysian private higher education sector) who are experienced in dealing with the market, husbanding and accounting for financial resources; tackling disruptive global challenges characterized by accelerating technological changes; making innovative decisions independently without concerns about a hierarchical chain of command; and effectively guiding their institutions towards achieving internal and external efficiencies.

Using Meritocracy to Increase Quality

Policymakers would do well to review the existing policies regarding student admissions in a bid to shift competition further down the education system. Admission into universities needs to be more competitive with the process of selection more transparent. The use of three entry routes inherently limits the quality of students unless admission is determined by being based on equivalent assessment criteria. By providing equal opportunities for access to public HEIs, the system would increase the competition which characterizes a vibrant and qualitatively strong higher education system. Besides, fostering interaction among ethnic groups at such a crucial period of their cognitive, affective and social development as Malaysians would contribute much towards mutual understanding and societal integration.

Notes

1. http://www.uitm.edu.my.
2. http://www.oecd.org/pisa/pisaproducts/46619703.pdf.
3. http://timss.bc.edu/timss2011/downloads/T11.
4. http://moe.gov.my/web_statistik/Indikator_PT 2009-2012.
5. http://www.mqa.gov.my/portal 2012/SETARA.
6. www.topuniversities/universityrankings/Asian-university rankings 2011-2013.

References

Department of Statistics, Malaysia. "Labour Force Surveys: Statistics of Graduates in the Labour Force, 2011". Ministry of Human Resources, Putra Jaya, 2011.
———. "Labour Force Report, 2013". Ministry of Human Resources, Putra Jaya, 2013.
———. "Population of Malaysia ages 19–24" via e-services, 24 July 2014.
Fernandez-Chung, Rozilini Mary, Cheong Kee Cheok, Leong Yin Ching and Chris Hill. "Employability of Graduates in Malaysia: The Perceptions of Selected Employers". Phase I Report of the TNE Employment Study, Manchester, British Council, 2014.
INPUMA. International Institute of Public Policy and Management, University of Malaya, Kuala Lumpur, 2000.
Lim Kim-Hwa, Dheepan Ratha Krishnan and Yap Jo-Yee. "The Economic Costs and Gains of Brain Drain: the case of Malaysia". Penang Institute, 2014.
Malaysia. Second Malaysia Plan. Kuala Lumpur: Government Printers, 1971.
———. Third Malaysia Plan. Kuala Lumpur: Government Printers, 1976.
———. Fifth Malaysia Plan. Kuala Lumpur: Government Printers, 1986.
———. "The New Economic Model (NEM)". Economic Planning Unit, Putra Jaya, 2010.
Marimuthu, T. "The Role of the Private Sector in Higher Education in Malaysia". In Teaching: Professionalization, Development and Leadership, edited by David Johnson and Rupert Maclean. Festschrift for Professor Eric Hoyle. Springer, 2008.
Ministry of Education (MOE), Malaysia. Educational Statistics of Malaysia. Various years. Kuala Lumpur, 1970 to 1995.
Ministry of Higher Education (MOHE). "The National Higher Education Strategic Plan Beyond 2020: The national higher education action Plan Phase 2, 2011–2015, MyBrain 15". Kuala Lumpur, 2006.

Ministry of Higher Education (MOHE), Malaysia. "Perangkaan Pengajian Tinggi Malaysia". Various issues. Bahagian Perancangan dan Penyelidikan, 2009 to 2012.

Mohamad, Mahathir. "The Way Forward — Vision 2020". Working paper presented at the Malaysian Business Council, 1991.

Nagaraj, Shyamala, Chew Sing Buan, Lee Kiang Hock and Rahimah Ahmad. *Education and Work: The World of Work*. Kuala Lumpur: University of Malaya Press, 2009.

Osman Zulkifly and Shahiri Hazrul. "Ethnic and Gender Inequality in Employment during the New Economic Policy". In *Institutions and Economies*, edited by Norma Mansor. (Faculty of Economics and Administration, University of Malaya), Vol. 6, No. 1 (2014): 57–72.

Parliamentary Q&A Session, Minister in Prime Minister's Department, Shahiddan Kassim, October 2013.

Public Services Department, Malaysia, Putra Jaya. November 2009.

Star, The. "100 more spots for medical students", 16 September 2014, p. 14.

Starbiz. "Malaysia's growth on track", 14 August 2014, p. 6.

Tapsir, Siti Hamisah. "Where are we today and where we aim to be tomorrow". Global Education Dialogue, The Asia Series, Transnational Education. Kuala Lumpur, 27–28 November 2012.

UNESCO Institute for Statistics (UIS). "Higher Education in Asia: Expanding Out Expanding Up". Montreal, Quebec, Canada, 2014.

Web of Science. Core Collections via Thomson Reuters Web of Science. 2014.

World Bank. "Affirmative Action Policies in Malaysian Higher Education". In "Commissioned report, East Asia and Pacific Region Human Development Unit", by Mukherjee, Hena, Jasbir S. Singh, Rozilini Mary Fernandez-Chung and T. Marimuthu. World Bank, Washington, D.C., 2011*a*.

———. "Malaysia Economic Report: Brain Drain". 2011*b*. <http://siteresources. worldbank.org/INTMALAYSIA/Resources/324392->.

———. "Malaysia Economic Monitor: Boosting trade competitiveness". World Bank Group, Washington, D.C., 2014.

5

INDONESIAN HIGHER EDUCATION
Gaps in Access and School Choice

Mohamad Fahmi

1. INTRODUCTION

Most research on school choice and academic achievement focus on the outcome in terms of either standardized exam scores or upper secondary graduation. However, instead of using these measures some economists place more emphasis on higher education attendance as an indicator of school performance. Using various methods, numerous studies have analysed the effect of school choice on secondary school and higher education or college attendance. A significant proportion of these studies focused on and evaluated the performance of Catholic, private and public secondary schools.

Some studies in developed countries have found that Catholic or private schooling has a positive effect on academic achievement or earnings. Evans and Schwab (1995) found that attending a Catholic high school increases the probability of graduating from high school or participating in a four-year college course by 13 percentage points. Likewise, Neal (1997) found that urban minorities benefit greatly from attending primary Catholic schools as their probability of high school and college graduate rates increased.

Vella (1998) also found that, despite the tuition fee being relatively low, attending an Australian Catholic School increases the probability of access to higher education and higher earnings. Using a quantile regression approach, Eide, Goldhaber and Showalter (2004) found that students attending a Catholic high school in the United States will more likely lead to attendance at a selective four-year college relative to students attending public high schools. Altonji, Elder and Taber (2005) developed a new technique of assessing selectivity bias in the absence of valid instruments based on measuring the ratio of selection on unobservable variables to estimate the effect of attending Catholic school on college attendance. They found that Catholic high school attendance substantially increases the probability of college attendance.

However, other research have found contradictory evidence. Akabayashi (2006) shows that in Japan public schools outperform private schools on college attendance rates when competition is increased. Cappellari (2004) found that general high school attendance increases the probability of access to university, whereas private high school students have lower academic performances. Similarly, Stevans and Sessions (2000) found that school choice has different implication for white, black or Hispanic students, as school choice is mostly taken advantage of by white urban residents. Moreover, white students perform better in private schools than in public schools, whereas a performance gain for private school minority students is found to be significant.

The superiority of public upper secondary schools over private schools in Indonesia on academic achievement alone has not been explored. However, there are some research which investigate the performance of public and private lower secondary schools with regard to academic achievement and future earnings. Bedi and Garg (2000) compared the effectiveness of four types of junior schools in Indonesia and found that individuals who studied at non-religious private schools earn 75 per cent higher than the public school group. Newhouse and Beegle (2006) using Indonesian data found that public school graduates score 0.17 to 0.3 standard deviations higher on national final exam scores than private school students.

In this chapter, I will investigate the effect of upper secondary school quality on higher education attendance in Indonesia using an extension of the Blinder-Oaxaca Decomposition for estimating a non-linear decomposition proposed by Fairlie (2005). This technique is useful for decomposing estimations coefficients from a logit or probit model which is used to model binary outcome. According to Fairlie (2005), the traditional Blinder-Oaxaca Decomposition (Blinder 1973; Oaxaca 1973) technique cannot directly quantify a model which has binary outcomes and its results are also difficult to interpret in terms of probability.

This chapter proceeds in the following direction. In the next section, I present some background on the Indonesia formal school system and higher education participation. The third section sets a model and empirical strategy. The fourth section presents details of the sample taken from the Indonesia Family Life Survey (IFLS). In the fifth section, I present the empirical result and interpret several empirical analyses, while the sixth and final section summarizes and concludes the discussion.

2. FORMAL SCHOOL SYSTEM AND INDONESIAN HIGHER EDUCATION

2.1 Formal School System

The formal school system in Indonesia is structured on three-tiers which include basic education followed by secondary education and higher education. Basic education consists of six years of primary school and three years of junior or lower secondary school. Secondary education consists of general upper secondary education and vocational upper secondary education, while higher education as the post-secondary level of education includes diploma, bachelor, master, specialized, and doctoral degrees. The institutions which provide higher education include academies, polytechnics, colleges, institutes and universities.

Based on sources of funding, schools in Indonesia are distinguished as either public or private schools. According to Oey-Gardiner (1997), many private schools are funded by the government in many financial forms and thus have to follow the government's set of rules, regulations and standards. Most public schools are non-religious schools, whereas many private schools are religious Islamic or Christian schools. Primary education is dominated by public schools. On the other hand, the private sector plays a larger role starting from junior secondary to the higher levels of education.

It is widely acknowledged that private schools provide places for students who cannot meet the public school entry test requirements and/or cannot afford public school tuition fees. Excluding a few very good private schools, the quality of most private schools is usually poor. According to Parker (2008), private schools are more cost-efficiently managed, but, however, they also have lower quality inputs. The educational attainment level of the average private school teacher and principal is usually lower and the availability of textbooks in private schools is much less than in public schools. The formal school system is managed by the Ministry of National Education (MNE), formerly known as the Ministry of Education and Culture (MEC), while the religious school system, mostly Islamic, is managed by the Ministry of Religious Affairs (MRA). Religious teaching makes up around 40 per cent of the religious schools' curriculum, and the other 60 per cent of the curriculum follows the non-religious formal school system set-up by MEC. Private Islamic schooling in Indonesia is regarded as second class, and the poor conditions in Islamic schools are admitted by the Indonesian government (Parker 2008).

In Indonesia, compulsory education begins at age seven and ends at age fifteen with the central government providing free basic education for each child. After graduating from basic education level 9 or junior secondary education, students may continue on to upper secondary school. At the end of primary, junior and upper secondary school, students have to take a national examination called Ujian Nasional (UN). Public schools and some of the elite private schools set some minimum level based on UN as their entry requirement.

2.2 Higher Education Participation

Higher education participation rate in Indonesia steadily increased between 2001 and 2005, from 0.14 to 0.17 (Nizam 2006). Although the participation rate in higher education is considerably lower than the primary and secondary education rates, the rate of enrolment is still higher than other countries such as India, Vietnam and Pakistan. Nizam (2006) attributes the rapid growth in the enrolment rate to the solid economic growth and the increasing global trend in participation rate in higher education. The higher education enrolment rate in Indonesia in 2002 is higher than some developing countries such as China (7.45 per cent) and Bangladesh (5.25 per cent).

Despite a steady increase in enrolment rates in the past five years, access and participation in higher education for rural populations and some minority groups remain a critical concern in Indonesia. Moreover, though Indonesia has a large number of private universities, competition for places in public universities remains very keen. While there are only 75,000 places available, the number of students taking the national public university entrance examination totalled about 450,000 each year (Nizam 2006). This means only one in every six applicants can obtain a public university place.

Thus the centralized public university admission examination system in Indonesia is highly competitive. Nizam (2006) argues that students typically need access to a high-quality upper secondary schooling and extra special training in a "private study centre" (known as *bimbingan belajar*) in order to gain admission into a public university. However, most high-quality secondary schools and *bimbingan belajar* are located in urban areas and only students from middle- and high-income families can afford the extra training. According to Nizam (2006), only 3.3 per cent of students from the lowest 20 per cent of income groups successfully passed the test. In contrast, the proportion of students from the highest income quintile who gain entry to public university places is 30.9 per cent.

Buchori and Malik (2004) note that most students who did not pass the public university admission test and afterwards choose to study at a private university are from the low socio-economic status (SES) backgrounds. The pattern of high SES students enrolling in high-quality public universities and low SES students enrolling in relatively low-quality private universities will likely continue to perpetuate social inequality.

3. MODEL AND EMPIRICAL STRATEGY

I will follow Rouse (1994), Epple and Romano (1998), Bedi and Garg (2000), Jacob (2002) and Edwards and Pasquale (2003) for multiple school choice sorting to model higher education participation choice using a random utility model. The model highlights several possible factors underlying the school choice gap and higher education participation. In my model, individual i graduates from lower secondary school type j jointly chooses with their parents to attend an upper secondary programme from among four available school choices: public, private non-religious, private Islamic, and private Christian.

I assume individuals and their parents have already decided to attend an upper secondary school as they are now searching for a possible school option. Moreover, students who choose to attend one of these upper secondary schools are assumed to graduate. This assumption is to simplify the view that an individual is able to choose a future level of education with no uncertainty about actually completing the current level.[1] I assume that the individual will choose alternative j that maximizes his or her utility. The individual utility function, U is

(1) $$U_{ij} = u_j (X_i, \varepsilon_i) \quad j = 1,...,J,$$

where X_i and ε_i are vectors of observable and unobservable variables, respectively, and j is upper secondary school alternatives.

I assume individuals will choose an alternative, j, if it maximizes their utility. Then the expression of a decision process of a student who chooses to attend one particular school is

(2) $$S_i = k \text{ iff } U_{ik} > \max U_{ij} \quad \forall_j \neq k$$

From Equations 1 and 2 the probability of individual i choosing to attend school type j may be obtained by estimating a multinomial discrete choice model. The model may be written as

(3) $$\Pr(S_i = j) = \frac{\exp (U_{ij})}{1 + \Sigma^J_{j=1} \exp(U_{ij})}$$

I will follow the estimation of the multinomial logit model above to not only investigate the determinants of the school choice decision by an individual, but also to construct selection correction variables, λ, that are included in the binary higher education participation choice model to detect the problem of selection bias. As in a linear regression model, selection bias is also a problem in the logit or probit model. According to Dubin and Rivers (1989) the treatment of the problem of selection bias in binary choice models is more difficult computationally. The problem of selection bias in upper secondary schools in Indonesia may appear since school choice is not random and may be influenced by unobservable characteristics.

Another potential factor that affects the decision is the school's selection criteria. According to Bedi and Garg (2000), this condition implies that school choice may be endogenous and students with higher ability may be more likely to attend public secondary schools. Furthermore, according to Vella (1998), when the relationship between school choice and higher education participation is purely through the observable variables, researchers can control by including the appropriate conditioning variables in the equation. However, if the unobservable characteristics affecting the school choice are correlated with unobservable characteristics affecting higher education participation, the failure to include an estimate of the unobservable characteristics will lead to sample selection bias.

The next step is the estimation of the logit model to explain an individual's choice with regard to higher education attendance. This logit model essentially estimates the probability that individual i will attend higher education or $H_i = 1$ and it may be written as

(4)
$$Pr(H_i = 1 \mid Z_i) = h((E_{ij} - C_{ij}), Z_{ij})$$
$$= h(X\hat{\beta})$$

where Z_{ij} are independent variables that include personal characteristics and family background, academic abilities, socio-economic status (SES), school quality, labour market incentives and regional variables. Personal characteristics and family background indicators include sex, religion, whether living in urban or rural areas when 12 years old, marital status and number of siblings under 16 years old. Students with more siblings aged less than 16 years are also expected to have a lower chance of attending higher education. Sex and religion are included in the model to control for sex and religious discrimination in higher education attendance. Moreover, it is hypothesized that residents of urban areas have a higher probability of access to higher education. The academic abilities variables include whether the individual has failed or passed a class in primary education and their standardized final exam score in lower and upper secondary education. SES indicators are parents' educational background and whether the student is working when studying in lower and upper secondary school. People who work while attending upper secondary are presumed also to come from a low socio-economic background as they have to contribute to family expenses. Hence, they have a lower chance of higher education attendance. The proxies for school quality consist of the number of classmates and the number of hours of activities in schools.

Labour market incentives or marginal benefits of extra education are denoted by E_{ij} and represent the extra lifetime earnings expected if students attend higher education. C_{ij} is the forgone earnings or opportunity cost of individuals aged 17–24 years old if they attend higher education.

To obtain lifetime earnings, I estimate the predicted earnings of the three age cohorts in the upper secondary and higher education group. The age cohorts are 25–34, 35–44 and 45–55 years old. I obtain the lifetime earnings predictions based on some of the regressors above. From these three separate estimations in each group, I obtain the average for each individual to estimate the predicted life cycle earnings.

To estimate forgone earnings, I follow Flanerry (2009) and use the gap between predicted earnings of those who do not continue to higher education and enter the labour market and predicted of expected income from any work while study in higher education. The earnings forgone maybe written as

(5) $C_i = (\hat{Y}_w - \hat{Y}_s)$

where $\hat{Y}_w$ is the predicted earnings of individuals who decide not to continue to higher education and $\hat{Y}_s$ is the predicted income of individuals from any kind of work when they study in higher education.

I follow Fairlie (2005) and use non-linear Blinder-Oaxaca Decomposition to estimate the gap from the binary choice model. The non-linear decomposition between public and private schools can be written as:

(6) $\bar{H}_j - \bar{H}_k = \left[\sum_{i=1}^{N_j} \frac{F(X_{ij}\hat{\beta}_j)}{N_j} - \sum_{i=1}^{N_k} \frac{F(X_{ik}\beta_j)}{N_k} \right] + \left[\sum_{i=1}^{N_k} \frac{F(X_{ik}\hat{\beta}_j)}{N_k} - \sum_{i=1}^{N_k} \frac{F(X_{ik}\beta_k)}{N_k} \right]$

where X_{ij} and X_{ik} are independent variables for school type j and k. β_j and β_k are vectors of coefficient estimates for school types j and k respectively. N_j and j are the sample sizes for school types j and k. Technically, I use *fairlie* a STATA module created by Jann (2006) to estimate the gap.

4. DATA

4.1 Description of Sample and Sampling Procedure

To estimate the probability of higher education participation in public and private school groups, I use data from the last three waves of the IFLS. The IFLS is a continuing longitudinal survey that provides rich information collected at the individual, household, and community level and contains a variety of economic and non-economic indicators. The IFLS is based on a stratified sample of provinces with random sampling of households within provinces. The stratified sampling of provinces was used not only to capture the cultural diversity of Indonesia but also to be cost effective.[2] The survey was conducted in thirteen provinces with the sample being representative of about 83 per cent of the Indonesian population. This chapter exploits waves 2–4 of the IFLS, omitting wave 1 to data differences between the later 3 waves and the first wave.

I follow the sample selection of Flanerry (2009) focusing on a sample of respondents whose age are from 17 to 24 years old, have finished upper secondary education and face the decision to participate in higher education. Adults over 24 years old are excluded since the decision for these respondents to participate in higher education may be influenced by a greater working opportunity and some other factors that are incorporated in the model. Some respondents in the 17–24 years age cohort were either still studying or did not finish upper secondary school and thus are also excluded from the sample.

Since the IFLS is a longitudinal survey, there may be multiple observations of individual respondent's probabilities that a respondent appears on more than one wave. I provide a particular treatment to classify those respondents. A respondent who was interviewed in all three waves is classified based on the wave which his or her age is within the 17–24 years old bracket. For instance, a respondent whose age is 9 years old in IFLS2 and 12 and 19 years old in IFLS3 and IFLS4 would be classified as being in the IFLS4 sample. If a respondent appears in two or three waves and his or her age is within the age cohort in two waves, then I focus on the latest wave on the assumption that the latest wave is the most up-to-date. Table 5.1 presents the number of respondents by IFLS wave.

The full sample consists of 88,030 observations from three waves. I reduced the sample to 1,400 observations by making the exclusions that

TABLE 5.1
Number in Sample by IFLS

Wave	Upper Secondary	Higher Education	Total
IFLS2 and IFLS3	49	30	79
IFLS2 and IFLS4	20	8	28
IFLS2, IFLS3, and IFLS4	187	96	283
IFLS3	23	2	25
IFLS3 and IFLS4	124	28	152
IFLS4	548	286	834
Total	951	449	1,400

are summarized in Table 5.2. A total of the 71,882 respondents are excluded as they are outside the age range of interest. Moreover, 11,120 respondents who did not graduate from upper secondary school are excluded. Some of respondents still attending upper secondary school are also excluded. A further 3,628 observations are dropped due to missing information on one or multiple variables. Most of the these respondents (1,935) are excluded due to missing information on place of residence when they were 12 years old, while 1,451 respondents are dropped due to missing information on results of final exams in either lower or upper secondary school. Another 242 observations are dropped due to missing information either on family income, number of students in the latest class attended in lower and upper secondary school, type of lower and upper secondary school, foregone income, whether working when studying in lower secondary school, or failed a grade in upper secondary school.

4.2 Descriptive Statistics

I present two descriptive statistics of the sample in Table 5.3 and Table 5.5. Table 5.3 presents the descriptive statistics of the sample by highest education undertaken by the respondents, while Table 5.5 presents the summary statistics by type of upper secondary school. The definitions of the variables are provided in Table 5.4.

In the sample, the number of students who attend higher education is lower than the number of students who do not continue to higher education. Only about 32 per cent of students continue on to higher education. The proportion of females is slightly higher than males in both groups. Based

TABLE 5.2
Number of Sample Deletions by Reason

No. of Obs.	Note
88,030	The initial full sample
–71,882	Age outside 17 and 24 years old
16,148	Age between 17 and 24 years old
–11,120	Has not graduated from upper secondary school
–3,628	Missing data on one or more variables
1,400	Remaining observations in the sample

TABLE 5.3
Descriptive Statistics by Highest Education Taken

	Not in Higher Education (N=1,445)		In Higher Education (N=659)	
	Mean	Std. Dev	Mean	Std. Dev
MALE	0.509	0.500	0.439	0.497
ISLAM	0.894	0.308	0.810	0.392
LANGINDO	0.387	0.487	0.475	0.500
URBAN	0.611	0.488	0.780	0.415
SIBLING	1.408	1.275	1.012	1.229
WORKSMA	0.111	0.315	0.065	0.247
WORKSMP	0.068	0.252	0.035	0.184
SMAFAIL	0.012	0.108	0.003	0.055
NEMSMP	35.153	13.859	38.256	13.97
NEMSMA	29.844	12.473	35.071	13.944
TSRATIO	0.091	0.084	0.086	0.073
FATHSHHE	0.144	0.351	0.347	0.477
MOTHSHHE	0.063	0.243	0.226	0.419
NSUMARES	0.059	0.235	0.062	0.242
WSUMARES	0.062	0.242	0.085	0.279
SSUMARES	0.056	0.23	0.068	0.252
LAMPUNGRES	0.043	0.203	0.026	0.159
JAKARTARES	0.143	0.350	0.167	0.373
WJAVARES	0.134	0.341	0.103	0.304
CJAVARES	0.114	0.318	0.091	0.288
JOGJARES	0.066	0.248	0.126	0.332
EJAVARES	0.134	0.341	0.099	0.298
BALIRES	0.044	0.204	0.061	0.239
NTBRES	0.045	0.207	0.052	0.221
KALSELRES	0.033	0.177	0.027	0.163
SULSELRES	0.055	0.229	0.033	0.180
OTHERRES	0.012	0.108	0.000	0.000

TABLE 5.4
Definitions of Variables

Variables	Description
HE	Higher education is the highest level education? yes=1, no=0
MALE	Male=1, female=0
ISLAM	Religion Islam? yes=1, no=0
LANGINDO	Do you speak Bahasa Indonesia in daily life? yes=1, no=0
URBAN	Live in urban? yes=1, no=0
SIBLING	How many siblings do you have?
WORKSMA	Did you work, when attending upper secondary school? yes=1, no=0
WORKSMP	Did you work, when attending junior secondary school? yes=1, no=0
SMAFAIL	Failed in upper secondary school? yes=1, no=0
NEMSMP	Final exam (Ebtana/UAN) score in junior secondary education
NEMSMA	Final exam (Ebtana/UAN) score in upper secondary education
FATHSHHE	Highest level education of father is uppersec. Or higher education? yes=1, no=0
MOTHSHHE	Highest level education of mother is uppersec. Or higher education? yes=1, no=0
PRIVATENRJH	Attend private non religious or secular lower/junior secondary school yes=1, no=0
PRIVATEISJH	Attend private Islam or lower/junior secondary school yes=1, no=0
PRIVATECPOJH	Attend private Christian lower/junior secondary school yes=1, no=0
NSUMARES	Reside in North Sumatra? yes=0, no=1
WSUMARES	Reside in West Sumatra? yes=0, no=1
SSUMARES	Reside in South Sumatra? yes=0, no=1
LAMPUNGRES	Reside in Lampung? yes=0, no=1
JAKARTARES	Reside in DKI Jakarta? yes=0, no=1
WJAVARES	Reside in West Java? yes=0, no=1
CJAVARES	Reside in Central Java? yes=0, no=1
JOGJARES	Reside in Jogjakarta? yes=0, no=1
EJAVARES	Reside in East Java? yes=0, no=1
BALIRES	Reside in Bali? yes=0, no=1
NTBRES	Reside in NTB? yes=0, no=1
KALSELRES	Reside in South Kalimantan? yes=0, no=1
SULSELRES	Reside in South Sulawesi? yes=0, no=1
OTHERRES	Reside in South Sulawesi? yes=0, no=1

on family background, the proportion of Muslim students in the higher education group is lower than the proportion of Muslim students in the upper secondary school group. The proportion of students who lived in a city or a town area when they were 12 years old is lower in the higher education group than in the upper secondary group. The higher education group has lower average number of siblings than the upper secondary group.

Students who participate in higher education generally come from higher SES families. The proxies for SES in this study are parents' education, family income, and a dummy variable indicating whether a student worked while studying in upper secondary education. The proportion of parents that attended upper secondary and higher education (FATHSHHE and MOTHSHHE) is larger for the higher education group than the upper secondary group. The proportion of fathers and mothers who attended upper secondary or higher education (FATHSHHE and MOTHSHHE) in the higher education group are 36.5 and 23.8 per cent respectively. The proportions of FATHSHHE and MOTHSHHE in this group are higher than in the upper secondary school group where the figures are only 15.2 and 8.1 per cent respectively. Moreover, the natural logarithm of family income in the higher education group is 16.594, whereas in the upper secondary group it is 16.362, and the proportion of students in the higher education group who worked while studying in upper secondary school is lower than for the upper secondary group.

In terms of academic achievement, students from the higher education group are superior to students from the upper secondary education group. The indicators of academic achievement are measured by final exam scores in upper and lower secondary education (SCORESMA and SCORESMP) and a dummy variable for whether the student failed a grade in primary education (PRIFAIL). Students who attend higher education had a higher average final exam scores in lower secondary education (SCORESMP) and upper secondary education (SCORESMA). The average final exam scores, SCORESMA and SCORESMP, of the higher education group are 38.595 and 32.366, respectively whereas the average scores for the upper secondary education group are 36.168 and 28.916, respectively. The higher education group also has a lower proportion of PRIFAIL than the upper secondary group. The rate of failure in one or more grades in primary school in the higher education group is 4.5 per cent, whereas the failure rate in the upper secondary education group is 12.5 per cent.

Table 5.5 shows the characteristics of individuals by the four types of upper secondary school. In terms of higher education participation, individuals from the private Christian group have the highest rate for higher education participation with more than half respondents (57.4 per cent) continuing on to higher education. Public schools considered to have better inputs than private schools have a 43 per cent participation rate. This rate is considerably higher than the other two private school groups, private non-religious and private Islamic with participation rates of only 13 per cent and 25.9 per cent respectively.

Female students outnumber male students in all schools, except in private Islamic schools. The proportion of male students in private Islamic, private non-religious, public and private Christian schools are 50.7, 47.0, 45.4 and 38.4 per cent, respectively. Muslim students are the majority in all schools including in private Christian schools. The proportion of Muslim students in private Christian schools is 57.5 per cent whereas in public schools and other private schools the proportion is higher than 85 per cent. Most of the private Islamic school students lived in a village area when they were 12 years old, whereas most of the students from public schools and other private schools lived in either a city or town area.

In terms of socio-economic status, public and private Christian school students mostly come from high SES families. About 30.1 per cent of fathers from the private Christian school group attended higher education, whereas 28.2 per cent of fathers from public school group attended higher education. On the other hand, the percentage of private non-religious and private Islamic students whose father attended higher education are only 13.5 and 16.9 per cent respectively. As with fathers' educational background, the education of mother in public and private Christian schools is higher than in the other two private school groups. The proportion of students in the public and private Christian school groups whose mother attended higher education are 17.3 and 20.5 per cent, whereas in the private non-religious and private Islamic school groups are 8.3 and 7.9 per cent respectively. Moreover, in terms of family income, public school and private Christian school groups have also higher incomes than the private non-religious school and private Islamic school groups. Despite the fact that students in private Christian schools come from high SES families, the proportion of students who worked while attending upper secondary school (WORKSMA) is the highest among all the groups. The proportion of students who worked while attending upper secondary education

TABLE 5.5
Summary Statistics by Type of School

Variables	Public		Private NR		Private Islam		Private Christian	
	Mean	Std.Dev	Mean	Std.Dev	Mean	Std.Dev	Mean	Std.Dev
HE	0.406	0.491	0.159	0.366	0.234	0.424	0.543	0.501
MALE	0.455	0.498	0.528	0.500	0.502	0.501	0.556	0.5
ISLAM	0.861	0.346	0.892	0.31	0.99	0.099	0.309	0.465
LANGINDO	0.398	0.490	0.514	0.500	0.267	0.443	0.420	0.497
URBAN	0.644	0.479	0.732	0.443	0.574	0.495	0.741	0.441
SIBLING	1.298	1.321	1.311	1.229	1.251	1.235	1.000	1.061
WORKSMA	0.079	0.27	0.109	0.312	0.129	0.335	0.123	0.331
WORKSMP	0.052	0.222	0.064	0.245	0.056	0.231	0.086	0.283
SMAFAIL	0.005	0.067	0.014	0.119	0.017	0.128	0.000	0.000
NEMSMP	38.091	14.242	33.143	12.193	35.273	15.953	35.627	10.285
NEMSMA	33.175	13.36	29.125	11.692	29.443	14.245	34.295	13.467
TSRATIO	0.086	0.071	0.091	0.086	0.098	0.102	0.095	0.077
FATHSHHE	0.262	0.440	0.149	0.357	0.122	0.328	0.247	0.434
MOTHSHHE	0.148	0.355	0.077	0.267	0.059	0.237	0.148	0.357
N	1,097		623		303		81	

in this group is 21.9 per cent, whereas the proportion of WORKSMA in public, private non-religious and private Islamic schools are 6.4, 12.2, and 12.9 per cent respectively.

Students from public and private Christian schools have also superior academic achievements. The mean of final exam score in lower secondary education is the highest for the public schools group. The average of this score among the public school group is 37.96, whereas the final exam scores in private non-religious, private Islamic and private Christian schools are 35.28, 36.75, and 35.88 respectively. The private Christian school group has the highest final exam score in upper secondary education (SCORESMA) or 33.31, whereas the upper secondary exam scores of public, private non-religious and private Islamic schools are 31.26, 29.65, and 28.31 respectively. The mean of PRIFAIL in public schools is also the lowest among these groups. Hence, public school students have higher average pass rate in primary education than students from private schools.

5. EMPIRICAL RESULT

5.1 Upper Secondary School Choice Estimation

Table 5.5 presents the multinomial logit model of choice among the four upper secondary school categories with 2,101 observations. I follow some previous studies about school choice effect (Bedi and Garg 2000; Le and Miller 2003; Newhouse and Beegle 2005) to assess whether selection bias is present in the probit model of the higher education participation using the multinomial logit estimation. The model's independent variables include: personal characteristics and family background (MALE, ISLAM, LANGINDO, URBAN, WORKSMP, and SIBLING), parents' education (FATHSHHE and MOTHSHHE), control variable for ability (PRIFAIL and NEMSMP), and junior secondary school choice (PRIVATENRJH, PRIVATEISSH, PRIVATECPOJH).

The positive coefficient on MALE in all estimation indicates that female student has higher odds to attend public lower secondary school as compared to male student. As expected, the positive and significant coefficient on ISLAM shows that a Muslim student is more likely to attend private Islamic school and private secular than public school. On the other hand, a non-Muslim student prefers to study at private Christian school than public school. Students who lived in urban area have higher odds to

TABLE 5.6
Multinomial Logit Estimates of School Choice Model

Variables	Private NR b/(t)	Private Islam b/(t)	Private Christian b/(t)
MALE	0.335***	0.197	0.360
	(0.111)	(0.146)	(0.295)
ISLAM	0.449**	2.349***	−1.982***
	(0.185)	(0.579)	(0.316)
LANGINDO	0.405***	−0.417***	−0.695**
	(0.115)	(0.160)	(0.326)
URBAN	0.438***	0.043	0.500
	(0.129)	(0.156)	(0.350)
SIBLING	0.004	−0.040	−0.085
	(0.042)	(0.057)	(0.115)
WORKSMP	0.221	0.036	0.662
	(0.248)	(0.336)	(0.589)
PRIFAIL	0.898***	0.767***	0.834**
	(0.164)	(0.207)	(0.404)
NEMSMP	−0.025***	−0.011**	−0.024*
	(0.005)	(0.005)	(0.012)
PRIVATENRJH	2.161***	1.110***	0.849
	(0.186)	(0.281)	(0.520)
PRIVATEISJH	1.079***	.353***	0.285
	(0.185)	(0.181)	(0.754)
PRIVATECPOJH	1.261***	−0.128	3.608***
	(0.385)	(1.031)	(0.431)
FATHSHHE	−0.582***	−0.615***	−0.202
	(0.159)	(0.231)	(0.407)
MOTHSHHE	−0.371*	−0.417	0.135
	(0.204)	(0.312)	(0.550)
CONSTANT	−1.100***	−3.525***	−1.402**
	(0.275)	(0.599)	(0.611)
Pseudo R-Square	0.189		
N	2101		
Chi2	714.333***		

Notes: Omitted category is public school group. T-statistics are in parenthesis and heteroscedasticity consistent.
* Significance at 10 per cent level, ** Significance at 5 per cent level, and *** Significance at 1 per cent level. Dummies representing the province where individual was lived were also included in the model.

attend private schools than public schools. Students who help finance the family by working when attending lower secondary school have lower odds to attend public school. This result suggests that students from poor family background are unlikely to attend public schools, usually considered the best schools in the country, than with private Islamic schools.

Based on positive and statistically significant on father education background, students whose father that have upper secondary or higher education background (FATHSHHE) have higher odds to attend public schools than private schools. Moreover, students whose mother has upper secondary or higher education background (MOTHSHHE) is most likely to attend public school than private Islamic or private secular school.

Based on control variable for ability, students who have good early academics ability or never failed in lower primary school have higher odds to attend public schools than private schools. NEMSMP has a statistically significant negative coefficient in all estimations as the higher score of final exam means the higher odds of student attending public school. This result is supported by the summary statistics by school type in Table 5.5 which indicates that students from private schools have lower scores on national final exam (NEM) than the students from public schools. These conditions occur as admission into most public schools require a minimum grade on national final exam score.

Lower secondary school type coefficients are significant in terms of the probability to choose upper secondary school. Students from private secular and private Islamic schools are less likely to attend public schools as compared to private schools. On the other hand, a student in private Christian school prefers to attend public school than private Islamic school even though he still has higher odds to attend private secular and private Christian as compared to public school.

5.2 Higher Education Participation with Correction of Selectivity Bias

As mentioned earlier, the selection of school particularly in public school is not random and thus consequently there is a possibility of selection bias in school choice. This chapter, following Lee (1983), will use the two step technique to overcome the selection bias problem. The first step to verify the selection is by creating selectivity variables. I use the results from multinomial logit to calculate the selectivity variable, λ_{ij}. Table 5.7 shows the estimations of probit model for higher education participation or HEP which include λ_{ij} as a regressor. The HEP probit estimation use six exclusion restrictions in the structural equation: PRIFAIL, WORKSMP,

TABLE 5.7
Probit Estimation with Selectivity Correction

Variables	Public Coeff./(t-stat)	Private NR Coeff./(t-stat)	Private Islam Coeff./(t-stat)	Private Christian Coeff./(t-stat)
FOREGONE	-0.221	-0.143	-0.157	-0.419
	(0.012)***	(0.013)***	(0.019)***	(0.040)***
TSRATIO	-0.206	0.106	0.815	-0.663
	(0.177)	(0.152)	(0.231)***	(0.440)
MALE	0.113	0.0921	0.032	0.348
	(0.0252)***	(0.027)***	(0.046)	(0.076)***
ISLAM	-0.022	-0.197	-0.037	0.022
	(0.045)	(0.052)***	(0.232)	(0.076)
LANGINDO	0.120	0.065	0.056	0.234
	(0.031)***	(0.031)**	(0.065)	(0.098)**
URBAN	-0.009	-0.023	0.135	-0.255
	(0.029)	(0.032)	(0.053)**	(0.089)***
SIBLING	-0.034	-0.039	-0.035	-0.069
	(0.010)***	(0.010)***	(0.018)*	(0.040)*
WORKSMA	-0.026	-0.038	0.039	-0.104
	(0.046)	(0.041)	(0.066)	(0.100)
SMAFAIL	-0.090	-0.036	-0.638	0.000
	(0.175)	(0.107)	(0.195)***	(0.000)
ZNEMSMA	0.048	0.046	0.063	-0.002
	(0.013)***	(0.015)***	(0.022)***	(0.038)
FATHSHHE	0.178	0.026	0.081	0.154
	(0.033)***	(0.040)	(0.070)	(0.096)
MOTHSHHE	0.165	0.189	0.003	0.161
	(0.041)***	(0.053)***	(0.098)	(0.120)
CONSTANT	0.176	0.527	0.183	0.772
	(0.075)**	(0.083)***	(0.256)	(0.219)***
λ	-0.113	0.127	0.040	-0.006
	(0.045)**	(0.039)***	(0.049)	(0.043)
Adjusted R2	0.345	0.300	0.235	0.730
N	1095	622	303	81

Notes: Standard errors are in parenthesis and heteroscedasticity consistent. * Significance at 10 per cent level, ** Significance at 5 per cent level, and *** Significance at 1 per cent level. Dummies representing the province where individual was lived were also included in the model.

ZNEMSMP, PRIVATENRJH, PRIVATEISJH, and PRIVATECPOJH. Following Wooldridge (2001), I will exclude all variables in the selection equation from the structural equation or the probit higher education participation equation. The objective of this exclusion is to avoid the estimation from becoming very imprecise.

The coefficients on λ_{ij} are statistically significant for public, private secular, and private Islamic schools. These evidence imply that there are selection biases in upper secondary school choice. Coefficients on selectivity variable for public schools and private Christian schools are negative which indicate that unobservable characteristics of students in these school types tend to have lower probability to participate in higher education. On the other hand, the negative coefficient on λ_{ij} in private secular and private Islamic schools imply that unobservable characteristics of students in these schools tend to have higher probability to participate in higher education.

Prior to discussing the results in probit model with selectivity correction, I compare the results to the probit model without selectivity bias. The results of probit model without selectivity bias correction are presented in Table 5.8. Whether or not the selectivity bias coefficients are significant, the insertion of these variables tends to alter other coefficient estimates. Generally, coefficients in all estimations decreased. Some of the estimations have more significant variables. One that changed dramatically is the private Christian group; the probit estimation without the selection bias treatment has only three significant variables, but, however, after the addition by selection variable the significant variables increased to nine.[3] In contrast, in the private secular group the number of significant variables decreases from 10 to 9. One variable that changed from significant at 1 per cent level to insignificant is SMAFAIL.

The results of probit estimation with selectivity correction provide important findings about the determinants of higher education participation of students from each type of school. Some of the determinants have the same effect as the decision of student from different type of school whereas some others do not. The variables that have same effect to the student across different type of school are earnings forgone (FOREGONE), parents' upper secondary and higher education background (FATHSHHE and MOTHSHE), number of sibling (SIBLING), sex (MALE), and use of language (LANGINDO).

The coefficients on earning foregone (FOREGONE), as expected, are negative and significant in all type of schools which means that students have disincentives to attend higher education from positive change on earnings forgone. Students from private Christian school are the most sensitive to the change in earnings foregone as its coefficient on FORGONE is the lowest or –0.419.

Probit Estimation of Higher Education Participation

Variables	Public coeff./(se)	Pr-NR coeff./(se)	Pr-Islam coeff./(se)	Pr-Christ coeff./(se)	All Sample coeff./(se)
FOREGONE	-0.703***	-0.683***	-0.660***	-20.781	-0.679***
	(0.064)	(0.109)	(0.105)	(.)	(0.050)
TSRATIO	-0.785	0.117	2.996***	16.353	0.293
	(0.648)	(0.727)	(1.035)	(.)	(0.404)
MALE	0.348***	0.358**	0.226	19.283	0.322***
	(0.098)	(0.176)	(0.188)	(.)	(0.076)
ISLAM	-0.112	-0.890***	-0.287	-2.791***	-0.428***
	(0.151)	(0.275)	(0.735)	(0.272)	(0.106)
LANGINDO	0.461***	0.291	0.264	13.674	0.390***
	(0.116)	(0.187)	(0.255)	(.)	(0.084)
URBAN	0.046	-0.035	0.621**	-15.621***	0.122
	(0.117)	(0.230)	(0.242)	(0.248)	(0.091)
SIBLING	-0.125***	-0.278***	-0.176**	-2.571***	-0.162***
	(0.038)	(0.080)	(0.080)	(0.110)	(0.031)
WORKSMA	-0.105	-0.332	0.107	6.211	-0.138
	(0.178)	(0.265)	(0.315)	(.)	(0.126)
SMAFAIL	-0.550	0.059			-1.508
	(0.645)	(0.540)			(0.989)
ZNEMSMA	0.163***	0.192**	0.252***	5.001***	0.216***
	(0.049)	(0.083)	(0.084)	(0.277)	(0.035)
FATHSHHE	0.589***	0.036	0.469	5.802	0.525***
	(0.118)	(0.202)	(0.273)	(.)	(0.090)
MOTHSHHE	0.507***	0.860***	-0.077	7.605	0.555***
	(0.155)	(0.241)	(0.366)	(.)	(0.116)
CONSTANT	-0.860***	-0.116	-1.624	-2.189	-0.699***
	(0.238)	(0.403)	(0.871)	(.)	(0.174)
Pseudo R2	0.306	0.379	0.297	1	0.322
N	1089	614	297	72	2087
Chi2	252.820***	163.131***	66.376***	.	449.246***

Notes: Standard errors are in parenthesis and heteroscedasticity consistent. * Significance at 10 per cent level, ** Significance at 5 per cent level, and *** Significance at 1 per cent level. Dummies representing the province where individual was lived were also included in the model.

Parents education background (FATHSHHE and MOTHSHHE) have similar effect in all groups as the coefficients are positive and significant. Among the school group, students from private secular school have the most advantage when their mothers attend upper secondary education or higher education. On the other hand, father's education background (FATHSHHE) affects the probability of higher education access differently. Except in private secular group, father's education in upper secondary and higher education increases the probability of student to attend post-secondary education. The influence of father's education is strongest to students from private Christian school.

Male students in all type of school have higher probability to continue to higher education than female students. Male students in private Christian and public schools have more chance to attend post-secondary education than students from private Islam and private secular ones. Moreover, number of siblings (SIBLING) also significantly affects the higher education participation. The coefficients on SIBLING are all negative and significant in all type of school indicating that the more siblings under 16 year old living in a household the less probability of a student in that household continuing to higher education.

There are mix signals on coefficients teacher-student ratio (TSRATIO), score of final exam (ZNEMSMA), and failed in upper secondary school (SMAFAIL). TSRATIO is a variable that provides information about school quality. ZNEMSMA and SMAFAIL are variables that inform about student abilities. In public schools, coefficient of ZNEMSMA is positive, whereas coefficients of ZNEMSMA and TSRATIO are negative. Intuitively, these results inform that the factors of ability are more important than school quality in higher education participation. On the contrary, positive coefficients on ZNEMSMA, TSRATIO and negative coefficient on SMAFAIL in private secular and private Islam schools inform that high ability and good school quality are important factor for student in those private schools to access higher education.

5.3 The Non-Linear Decomposition of the Logit of Higher Education Participation

In this subsection, I provide the result of non-linear decomposition estimation to identify the causes of the choice of school type differences on higher education participation. The summary statistics in Table 5.5 indicates that 54.3 per cent and 40.6 per cent students from private Christian and public schools continue to post-secondary education. On the other hand, only 23.4 per cent and 15.9 per cent students from private Islam and secular school participate in higher education. I use the non-linear decomposition as a technique to find the strongest determinant of group differences that contribute to higher education access.

The appraisals of non-linear decomposition estimation for school choice gap on higher education participation between public, private secular, private Islam and private Christian schools are in Table 5.9 and Table 5.10. The independent variables consist of all variables from the previous probit with selectivity correction, which are earnings foregone (FOREGONE), school quality (TSRATIO), differences in sex (MALE), religion (ISLAM), language (LANGINDO), household location (URBAN), number of siblings (SIBLING), whether working in upper secondary school or not (WORKSMA), academic performance (ZNEMSMA and SMAFAIL), parent education background (FATHSHHE and MOTHSHHE), and a set of dummies of province where individual was educated in upper secondary school.

The results of the decomposition for private secular schools are reported in column 2 in Tables 5.9 and 5.10. The gap between public and private secular group on higher education participation is the largest or 0.249. There are four determinants that contribute statistically significant to the gap; personal characteristics (PERSONAL), earning foregone (INCOME), academics performance (ABILITY) and parents' education background (PARENTS). All indicators are both significant at 1 per cent level. The other two determinants FAMILY and SCHOOL are not significant. Earning foregone (INCOME) is the highest contributor to the gap between public and private secular school as it contributes 0.114 or 11.4 percentage points to the gap. The second largest gap between public and private secular is contributed by parents' educational backgrounds. The difference of parents' educational background is 0.033 and significant at 1 per cent level. Both variables on parents' education determinant, FATHSHHE and MOTHSHHE, are statistically significant at 1 per cent and the influence of father's education is stronger than mother's education background. This result support the evidence from the summary statistics in Table 5.3. In public school, the percentage of father that attends upper secondary or higher education background is 26.2 per cent whereas private secular students are almost half of the public school group or 14.9 per cent. The

TABLE 5.9
Non-Linear Decomposition of Higher Education Participation with Selectivity Bias Correction

	Private NR	Private Islam	Private Christian
Higher Ed. Participation Diff.I	0.249	0.172	−0.136
From school choice differences in:			
FOREGONE	0.114***	0.067***	0.037***
	(0.005)	(0.004)	(0.004)
TSRATIO	0.000	0.002	0.001
	(0.000)	(0.002)	(0.002)
MALE	−0.000	−0.001	−0.008***
	(0.001)	(0.001)	(0.003)
ISLAM	0.001	0.003	−0.013
	(0.001)	(0.005)	(0.024)
LANGINDO	−0.010***	0.013***	−0.004
	(0.003)	(0.003)	(0.003)
URBAN	−0.001	0.000	−0.001
	(0.003)	(0.001)	(0.004)
SIBLING	0.003***	−0.001	−0.009***
	(0.001)	(0.001)	(0.003)
WORKSMA	0.001	0.001	0.000
	(0.001)	(0.002)	(0.001)
SMAFAIL	0.001	0.001	−0.001
	(0.000)	(0.001)	(0.002)
ZNEMSMA	0.010***	0.007***	−0.006**
	(0.003)	(0.002)	(0.002)
FATHSHHE	0.021***	0.025***	−0.004
	(0.005)	(0.005)	(0.003)
MOTHSHHE	0.012***	0.013***	0.001
	(0.003)	(0.004)	(0.002)
N	1,717	1,398	1,176

Standard errors are in parenthesis and heteroscedasticity consistent. * Significance at 10 per cent level, ** Significance at 5 per cent level, and *** Significance at 1 per cent level. Dummies representing the province where individual was lived and selectivity variables were also included in the model.

proportion of mother that attends upper secondary or higher education in public school (14.8 per cent) is more than twice that of the private secular school (7.7 per cent). ABILITY also plays a role in higher education participation gap. Even though ABILITY is not as strong as parent education and income, it contributes 0.011 to the total gap. As expected, the academic ability of student from public school is higher than private secular school.

TABLE 5.10
Non-Linear Decomposition of Higher Education Participation with Selectivity Bias Correction between Public School and Private Schools

	Private NR	Private Islam	Private Christian
Higher Education Participation Differential	0.172	–0.136	0.249
Contributions from school choice differences in:			
INCOME	0.114***	0.067***	0.042***
	(0.005)	(0.004)	(0.004)
SCHOOL	0.000	0.002	0.001
	(0.000)	(0.002)	(0.002)
PERSONAL	–0.010**	0.016***	–0.025
	(0.004)	(0.006)	(0.024)
FAMILY	0.002	0.000	–0.010*
	(0.003)	(0.002)	(0.005)
ABILITY	0.011***	0.008***	–0.007**
	(0.003)	(0.003)	(0.003)
PARENTS	0.033***	0.037***	–0.002
	(0.004)	(0.004)	(0.003)
N	1,717	1,398	1,176

Notes: Standard errors are in parenthesis and heteroscedasticity consistent. * Significance at 10 per cent level, ** Significance at 5 per cent level, and *** Significance at 1 per cent level. Dummies representing the province where individual was lived and selectivity variables were also included in the model.

The smallest contributor to the gap is personal characteristics and, in fact, this variable contributes negatively to the gap. The higher number of non-Muslim students from wealthy family in private secular school than public school could be one of the reasons for this gap is negative.

The family background (FAMILY), and school quality (SCHOOL) do not play a major role in explaining public and private secular differences in higher education participation. FAMILY contributes 0.002 to the gap whereas SCHOOL only contributes a little bit more than –0.000. SIBLING and WORKSMA have positive contribution whereas URBAN contributes negatively to the gap.

The disparity of probability of higher education participation between public and private Islam school group is smaller than private secular gap, but still quite large or 0.172. The non-linear decomposition results between public and private Islam group are in column 3 of Tables 5.9 and 5.10. There are four determinants that statistically significantly contribute to the difference on higher education participation between public and private Islam. Those determinants are, from the largest to the smallest, earning foregone (INCOME), parents' education background (PARENTS), personal characteristics (PERSONAL), and academic performance (ABILITY). All gaps are significant at level 1 per cent. The other two gaps, school quality and family background (FAMILY), are small and not significant.

Similar to the result on private secular decomposition, INCOME is the highest contributor to the difference between public and private Islam schools; it contributes 0.067, or 6.7 percentage points gap. Also similar to private secular decomposition, parents' education contribute significantly to the gap; FATHSSHE contributes 0.025 which is higher than MOTHSHHE that contributes 0.013. The other big gap is contributed by PERSONAL or personal characteristics. LANGINDO is the biggest contributor and significant in PERSONAL. However, unlike the private secular gap, LANGINDO has a positive contribution as it is evident that socio economic background has an important role in the gap between public and private Islam school. The last significant gap is the difference in ABILITY. The gap on ABILTY mostly comes from the normal score of national test or ZNEMSMA (0.007) that is significant at level 1 per cent. Again, similar to the private secular decomposition, the large contribution in ABILITY is primarily due to large gap in the average score; the average of national test score of public school is 33.175 whereas the average score of private Islam students is only 29.443.

PARENT is the second strongest determinants that contribute to the gap between public and private Islam school. It contributes 0.074 as only two variables are significant statistically; FATHSHHE and MOTHSHHE. The share of FATHSHHE to the gap is 0.038 whereas that of MOTHSHHE is 0.030. The strong influence of FATHSHHE and MOTHSHHE to the gap is expected since mean of FATHSSHE and MOTHSSHE of private Islam group is lower than public school. The mean of FATHSHHE and MOTHSHHE in private Islam are 0.282 and 0.194 whereas in public school they 0.474 and 0.308 respectively.

The third determinant that statistically significantly contribute to the gap between public and private Islam group is FAMILY as it is significant at 5 per cent. Despite the significance of FAMILY, all variables in FAMILY are not statistically significant. LANGINDO and SIBLIG contribute lower than 0.000 to the gap whereas URBAN and WORKSMA contribute 0.003 and 0.006 respectively. Moreover, SCHOOL or school quality gap is small

TABLE 5.11
Non-Student Earnings and Student Earning Estimation
Aged 17–22

Variables	Non-Student	Student
ZNEMSMP	0.163	0.698*
	(0.119)	(0.423)
EDUC	0.030	0.163
	(0.103)	(0.150)
AGE	−0.159	−1.272
	(0.833)	(3.477)
AGE2	0.006	0.036
	(0.021)	(0.089)
MALE	0.587***	
	(0.110)	
ISLAM	−0.046	
	(0.161)	
PRIFAIL	0.045	−0.219
	(0.136)	(0.743)
LANGINDO	0.317***	
	(0.111)	
FATHSHHE	0.243	
	(0.161)	
MOTHSHHE	0.119	
	(0.227)	
URBAN	0.003	0.559
	(0.131)	(0.511)
LAMBDA	0.775	0.244
	(0.341)	(0.956)
CONSTANT	8.437	16.130
	(8.252)	(33.808)
N	1142	74
Wald Chi2	44.038***	9.830

Notes: Standard errors are in parenthesis and heteroscedasticity consistent.
* Significance at 10 per cent level, ** Significance at 5 per cent level, and
*** Significance at 1 per cent level. Dummies representing the province where
individual was lived were also included in the model.

insignificant statistically but positive. The positive gap informs that the better quality of public school still has a role in increasing the higher education attendances.

Contrary to the two decomposition result, the gap between public and private Christian school is negative as the difference is −1.136. This evidence confirmed that the private Christian group has higher chance to access higher education than public school group.

There are three determinants that are statistically significant to the gap between public-private Christian. They are INCOME, FAMILY and ABILITY. INCOME or earnings forgone contributes to the positive 0.042 difference to the gap. However this positive gap is compensated by the dummy variables of province of the household lived and selectivity variables gap.[4] The gap in ABILITY is –0.007 and significant at level 0.05 per cent. The gap in ABILITY is mostly contributed by ZNEMSMA as it confirms that the academic ability of private Christian is higher than public school group. This result supports Bedi and Garg (2000) that considers private Christian or Catholic school as the best school in Indonesia. The negative gap on FAMILY and PARENTS also confirms that students from private Christian school have higher SES status and their parents, particularly the father, are more educated.

6. CONCLUSION

This chapter discusses the effect of school quality on higher education participation in Indonesia. Using Fairlie's (2005) non-linear decomposition technique, I find that individuals who studied in public secondary schools have higher probabilities to attend higher education than private non-religious school and private Islamic school group. On the other hand, private Christian schools are superior to public school in terms of higher education participation.

The results of the higher education probability decomposition have some implications. First, Indonesian public school students are likely to attend higher education than students from private non-religious and private Islamic schools. The probability of the public school group attending higher education is 27.5 percentage points more than the private non-religious school group, whereas it is 19.5 percentage points more than the private Islamic school group. On the other hand, the negative disparity between public schools and private Christian schools confirms the superiority of private Christian schools with respect to higher education access. The probability of private Christian schools students of attending higher education is 8.8 per cent higher than the public school group.

The evidence also indicates that there are considerable differences between public school, private non-religious school and Islamic school graduates in terms of academic achievement and socio-economic status. I find that school quality differences of these schools and unobservable variables explain the difference of higher education participation among these groups. Specifically, a low level of parents' education and academic achievement provides an important contribution to a low probability of entering higher education for private non-religious school graduates. On the other hand, a low level of father's education and family income contribute substantially to a low probability of accessing higher education for the private non-religious group.

Failing a grade in primary education reduces the probability of higher education attendance of public and private Islamic school graduates by 0.288 and 0.149 log points respectively. The significant effect on early academic achievement in earnings formation supports the investing in early childhood argument by Heckman (2006). Investing in early childhood education programme creates higher returns than later interventions such as public job training programme, reduced teacher-pupil ratio, convict rehabilitation programs or expenditure on police (Heckman 2006).

Notes

1. See Altonji (1993) for a model that explicitly estimates the uncertainty that is inherent in the higher education participation decision.
2. For detail sampling method, see "The 1993 Indonesian Family Life Survey", DRU-1195/1-6-NICHD/AID, The RAND Corporation, December 1995.
3. Note that the significant coefficient on constant and selectivity variable are ignored.
4. The gap on dummy province and selectivity variable are not shown in the table since I do not focus for those determinants. The gap on dummy province is xxx and for xxx selectivity variable in private Christian group.

References

Akabayashi, H. "Average effects of school choice on educational attainment: Evidence from Japanese high school attendance zones". Unpublished manuscript, 2006 <http://www.econ.keio.ac.jp/staff/hakab/akabayashijsa.pdf>.

Altonji, J.G. "The demand for and return to education when education outcomes are uncertain". *Journal of Labor Economics* 11, no. 1 (1993): 48–83.

———, T. Elder and C. Taber. "Selection on observed and unobserved variables:

Assessing the effectiveness of catholic schools". *Journal of Political Economy* 113, no. 1 (2005): 151–84.

Becker, G.S. and H.G. Lewis. "On the interaction between the quantity and quality of children". *Journal of Political Economy* 81, no. 2 (1973): S279–88.

Bedi, A.S. and A. Garg. "The effectiveness of private versus public schools: The case of Indonesia". *Journal of Development Economics* 61, issue 2 (2000): 463–94.

Blinder, A.S. "Wage Discrimination: Reduced Form and Structural Estimates". *Journal of Human Resources* 8, no. 4 (1973): 436–55.

Buchori, M. and Malik, A. "The Evolution of Higher Education in Indonesia". In *Asian Universities: Historical Perspectives and Contemporary Challenges*, edited by P. Altbach and T. Umakoshio. Baltimore: John Hopkins University Press, 2004.

Cappellari, L. "High school types, academic performance and early labour market outcomes". Technical report, Universita del Piemonte Orientale, CHILD and IZA Bonn, 2004.

Dubin, J. and D. Rivers. "Selection bias in linear regression, logit and probit models". *Sociological Methods and Research* 18, no. 2 (1989): 360–90.

Edwards, L.N. and M.K. Pasquale. "Women's higher education in Japan: Family background, economic factors, and the equal employment opportunity law". *Journal of the Japanese and International Economies* 17, no. 1 (2003): 1–32.

Eide, E., D. Goldhaber and M. Showalter. "Does Catholic High School Attendance Lead to Attendance at a More Selective College?". *Social Science Quarterly* 85, no. 5 (2004): 1335–52.

Epple, D. and R.E. Romano. "Competition between private and public schools, vouchers, and peer-group effects". *American Economic Review* 88, no. 1 (1998): 33–62.

Evans, W.N. and R.M. Schwab. "Finishing high school and starting college: Do catholic schools make a difference?". *Quarterly Journal of Economics* 110, no. 4 (1995): 941–74.

Fairlie, R.W. "An extension of the Blinder-Oaxaca decomposition technique to Logit and Probit models". *Journal of Economic and Social Measurement* 30, no. 4 (2005): 305.

Flannerry, Darragh and C. O'Donoghue. "The determinants of higher education participation in Ireland: A micro analysis". *Economic and Social Review* 40, no. 1 (Spring 2009): 73–107.

Heckman, J. "Skill Formation and the Economics of Investing in Disadvantaged Children". *Science*, vol. 312, 30 June 2006: 1900–902.

Jacob, B.A. "Where the boys aren't: Non-cognitive skills, returns to school and the gender gap in higher education". *Economics of Education Review* 21, no. 6 (2002): 589–98.

Jann, B. "Fairlie: Stata module to generate nonlinear decomposition of binary outcome differentials". Statistical Software Components, Boston College Department of Economics, 2006.

Lee, L.F. "Generalized econometric models with selectivity". *Econometrica* 51 (1983): 507.

Neal, D. "The effects of Catholic secondary schooling on educational achievement". *Journal of Labor Economics* 15, no. 1 (1997): 98–123.

Newhouse, D. and K. Beegle. "The effect of school type on academic achievement: Evidence from Indonesia". *Journal of Human Resources* 41, no. 3 (2006): 529–57.

Nizam. "The Need for Higher Education Reform". In *Higher Education in East-Asia*, pp. 35–68. Bangkok: UNESCO Asia and Pacific Regional Bureau for Education, 2006.

Oaxaca, R. "Male-Female Wage Differentials in Urban Labor Markets". *International Economic Review* 14, no. 3 (1973): 693–709.

Oey-Gardiner, M. "Educational developments, achievements and challenges". In *Indonesia Assessment: Population and Human Resources*, edited by G.W. Jones and T.H. Hull. Singapore: Institute of Southeast Asian Studies, 1997.

Parker, L. "Introduction: Islamic education in Indonesia" [online]. *RIMA: Review of Indonesian and Malaysian Affairs* 42, no. 1 (2008): 1–8.

Rouse, C.E. "What to do after high school: The two-year versus four-year college enrollment decision". In *Choices and Consequences*, pp. 59–88. Ithaca: ILR Press, 1994.

Stevans, L.K. and D.N. Sessions. "Private/public school choice and student performance revisited". *Education Economics* 8, no. 2 (2000): 169–84.

Vella, F. "Estimating models with sample selection bias: A survey". *Journal of Human Resources* 33, no. 1 (1998): 127–69.

Wooldridge, J.M. *Econometric Analysis of Cross Section and Panel Data*. The MIT Press, 2001.

6

INCREASING ACCESS TO AND RETENTION IN PRIMARY EDUCATION IN MALAYSIA

Lorraine Pe Symaco

INTRODUCTION

Access to and quality of education have been key agendas of the Malaysian government to foster national unity and enhance economic growth. The First Malaysia Plan (1966–70) and the subsequent plans give much importance to education: "unless the education system is geared to meet the development needs of the country, there will be a misallocation of an important economic resource, which will slow down the rate of economic and social advance" (Government of Malaysia 1965, p. 163). The government allocates substantial financial resources to education annually, constituting about 17 per cent of the total public expenditure.

The Malaysian Ministry of Education has worked closely with state and district education offices, international organizations (e.g., United Nations Children's Fund (UNICEF) and United Nations High Commissioner for Refugees (UNHCR)), and non-governmental organizations (NGOs), such as Child Aid Borneo and Human Rights Commission, to expand access to primary schooling to all children. However, access to education remains lower for children who are poor, live in remote and sparsely populated area and without citizenship documentation. It should be noted that children without citizenship documents are not captured in the calculations of Net Enrolment Ratio (NER), and thus represents an additional population of out-of-school children and youth.

The following sections will discuss patterns of primary school access and retention, quality and equity in Malaysia, and policies affecting access and retention in the sector.

WHAT HAS BEEN ACHIEVED?

Patterns of Primary School Access and Retention in Malaysia

Figure 6.1 shows the primary school NER for selected years (indicated by dots) between 1970 and 1972 as well as between 1994 and 2005. This rate measures the proportion of children aged 7 to 13 who were enrolled

FIGURE 6.1
Primary School Net Enrolment Rate, 1970–2005

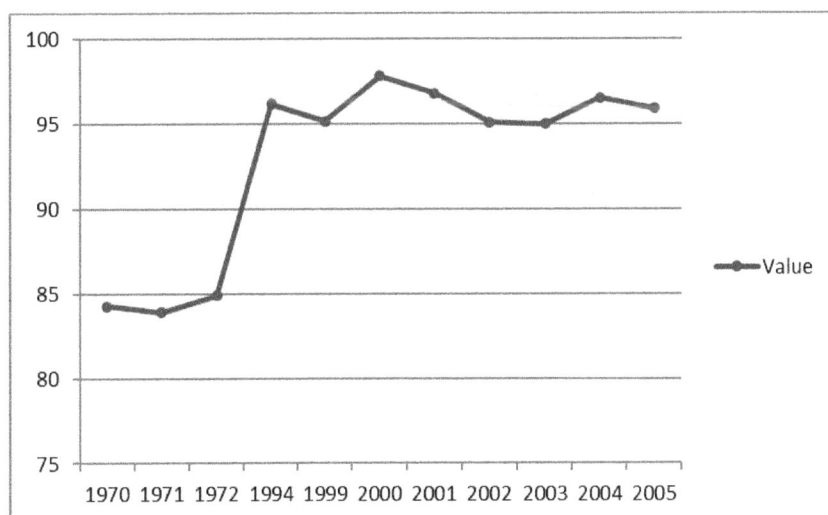

Source: World Bank data.

in primary school. One notes that this rate was already relatively high in 1970 (84.3 per cent) and had increased to 96.2 per cent in 1994. Between 1999 and 2005, although minor fluctuations occurred, the percentage of primary school-aged children enrolled remained at or above 95 per cent but did not reach 100 per cent (with the highest net enrolment of 97.8 per cent, recorded in 2000). It is important to note that the figures — both the numerators and denominators of these percentages — exclude undocumented children (e.g., those whose parents are refugees or migrant workers), who face special challenges in gaining access to public schools.

That the NER has remained below 100 per cent points to a relatively small, but nonetheless important problem of access and retention. That is, some children do not enter the first grade as well as some children who enter the first grade drop out before completing six years of primary schooling. Figure 6.2, which displays the primary school net intake rate (NIR) for the years 1970 to 2005,[1] addresses the question of access. As can be seen, the proportion of seven-year-olds who enter the first grade was already relatively high in 1970 (84.8 per cent). However, it took more than a decade (in 1982) to increase by 10 per cent and thus more than 95 per cent of seven-year-olds were enrolled in primary school. Since 1982 the NIR

FIGURE 6.2
Primary School Net Intake Rates, 1970–2005

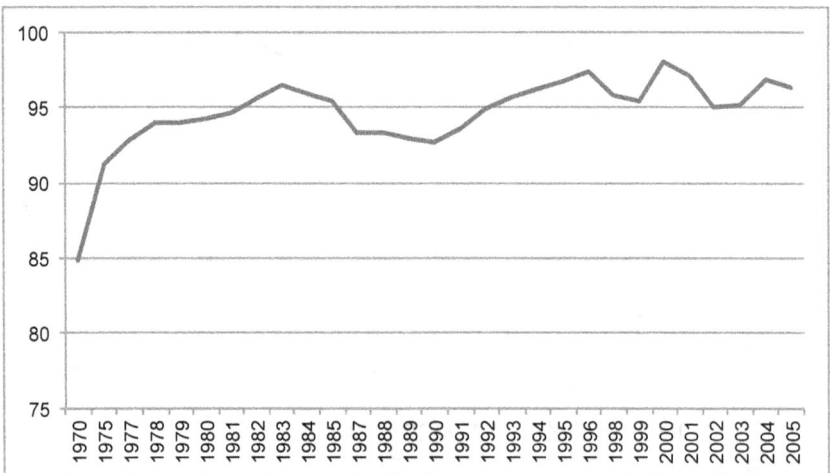

Source: UIS (2011).

has ranged from 92.7 per cent (in 1990) to 98.1 per cent (in 2000), with it being 96.3 per cent in 2005, the latest year for which statistics are available. Thus, even ignoring those children without documents (to be discussed below), we see that some seven-year-olds do not enter the first grade.

That drop-out also contributes to keeping the NER below 100 per cent is evidenced in Figure 6.3, which presents primary school survival rates and drop-out numbers for some of the relevant years, 1989 and 2000–04. For instance, one notes that the primary school survival rate was relatively high in 1989 (96.7 per cent), though not equal to 100 per cent, which would be the case if there were no dropouts. Moreover, with the exception of the years 2002 and 2003, the survival rate gradually increased between 2000 and 2004, when the figure was 98.3 per cent.

EQUITY OF ACCESS AND RETENTION, 1980–2010

Malaysia has been on track to providing equitable learning opportunities to all Malaysian children since its Independence in 1957. The country has a vested interest in bridging the gap in access to education of the various subgroups, given that those without the competencies to participate fully in the society can bring a bigger cost to the country and affect achieving its economic goals. The following sections will examine issues of access

FIGURE 6.3
Survival Rates to Year 6 and Primary School Drop-outs, 1989–2004

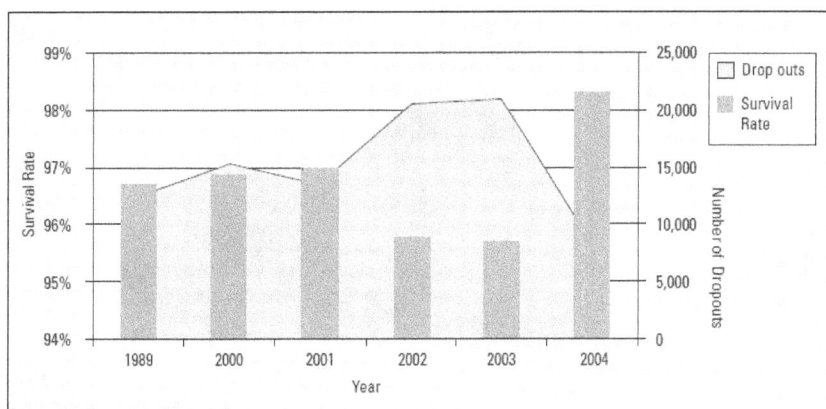

Source: MOE (2008).

and retention for socio-economic groups, urban/rural residents, genders, indigenous and other minority groups, and special needs populations.

Socio-economic Status of Families

The socio-economic condition of families is still the strongest predictor for primary school access and retention in Malaysia. Poverty remains a factor limiting access and retention in primary schooling. To illustrate, while 5 per cent of primary school-aged children of "poor" families were out of school in 2007, the corresponding figure for "non-poor" was at most 1 per cent (United Nations 2011). The Penan community in Sarawak, a tribe still living a nomadic life, is also greatly affected by poverty such that the cost of books, uniforms and transportation demotivates Penan families from sending their children to school. It is interesting to note that the same pattern is recorded in the Drop Out Study of 1973 (MOE 1973) which indicated that, at the primary level, 99 per cent of children from high SES families were enrolled in schools as opposed to only 71 per cent from lower SES families.

As previously noted, Malaysia has been largely successful at tackling poverty. The poverty rate declined from 49.3 per cent in 1970 to 5.5 per cent in 2000 and 4.2 per cent in 2010 (Department of Statistics Malaysia 2011).[2] However, economic development has not been equal in all states, with Kedah, Kelantan and Perlis remaining relatively poorer compared to other states in West Malaysia. As can be seen in Figure 6.4, Sabah, followed by Kelantan and Perak (located in Peninsular Malaysia), were the states with the highest number of children not in schools in 2000 and 2005. The higher number of out-of-school children in these states is primarily a function of family poverty levels, with Kelantan and Sabah having two to three times the rates of poverty as other states (UNESCO 2005).[3]

Rural/Urban Residence

Malaysia faced greater challenges in increasing primary school access and retention in the more remote, rural areas of Peninsular Malaysia, Sabah and Sarawak. Approximately 58.2 per cent of Malaysia's territory is covered by forest. In the Peninsular region, numerous mountains run parallel from north to south, with the main mountain range, Titiwangsa Mountains, dividing the region between the east and west coasts. Not only

FIGURE 6.4
Number of Children Not in Primary Schools, by State, 2000 and 2005

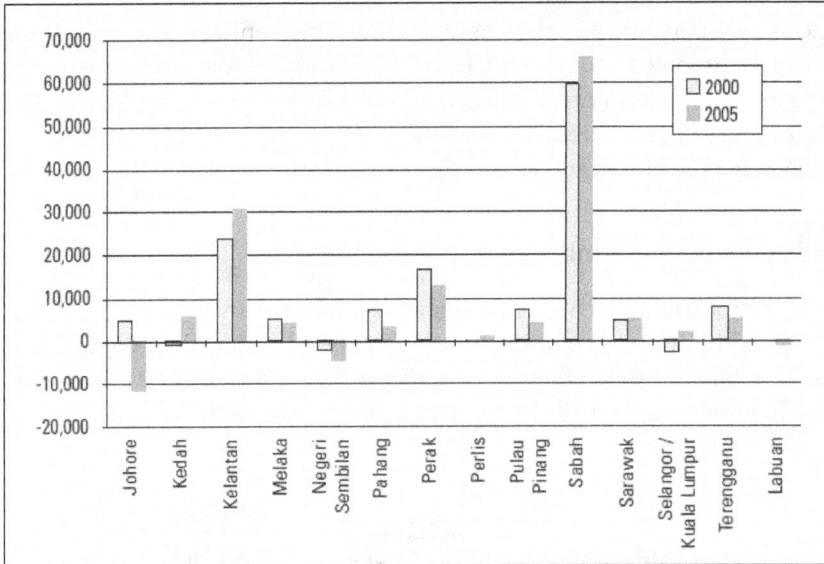

Source: MOE (2008).

are the children living closer to the mountains likely to be from poor rural families, but they also have to travel longer distances to get to school. As a result, many tend to fall behind in their academic performance, which leads them to drop out (Government of Malaysia 2012; interviews). A similar scenario is also faced by students in Sabah and Sarawak, where remote areas still lack clean water and electricity. There are no connecting roads to these remote places and the only mode of transportation is usually by boat or ferry. The schools in these remote areas also lack infrastructure and amenities (Government of Malaysia 2012; interviews). As noted by an interviewee from the Human Rights Commission of Malaysia:

> Again the access is not there, because the … school and the settlement are far away and the children travel in very dangerous condition to reach the schools. So other social problems come out. Although the schools are there, I don't think they actually meet the needs of the children. Yes, there they are set up, they run, but then the extended care and concern for all children is not there.

However, challenging circumstances in rural areas seem to affect access rather than retention. This point can be seen in Table 6.1 which presents drop-out rates for schools located in rural and urban areas during the 1998–2004 period. Although there is some variation across years and for different grade (or year) levels, the overall picture shows that drop-out is a bigger problem in urban areas than rural areas. That is, for the smaller percentage of rural children who make it into primary school there is a somewhat lower percentage that drop out before completing the six years.

Ethnic Group Membership

Ethnic group membership is a factor affecting access and retention. Chinese followed by Indians continue to have higher educational attainment and socio-economic status than Malays (Brown 2011; Khalid 2011). However, the historical differences in primary school access and retention among

TABLE 6.1
Dropout Rates in Rural and Urban Government Schools, 1998–2004 (%)

Rural	1998	1999	2000	2001	2002	2003	2004
Years 1–2	–0.7	–1.1	0.4	–0.7	–0.6	–0.1	0.6
Years 2–3	0.3	–0.2	0.7	–0.3	–0.2	0.6	0.3
Years 3–4	–0.6	–1.5	–0.1	–1.2	–0.5	–0.2	–0.1
Years 4–5	0.4	0.0	–0.2	–0.8	–0.8	–0.1	–0.2
Years 5–6	–2.2	–1.7	–1.5	–2.1	–2.2	–1.4	–0.8
% of total loss at primary level (rural)						–3.9	–3.7	–1.2

Urban	1998	1999	2000	2001	2002	2003	2004
Years 1–2	–1.2	–1.6	–0.1	–0.5	–1.3	–2.5	–0.5
Years 2–3	–0.5	–0.9	–0.4	–0.4	–1.2	0.3	–0.3
Years 3–4	–1.2	–3.5	–0.8	–1.6	–0.9	0.1	–0.2
Years 4–5	0.7	0.2	1.6	–0.5	–1.3	–0.1	–0.5
Years 5–6	–1.2	–2.0	–0.8	–1.2	–1.3	0.0	–0.4
% of total loss at primary level (urban)						–4.7	–4.8	–1.9

Source: United Nations, Malaysia, 2011.

these groups no longer exist, though some other ethnic groups have lower enrolment rates.

Non-Malay indigenous groups account for 4 per cent of the entire primary and secondary school students in Malaysia, of which 68 per cent live in rural areas and 80 per cent live in the states of Sarawak and Sabah (Government of Malaysia 2012). Educational access and achievements statistics for these groups are scant, except for some data on primary schools for the Orang Asli population. Generally, drop-out rates are higher for Orang Asli children. For example, Nicholas (2006) compiled statistics concerning drop-out rates for Orang Asli children in Malaysia. Although the drop-out rate declined between the 1980–85 and the 1995–2000 periods from 71.6 per cent to 42.9 per cent, the latter rate is still quite high.

Poverty is a critical factor for Orang Asli children's school attendance (Nicholas 2006). The poverty rate among Orang Asli in 1999, for example, was 50.9 per cent compared to the country's rate at 7.5 per cent (Government of Malaysia 2001). Although school fees were abolished in 1962 and scholarships, school uniforms, school bags, and stationery are provided by the government, other fees are assessed in school (e.g., for PTA, sports). Often Orang Asli parents cannot afford to pay these fees, especially when they have several school-going children. Free transportation is also provided for them, since most Orang Asli live in rural areas close to the forest. However, such transportation is not reliable and the distances they need to travel are generally great.

In addition, cultural differences also play a role in determining why these children often do not go or stay on in school. Orang Asli's traditional way of learning is through arts, crafts, songs and folklore, where they are taught by their family to be polite, considerate, creative, and proud of their identity (Nicholas 2006). Orang Asli children who enter school at the age of seven often find it difficult to adapt to the structured system, where the teacher is the primary person delivering the content, and to the new environment with people from different cultures. Language also poses a problem as not many Orang Asli children speak the Malay language when they enter primary school. Thus, many chose to withdraw as they were unable to cope with teaching and learning in the Malay language (Nicholas 2006).

Different groups of children will have different sets of barriers which would hinder their participation rate in school. Refugee children have been living invisibly in Malaysia for some years, in particular the Rohingya refugees who have been in Malaysia for almost three decades. The Rohingya children are not given access to free public schooling and have to study in learning centres run by UNHCR, NGOs and the communities themselves. There is no recognized certification for learning in such centres and the quality of education often is compromised due to lack of educational resources, trained teachers, and crowded classrooms (CRICE 2013).

Children living in plantations in both the peninsula (smaller number yet problem persists) and Sabah face similar issues of not being able to join the mainstream schooling. These children, many of whom have parents who are migrant workers from Indonesia, are without proper citizenship documents and at risk of being "stateless". In order to access government schools, proper citizenship documents are required. This leads to the exclusion of children of refugees and migrant workers as well as undocumented children in the calculations of the NER. Also, for them primary education does not promise a bright future since there are few post-primary educational opportunities for them.

> We have huge number of [undocumented] refugee children [in] Sabah. I have given up, and nothing has been done. So these children are going to become adults (...) [b]ut the refugee children are not going to go anywhere. (Interviewee, Human Rights Commission of Malaysia)

Other groups with similar fate, being undocumented, are street children and children in detention centres and prisons. It is reported that in Chow Kit, Kuala Lumpur alone there are more than 500 street children whose parents are sex workers or drug abusers (Fazli, Yusuf and Ramli 2012).

Special Needs Students

Part of the population of out-of-schools children are those with physical disabilities (e.g., having limitations in hearing, sight, or mobility). The government estimates that about 1 per cent of the population have special needs, though this is an underestimate as families rarely register their children as having special needs (Government of Malaysia 2012). The number of out-of-school children with physical disabilities likely declined when the government equipped some schools with special facilities (Government of Malaysia 2012). However, such schools with special facilities tend to be located in cities and towns, and thus rural children with physical disabilities are less likely to attend school. There is also a shortage of qualified professionals (e.g., occupational therapists). Additionally, while tailored curriculum for certain groups has been developed (e.g., the Bahasa Isyarat Komunikasi for deaf students), this has yet to be achieved for children with other disabilities such as autism.

QUALITY OF EDUCATION, 1980–2010

Access and retention cannot be separated from the quality of primary schooling in Malaysia. One indicator of educational quality — an input — is the student-teacher ratio. As shown in Figure 6.5, this indicator improved between 1970 and 2010; that is, it decreased from approximately thirty to less than fourteen during this period.

Another indicator of educational quality is students' performance on the national examination (Ujian Penilaian Sekolah Rendah or UPSR) taken at the end of year 6 of primary school. Students in national schools are tested in four subjects: Malay (Comprehension and Writing), English, Mathematics and Science. Students in national-type schools are also examined in Chinese (Comprehension and Writing) or Tamil (Comprehension and Writing).

FIGURE 6.5
Primary School Student-Teacher Ratio, 1970–2010

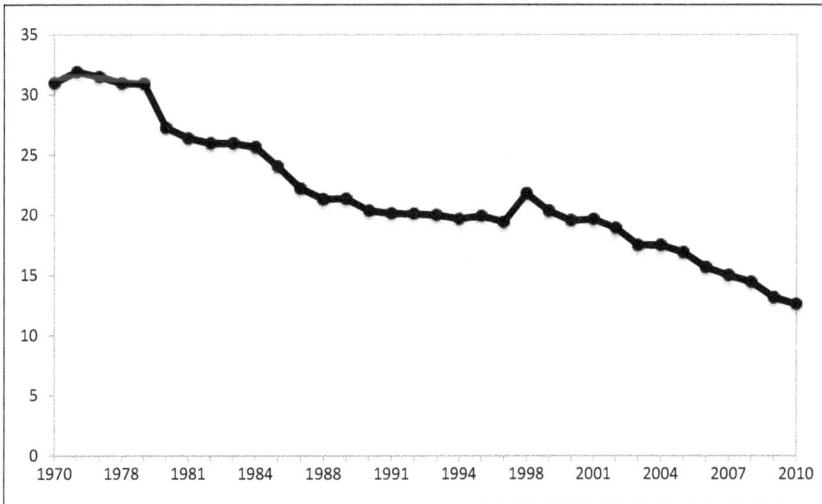

Source: UNESCO, Institute for Statistics.

Other exams are administered to secondary students: (1) the PMR (Penilaian Menengah Rendah or Lower Secondary Assessment); and (2) the SPM (Sijil Pelajaran Malaysia or Malaysian Certificate of Education, taken by the fifth year secondary students).

We observe that during the period 2000–11 there is a trend of increasing percentages for both statistics for the UPSR as well as the other two exams. For example, the percentage passing the UPSR rose from just below 76 per cent in 2000 to over 84 per cent in 2011 (Government of Malaysia 2012). And with respect to the percentage of students being graded "A" on the UPSR, that figure increased from about 25 per cent in 2000 to over 30 per cent in 2011.

A comparison across states of the GPS (Gred Purata Sekolah or Grade Point Average) for the UPSR in 2011 shows that the two worst performing states are Sabah followed by Sarawak (see Figure 6.6). These states' GPS across subjects are 54.3 per cent and 60.8 per cent, respectively. We also note that W.P. Putrajaya has by far the best performance, with a GPS

FIGURE 6.6
Comparison of Performance across State for UPSR in 2011

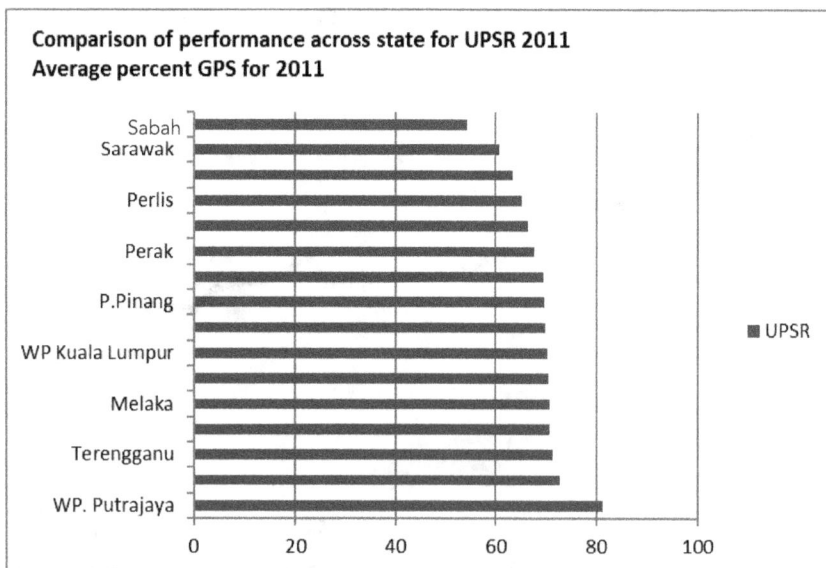

Comparison of performance across state for UPSR 2011
Average percent GPS for 2011

Source: Government of Malaysia (2012).

across subjects of over 80 per cent. As discussed above, there are a number of factors that may contribute to the lower performance in Sabah and Sarawak, including historical residue from less provision of schooling during the colonial period, high poverty rates, and the rural nature of the population in these states. In contrast, the population in W.P. Putrajaya is highly urbanized and has a greater proportion of middle- to upper-income families (Government of Malaysia, 2012).

Students in rural areas perform less well than their urban peers. Note, however, that while the rural–urban gap in exam performance remained visible, it narrowed between 2005 and 2011 from more than 7.0 per cent to 3.8 per cent. States with more rural schools, like Sabah and Sarawak, usually underperform states with fewer rural schools (Government of Malaysia 2012).

Studies reveal that, from 2006 to 2011, girls consistently outperformed boys on UPSR and other learning outcome measures, though the details have not been provided (Government of Malaysia 2012).

Finally, educational outcomes are poorer for the Orang Asli group as compared to the national average. For instance, in 2011, while 61 per cent of students in Orang Asli schools passed the core subjects in the UPSR, the national average was 87 per cent. Additionally, 35 per cent of the schools primarily attended by Orang Asli are identified as being in the "poor performance" band, although this is the case for only 1 per cent of public schools generally (Government of Malaysia, 2012).

DRIVERS AND IMPEDIMENTS OF CHANGE

Policies Affecting Access and Retention

The dramatic rise in the NER between 1972 and 1994 can be attributed to the policies set by the government that placed priority on educational development. It is commonplace to argue that the political will of government officials is a key factor shaping progress in achieving universal primary education (e.g., see Kozack 2009). Evidence of Malaysian government officials' political will can be seen in the First Malaysia Plan (1955–60), which gave priority to access in education. It was during this period that the government implemented double shifting so that more students could use the existing school buildings (UNDP 2005). In addition, the New Economic Policy, adopted in 1971 in the wake of the May 1969 inter-ethnic group riots, was aimed at reducing inequalities especially between Malay and Chinese ethnic groups, and education was one of the vehicles used by the government for this purpose.

Another indicator of political will is the level of financial resources devoted to building schools and employing teachers,[4] among others. Of course, Malaysia was in a position to increase educational expenditure because of the strength of its economy. As mentioned above, Malaysia's GDP grew annually by an average of 5 per cent over the period of 1970 and 2000, and 5.5 per cent between 2000 and 2010 (UNDP 2005; UN 2011).

In particular after the 13 May 1969 riots, the government's nationwide effort to foster unity and bridge the economic gap resulted in many schools being built in rural areas and villages and existing schools being equipped with better facilities and resources to equally enhance the quality of education. Moreover, during the 1980s additional efforts were undertaken to expand and improve educational infrastructure, especially in rural areas. And under the Ninth and Tenth Malaysia Plan (2006–10 and 2011–15) the building and upgrading of infrastructure continued, especially in schools in Sabah and Sarawak.

In Figure 6.7 we observe that government expenditure on education increased fairly steadily between 1970 and 2010, with the slope of increase somewhat steeper between 1988 and 1998 and, even more so between 1998 and 2010. Furthermore, public expenditures as a percentage of GDP rose

FIGURE 6.7
Government Expenditure on Education

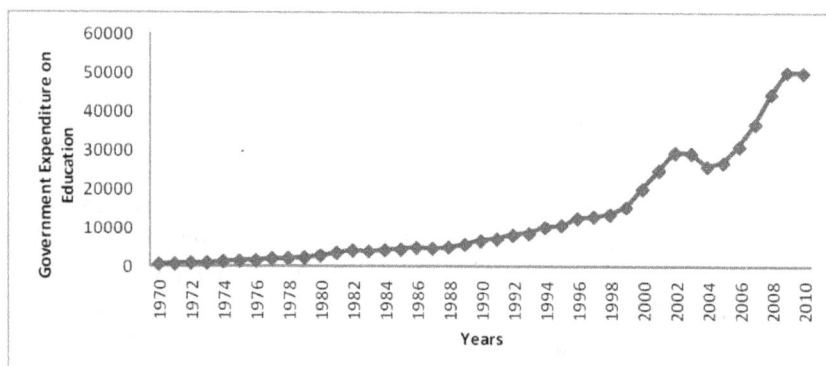

Source: Mohd Yahya, Fidlizah and Azilah (2012).

from 4.3 per cent in 1971 to 6.9 per cent in 1982. From then until 2010 this figure fluctuated, with a low of 4.3 per cent in 1982 and a high of 7.7 per cent in 2002, but remained relatively high compared to other countries (UIS 2011). For instance, in 2008 Malaysia ranked seventeenth (out of 102 countries) in terms of education expenditure for all levels (as a percentage of total government expenditure), only second to Thailand in the region (Government of Malaysia, 2012).

Another financial indicator of political will is that the Malaysian government has invested greatly in pre-schools since the 1990s. Pre-schools have been established in all national and national-type primary schools, with teachers specially trained in pre-primary education. Children who attend pre-schools are less likely to drop out from primary schools (MOE 2008). And especially, children whose first language is not the language of instruction benefit from attending the pre-schools for one to two years (MOE 2008).

The political will of government authorities was also evidenced by implementing the policy of no school fees (specified in the Education Act of 1961). This policy undoubtedly was crucial for promoting access to and retention in primary school among children who live in poverty.

Although the 1961 Education Act stipulated that primary education would be free, this legislative provision only applies to children with proper registration documents. The policy requiring such documents to enrol in government schools hinders access and retention for refugee and other undocumented children. These undocumented children include: (a) children who are born in Malaysia to Indonesian migrants (e.g., those working on plantations); and (b) children of Malaysian parents who, due to lack of knowledge, failed to register them (at birth) with the National Registration Department. There are also street children, orphans and children born to prostitutes who are undocumented. Because of their families' socio-economic status, these children do not have the means to attend private schools, although some attend learning centres run by communities and NGOs (see discussion below).

It is important to stress that children without documents, if they were included in the calculations of the NER, would likely reduce this statistic below what is reported officially. That is, while approximately 96 per cent of registered Malaysian children attend primary, the percentage of all primary school-aged children (registered and not registered) living in Malaysia who attend school would be less than 96 per cent.

Additionally, policies affecting access and retention such as the Razak Report of 1956 resulted in the incorporation into the government education system most of the previously created schools. The Razak Report is a compromise between the Barnes Report, which was favoured by the Malays, and the Fenn-Wu Report, favoured by the Chinese and Indians. The Razak Report was incorporated in the Education Ordinance of 1957 and serves as a basis for the present educational framework in Malaysia. Based on this report, the large majority of previously existing schools became part of the state education system, with Malay-medium schools being labelled as national schools and Chinese-, English-, and Tamil-medium schools being labelled as national-type schools.

Programmes Affecting Access and Retention

> If we just talk about primary education, in terms of access, I think the MOE can provide primary schools no matter where you are in this country, meaning that the access in terms of distance shouldn't be a problem, except in some very, very rural places. Access to primary education has improved in terms of finance. The government supports the poor by giving free food, transportation, uniform, tuition and scholarships. (Interviewee, UNICEF Malaysia)

In order to achieve universal primary education, the Malaysian government has embarked on numerous interventions to increase the access and survival rates in primary school in the country.[5] For example, since 1976 the government has given supplementary food to students from low income families who come to school without breakfast and are malnourished. Additionally, since 1975 there has been a government programme of loaning textbooks to students from low-income families. More than 75 per cent of children enrolled in primary school benefit from this textbook-on-loan scheme.[6]

Also contributing to increasing access and retention among students from poorer families is the Supplementary Food Programme. Administered by the Ministry of Education since 1980, this programme seeks to improve the nutritional level of primary students from poor households to advance retention in schools. For example, the programme supplied breakfast to nearly 707,000 primary school students in 2006. This programme has led to improved rate attendance for children from poor households (MOE 2008; UN 2011; UNDP 2005).

More recently, the Government of Malaysia initiated the Poor Students Trust Fund 2003, which gives funds directly to lower socio-economic status families and has reduced the number of their children dropping out of school (UN 2011). Then, in 2004 the government launched a Tuition Aid Scheme that provides extra lessons during the weekends or after school for government school students with low achievement and who belong to households that fall below the poverty line. In 2006, about half a million primary school children received aid under this scheme amounting to about US$52 million (MOE 2008). Furthermore, the School Milk Programme benefited more than half a million primary students in 2006, with the Ministry allotting some RM20 million annually to that programme. These programmes have likely reduced the financial pressures that may cause children and youth to drop out (UN 2011), thus enabling Malaysia to maintain its relatively high primary school net enrolment rate remains high (96 per cent in 2005) and its relatively high rate of survival to Year 6 (96 per cent from 2005 to 2010).

With regard to promoting access and retention of children with special needs, the Ministry of Education developed the Integrated Special Education Programmes in 1981 to cater to this population. Children with special needs have three options for schooling: (a) *special education schools* primarily catering to children with special needs, such as the visually impaired or other similar disabilities such as auditory impairment and physical/mobility handicap; (b) *mainstream integrated schools* with specific classes dedicated to children with special needs; and (c) *inclusive education programmes*, or mainstream schools that integrate one to five children with special needs into mainstream classes. Overall, the government estimates that of children identified as having disabilities, about 6 per cent of children are enrolled in inclusive education programmes, about 5 per cent attend *special education schools*, and most (89 per cent) are enrolled in mainstream integrated schools (Government of Malaysia 2012). Further, retention is pursued through the introduction of the Early Intervention Reading and Writing Class, implemented in all government primary schools beginning in 2006, which aims to identify children with difficulties in reading and writing (as evidenced in the first year of primary school). Intensive tutoring is provided through this programme to ensure retention.

As previously mentioned, Sabah has the lowest NER compared to other states in the country. Sabah is also one of the poorest states in Malaysia.

In addition to other previously initiated programmes, the Sabah State Education Department began an initiative in 2008 to develop more practical class lessons. The Department organizes activities (such as literacy classes and vocational courses) in collaboration with higher learning institutions for children who are out of school. For example, there are classes to teach children from the Bajau Laut, known also as the "sea gypsy" people, how to create crafts from materials they can gather from the sea. As a result of increasing students' interest in learning the practical class lessons have likely increased school attendance.

More recently, in 2012 the State Education Department began organizing weekly meetings known as "Hari Bertemu Pelanggan" (Client Interface Day), to help people from poor households. This programme has attracted many parents to bring their children who have not attended school to the department office. The children are enrolled in normal classes according to their age groups (regardless of how many years of school they have attended). These students are then given remedial classes to help them follow through the lessons taught in school.

Furthermore, the Malaysian government recently reached an agreement with the Indonesian government for the latter to send 109 Indonesian teachers to work on plantations to teach children in the learning centres operated by the NGO Humana Child Aid Society Sabah. There is also potential collaboration with the Government of Thailand to enhance education for children across the region (Humana interview).

As for the Orang Asli community,[7] the Malaysian government initiated in 2007 a Special Comprehensive Model School, which incorporates residential education (from Year 1 to Form 3) to reduce the drop-out rate. It was reported that attendance rates have been improving from 85.7 per cent in 2007 to 97.6 per cent in 2010 (Government of Malaysia 2012). Furthermore, the government is supporting primary school access and retention among the Orang Asli through providing school uniforms, food allowances, and scholarships, at a cost of more than US$3 million in 2005 (MOE 2008).

Additionally, as noted by an interviewee from UNICEF Malaysia: "To say that they [the Orang Asli] have no access [to education] would be wrong because they do have support from the community, churches, mosque and temples, also private individuals who provide some basic education." Similarly, in 2000, the Rotary Club of Kota Kinabalu, in collaboration with the Roman Catholic Church, built a hostel for students from interior Keningau who would otherwise have to walk for miles to reach schools in and around Keningau town (FSIC 2013).

Other NGOs also assist in helping children to have access to primary education by providing various supports. One such NGO is Borneo Child Aid Society, also known as NGO Humana Child Aid Society Sabah, which was established in 1991 and registered as a society in 1996. It provides pre-primary and primary education to children living in plantations in Sabah, of which 90–100 per cent of school-aged children attend the learning centres in a given plantation. To date, Humana has 130 projects which cater to 12,500 children in Sabah. Of these, 10,000 are plantation children, another 1,500 are migrant children who live in the town areas and the remaining are the Bajau Laut (sea gypsies) children. Of the plantation children, 90 per cent are born in Sabah to Indonesian parents who are plantation workers in this state. The remaining 10 per cent are Filipino migrants. However, while these initiatives clearly benefit the children involved, their impact on enrolment is not captured in officially calculated NERs, because the students involved do not have documents and are thus not counted in the official statistics.

Humana runs learning centres in these plantations in collaboration with the plantation companies and other organizations. The Malaysian Ministry of Education has approved Humana to provide free education to these children as an effort towards achieving the EFA and MDG goals. Humana organizes education for pre-school for two years and primary school until grade 6. It employs teachers, mostly Sabahans who have a minimum of SPM (Sijil Pelajaran Malaysia or Malaysia Certificate of Education; equivalent to GCE "O" level) qualification. These teachers receive basic preparation in pedagogical methods in teacher training institutes in Sabah for three months. Currently, there are 300 Malaysian teachers and 109 Indonesian teachers, with the Indonesian teachers sponsored by the Government of Indonesia. In the learning centres the children are taught the Malaysian curriculum and some knowledge of Indonesia and Bahasa Indonesia. They are enrolled and promoted based on ability, not age.

However, the then Humana's Director admitted that it is difficult to monitor the rate of students in these learning centres completing grade 6, because many plantation workers move to different plantations or simply return to Indonesia in the middle of their children's schooling. However, absenteeism and dropout in the learning centres are not major issues. Less than 5 per cent of children in the plantations served by Humana do not attend these learning centres, mainly because they work (interview). The main challenge faced by Humana is the lack of educational facilities (e.g., classrooms) in the majority of the plantations which makes it virtually impossible to organize lessons for the children. Apart from that, transportation is also a problem for children who live in rural areas who are required to commute daily to the learning centre. Regrettably, Humana is unable to open new learning centres due to limited financial resources. The organization also has to constantly monitor and ensure that plantation companies pay for the cost in order to provide the teachers a reasonable salary. Humana, however, receives financial support from the Malaysian Ministry of Education and the Sabah State Education Department to ease the process of opening up more learning centres.

Supplementing efforts undertaken in the past, in 2010 UNICEF began to assist the Ministry of Education in developing and implementing Individual Education Plans (IEPs) for children with special needs. It is estimated that more than 23,000 primary and secondary students benefit from this. Tailoring curriculum and assessment for children and improving special education service facilities in schools are promoted by the government. These initiatives are endorsed to ensure better access for students with special needs (Government of Malaysia 2012).

CONCLUSION

Malaysia's primary school net enrolment rate has remained high (95.8 per cent in 2005) since achieving this rate in the mid-1990s. Moreover, its survival rate to year 6 in primary school also remained relatively high, averaging 96 per cent from 2005 to 2010. Moreover, there is no significant gender disparity in enrolment and completion of primary schooling. This has resulted in significant increase in youth literacy rate from 88 per cent in 1980 to near-universal literacy of 99 per cent today and a significant increase in NER between 1970 and 1994. It is also important to note that these positive indicators of access and equity coexist with improvements in the quality of education, as evidenced in pupil-teacher ratios and test scores. This improvement can be attributed to the strong political commitment of the government to focus on — and provide resources for — education, alongside the assistance provided by various organizations.

However, despite the progress shown by the country having come near achieving the Education for All (EFA) and Millennium Development Goals

(MDG) education goals — ensuring all children have access to primary schooling by 2015 — a number of issues persist that need to be addressed. In addressing these it may be possible for Malaysia to incorporate the remaining 4 per cent who do not currently obtain a full six years of primary education. The 4 per cent are comprised disproportionately of children of poorer families, rural residents, and minority groups. Ideally, future efforts can reach all primary school-aged children, while continuing to maintain the quality of education, as measured by pupil-teacher ratios or test scores (Government of Malaysia 2012).

There are signs that the government will continue to pursue the goals of access, retention, and quality. For instance, the Tenth Malaysia Plans (2011–15) focuses heavily on rural areas to reduce, if not eliminate, the remaining gap between rural and urban in access, retention and quality of education. The plan also focuses on bridging the gap between children in Peninsular Malaysia and those in Sabah and Sarawak in Borneo Malaysia.

The School Improvement Programme launched in 2010 also aims to support all public schools to improve student outcomes. Under this scheme, basic infrastructure and amenities (e.g., electricity, water) are prioritized by the government for all public schools, especially in rural areas schools located in Sabah and Sarawak (EPU 2010). The government aims to ensure that schools meet 100 per cent basic infrastructure requirements by 2015 (Government of Malaysia 2012).

As part of its initiative to improve retention, the government in 2010 began implementing the Literacy and Numeracy Screening (LINUS),[8] which is an early intervention initiative (i.e., first three years of primary school) that focused on developing literacy and numeracy among all students. Interventions include improved remedial teacher-to-student ratio, and training support for teachers to improve pedagogical skills. A total of RM400 million was allocated to promote this for the period 2010–12.

Also in 2010, the Ministry launched the trust schools. These are public schools that are managed jointly by private organizations/civil society school leaders under the authority of the Ministry of Education with the objective of increasing access and quality in schools. By 2025, this programme is to expand to 500 schools, targeting public schools in rural areas and those with enrolments of minority (i.e., indigenous group) students as well as students with special needs (EPU 2010; Government of Malaysia 2012).

Private and international organizations will also continue to play a significant role in improving access to education in the country. A key organization involved is UNICEF, which in 2010 launched a Supplementary Reading Programme to ensure that children in vulnerable communities have access to learning resources. Children living in these communities in Sabah and Sarawak (e.g., migrants, plantation workers, refugees and the poor) are provided with books of different levels and genre to cater to the different reading abilities and interest. Approximately, 13,000 students from ninety schools are involved in this programme, which also provides remedial activities, story-telling competitions, and reading camps.

UNICEF also collaborates with the Sabah Special Task Force to provide education for out-of-school children in this state. The Sabah Special Task Force manages thirty-three gazetted centres for refugees and illegal immigrants (UNICEF 2012). Education is not provided in most of these centres, and the few which do tend to have overcrowded classrooms with poor facilities and a lack of clean water and sanitation. However, the education centre in Kampung Numbak in Sabah was established in 2011 to cater to refugee and undocumented children. To date, the centre has over 300 children who otherwise will not be receiving any sort of formal or non-formal education.

In line with the government's support to uplift the education sector of the country, an education transformation plan has been recently proposed that will improve access, equity, and quality of education for the children of Malaysia. The transformation plan will take place in thirteen years (2013–25) which has the following initiatives (Government of Malaysia 2012, p. 208):

a. Phase 1 (2013–15), this first phase focuses on supporting teachers and core skills. It is envisioned that there will be 98 per cent enrolment in primary level and that 25 per cent reduction in the urban-rural gap will be achieved.

b. Phase 2 (2016–20) focuses on accelerating system improvement and envisions a 100 per cent pre-school to lower secondary enrolment. Reduction in the urban–rural gap at 50 per cent and additional 25 per cent reduction in the socio-economic and gender gap.

c. Phase 3 (2021–25) focuses on excellence with increased operational flexibility while maintaining and improving the enrolment rates; urban–rural gap of the prior phases and a 50 per cent reduction in the socio-economic and gender gaps.

Investment in education remains to be a critical factor in Malaysia's development plans in line with the country's Vision 2020. Despite the inadequacies in providing education to some communities, it is evident that the education sector will remain one of the top priorities of the country. Perhaps what we can learn from this case study, given that the primary school participation and survival rates in Malaysia are indeed admirable, children unable to access mainstream education still exist. Poverty, as in other context, continues to be a main detriment to school access and undocumented children (e.g., refugees and illegal migrants) are not captured in education system statistics. This poses a set of challenges and demands for Malaysia. The children who are not in school have to be located and their barriers to access to schooling identified.

Notes

Note: The idea and funding for this work was provided by the Educate A Child programme in Doha, Qatar. The opinions are those of the author and do not necessarily represent Educate A Child policy. The original published version of this case study is available at <http://educateachild.org/library>. Appreciation is also expressed to Mark Ginsburg (FHI 360, Washington, D.C., USA) for his guidance and feedback during the development of the case study.

1. This rate measures the proportion of children aged seven who were enrolled in grade one of primary school.
2. In 2010, the poverty rate in Peninsular Malaysia was 4.1 per cent, in Sabah 4.9 per cent and in Sarawak 4.5 per cent. Nationally, hard core poverty or extreme poverty — those whose household income is below half the poverty line was at 0.7 per cent in 2009.
3. As we will discuss below, Sabah also has a sizeable population of immigrants and undocumented children, who are not allowed to enrol in public schools in this country. In 2012, the hard core poverty rate was recorded at 1.6 per cent in Sabah, the highest in the country, followed by Perlis (0.5 per cent), Kelantan and Sarawak (0.3 per cent) (Department of Statistics, Malaysia 2011).
4. In order to ensure that all teachers in primary schools are qualified (i.e., possess a Bachelor's degree), the Teacher Education Division of the Ministry of Education has offered scholarships to in service teachers to pursue a diploma or degree in education through distance learning.
5. Such efforts have been renewed in recent years. For instance, the 10th Malaysia Plan (2011–15) emphasized providing special assistance to children in families in the bottom 40 per cent of households in terms of income. The assistance includes placement in boarding schools and scholarships.

6. In 2008, the Ministry of Education made a provision of providing free textbooks for children regardless of socio-economic status.
7. The Ministry of Education has also commenced a five-year transformation plan (2013–18) to address access, retention and learning outcomes of the Orang Asli. Using tailored interventions and introducing ICT education programmes that will promote culturally relevant content, the Ministry envisions that the academic performance of the Orang Asli students will improve.
8. LINUS incorporates both literacy and numeracy programmes while previous programmes focused on literacy (2006) and numeracy (2008) separately.

References

Brown, G.K. "Rectifying inequality, reifying identity? The political economy of education and ethnic relations in Malaysia". In *The Political Function of Education in Deeply Divided Countries*, edited by T. Hanf, pp. 159–78. Baden-Baden: Nomos, 2011.
CRICE. "Education of refugees". Unpublished research report, 2013.
Departments of Statistics, Malaysia. "Monthly statistical bulletin". 2011 <http://www.statistics.gov.my> (accessed 6 May 2013).
Economic Planning Unite (EPU). *Tenth Malaysia Plan*. Putrajaya: EPU, 2010.
Fazli, I., A. Mohamad Yusuf and A. Ramli. "Stories Untold: The Street Children of Chow Kit — An architectural intervention". 2012 <http://fspu.uitm.edu.my/cebs/images/stories/cebs/ajebsv3n9c6p75to89.pdf> (accessed 1 August 2013).
FSIC. "St Maria Goretti Convent and Hostel, Keningau". 2013 <http://www.fsicmalaysia.com/st-maria-goretti.html> (accessed 5 September 2013).
Government of Malaysia. "First Malaysia Plan 1966–1970". Kuala Lumpur, 1965.
———. "Eighth Malaysia Plan 2001–2005". Putrajaya: EPU, 2001.
———. "Malaysia Education Blueprint". 2012 <http://www.moe.gov.my/userfiles/file/PPP/Preliminary-Blueprint-Eng.pdf> (accessed 26 June 2013).
Khalid, Muhammed Abdul. "Household Wealth in Malaysia: Composition and Inequality among Ethnic Groups". *Jurnal Ekonomi Malaysia* 45 (2011): 71–80.
Kosack, S. "Realising Education for All: Defining and using the political will to invest in primary education". *Comparative Education* 45, no. 4 (2009): 495–523.
Ministry of Education (MOE). "Kajian Keciciran" [Drop-out Study]. Kuala Lumpur: MOE, 1973.
———. "Education for All: Mid-decade assessment report 2000-2007". Putrajaya: Ministry of Education, Malaysia, 2008.
Mohd Yahya, M., M. Fidlizah and R. Azila. "Education expenditure and economic growth: A causal analysis for Malaysia". *Journal of Economics and Sustainable Development* 3, no. 7 (2012): 71–81.

Nicholas, C. "The State of Orang Asli Education and Its Root Problems. Orang Asli: Rights, problems, solutions". A consultancy report prepared for the Human Rights Commission of Malaysia (SUHAKAM), 2006.

UN Data. "Net enrolment". 2013 <http://data.un.org/Data.aspx?d= UNESCO&f=series%3ANER_1> (accessed 26 August 2013).

UNDP. "Malaysia — Achieving The Millennium Development Goals". Kuala Lumpur: United Nations Development Programme (UNDP), 2005.

UNESCO. "Education for all: The quality imperative". 2005 <http://unesdoc. unesco.org/images/0013/001373/137333e.pdf> (accessed 20 June 2013).

———. "Education Statistics". 2011 <http://web.worldbank.org/WBSITE/ EXTERNAL/TOPICS/EXTEDUCATION/EXTDATASTATISTICS/ EXTEDSTATS/0,,contentMDK:22614780~menuPK:7196605~page PK:64168445~piPK:64168309~the SitePK:3232764,00.html> (accessed 2 July 2013).

UNICEF. "Reaching the Unreached: An Evaluation of the Alternative Education Programme for Refugee, Undocumented and Stateless Children in Kampung Numbak, Kota Kinabalu, Sabah". 2012 <http://www.unicef.org/malaysia/ TOR_Evaluation_Education_for_Children_in_Kg._Numbak_Sabah.pdf> (accessed 30 July 2013).

United Nations (Malaysia). *Malaysia — The Millennium Development Goals at 2010*. Kuala Lumpur: United Nations Country Team, Malaysia, 2011.

World Bank. "World development indicators". 2013 <http://databank.worldbank. org/data/views/reports/tableview.aspx> (accessed 21 October 2013).

7

PRIMARY AND SECONDARY EDUCATION IN MYANMAR
Challenges Facing Current Reforms

Brooke Zobrist and Patrick McCormick[1]

INTRODUCTION

Since the political changes starting in 2011, the new quasi-civilian Myanmar government has announced a number of reforms to the education sector. For several decades before that, Myanmar had spent far less on education than any of its neighbours. When a government has failed to provide adequate education to enough citizens, many embrace decentralization as a strategy to improve their education system, often with the encouragement of international advisors and donors. The Myanmar government has stated that decentralization is a goal for their provision of basic education. It has also stated its intention to increase funding and the number of schools and teachers, increase the number of years of compulsory education, reform the curriculum, draft an education law, and reach out to non-state actors that have signed ceasefire agreements with the central government.

Against this background of long-term underfunding and neglect, what is the nature of, and prospects for, decentralization in education in

Myanmar? Can decentralization be effective in addressing the deep-seated problems in the Myanmar education sector? To explore answers to these questions, we have examined relationships within the formal education system in the Ministry of Education across various levels of government, from the national down to the state or region, and below that to the district and township. We describe the provision of education starting from the colonial era in the late nineteenth century through to the present. We have also reviewed some of the non-state actors involved in the provision of education, especially as their involvement throws into relief challenges that the formal education system faces. We then present our findings, which suggest that of this writing (2014), decentralization, to the extent that is has happened at all, is limited. The institutional culture of the Ministry of Education, together with societal attitudes towards education and perceptions of the proper roles of students, teachers, and Ministry staff, all limit decentralization.

METHODOLOGY

We have based our findings on a literature review and on interviews with key participants and decision-makers in two regions, Mon State and Yangon Region. The purpose of this review and interviews was to gauge how people involved with the provision of education understand "decentralization", what decisions and responsibilities have been handed down from higher to lower levels of administration, and how they understand their own role in the process. We have examined the formal arrangements between the central Ministry of Education and the various states and regions providing education; and arrangements between the centre and the states for the management of education, for example, budgeting, human resources, curriculum development, policy frameworks, and overall decision-making authority.[2] At the same time, our research gave insight into what we have called the institutional culture or "ethos" of education. While our focus was primarily on the Ministry of Education, it appears that this ethos reflects views on society more widely.

We carried out twelve interviews with members of the Ministry of Education and leaders of the Mon National Education Committee, an "ethnic" education department active largely in ceasefire areas of Lower Myanmar.[3] We chose Yangon Region and Mon State as our research sites for breadth of comparison. Mon State has a long history of armed conflict between the central government and various armed Mon groups, whose goals have been greater autonomy if not some kind of independence. Within Mon State, there were until recently a number of so-called "brown" areas, those under partial government control, and "black" areas, which were not under government control. Mon State is fairly prosperous, with high levels of emigration to neighboring Thailand. A number of international organizations, such as UNICEF, the Myanmar Peace Support Initiative (MPSI), and Norwegian People's Aid, have funded education programmes there. In Yangon Region we conducted interviews with the Ministry of Education officials. Yangon Region has the country's largest city and a great diversity of socio-economic backgrounds among its population.

BACKGROUND

Government in Burma/Myanmar

After the elections of October 2010 and the subsequent change to a quasi-civilian government, President Thein Sein announced plans to change the structure and practices of the government.[4] The national houses of the *hluttaw* (parliament) convened regularly, for the first time in decades. Substantive parliamentary debate is part of the political process and the *hluttaws* had proposed new legislation, although not all of this have been implemented. The central government also stated that they would hand down some responsibilities to the state-level *hluttaws* and below.

When discussing "the government" in Myanmar, it is important to keep in mind that, despite its internationally recognized borders, the central government is not necessarily sovereign throughout its entire geographical area, nor does the power of the central government extend with the same force everywhere. Large areas of the "border" are out of *de facto* government control. Here the reach of central government services is poor. Local non-state actors may provide some such services, or citizens avail themselves of the services of nearby countries. However, the central government and most non-state armed groups have signed ceasefire agreements.[5] This process is bringing many areas that were formerly outside the control of the central government under its purview, or at least into closer association with it.

These are radical changes for Myanmar. Beginning with independence from the British in 1948, but especially since the first military coup in

1962, the political culture of government has been top-down, perhaps building upon earlier authoritarian practices that had been in place before the British began to take over the country in the early nineteenth century. This top-down political culture has done little to foster accountability, responsiveness to local needs, or flexibility. It has often been difficult for information to flow upwards. Top-level decision-makers tended to make pronouncements often based on the ideology or short-term agendas. Officials and bureaucrats lower down carry out orders, even if they do not always have the ability to do so. Proper funding for projects has often not been provided. Despite the fact that a majority in the bureaucracy take pride in their work and have the interests — however understood — of the nation at heart, governance is not efficient. The degree of openness and flexibility vary widely among ministries. Personal relationships are central to the exercise of power, so that patronage ties between superiors and inferiors are more important than formal procedures. In quotidian terms, this dynamic means that officials usually do not do anything unless the action is a completely routine matter for which there is a clear precedent, or unless an immediate superior directs them to do so.[6]

Both as researchers and as long-term residents who have interacted with Myanmar officialdom in various capacities, we have observed that many throughout the administration want there to be change in how things are done. Yet the hierarchical nature of social relations and power structures has had a profound influence on the practices of governance.

Governance in Education

Our research focuses largely on, but is not wholly limited to, the Ministry of Education, which is the second largest department in the government of Myanmar after the military. It has the second largest number of personnel, and an extensive geographic reach. While the Ministry of Education is the largest education provider, other ministries and departments are also involved with providing education, albeit with more specialized purviews. These include the Department of Education Planning and Training, the Ministry of Border Areas, the Ministry of Religious Affairs, under which fall Buddhist monastic schools, and the Ministry of Trade for private schools.

Planning, budgeting and decision-making are highly centralized in the Ministry of Education. The administrative divisions relevant to primary and secondary education are three Departments of Basic Education, under which is either the appropriate State or Region Education Office.[7] Within each state or region are several of the newly created *khayaing,* or District Education Offices, below which there are several Township Education Offices in each of the 325 townships of the country. Additional administrative units include six self-administered zones representing six different minority ethnic groups. These self-administered zones were mandated by the new 2008 Constitution and hold the authority and responsibility to provide education in their zones.

During the past several decades, the levels with the most administrative responsibilities have been the three Departments of Basic Education and the Township Education offices. According to our interviewees, the District Education Offices were only created in September 2012, which are

FIGURE 7.1
Simplified Administrative Structure — Ministry of Education

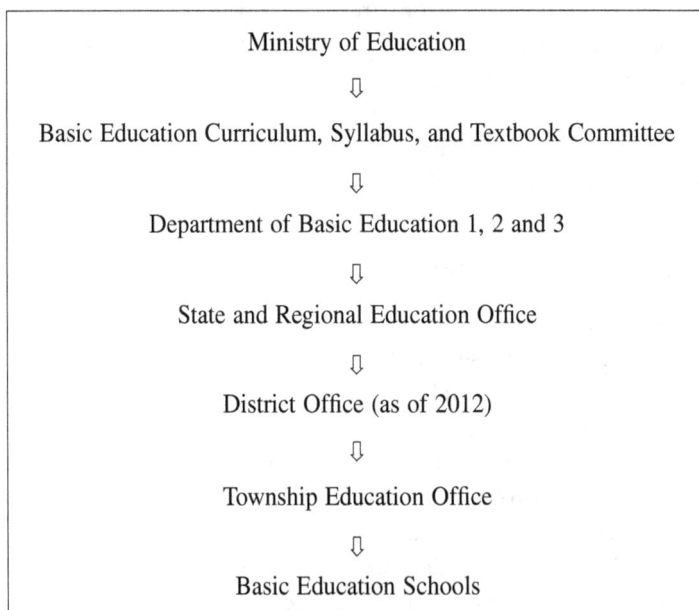

Ministry of Education

⇩

Basic Education Curriculum, Syllabus, and Textbook Committee

⇩

Department of Basic Education 1, 2 and 3

⇩

State and Regional Education Office

⇩

District Office (as of 2012)

⇩

Township Education Office

⇩

Basic Education Schools

Note: This figure shows only the most salient levels of administration. Ministry of Education Department of Higher Education (Lower Myanmar), *Administrative Structure of Basic Education Sector* <http://www. myanmar-education.edu.mm/dhel/education-system-in-myanmar/education-structure/>.

still in the process of being set up and taking on their duties. Township Education Offices still perform many of the responsibilities that the District Education Offices are meant to take on. As in other government ministries, administration and implementation flow from the Ministry down to the townships.

In terms of the legal framework for education, the current law guiding Basic Education was enacted in 1964 and has been amended several times, most recently in 1989. This law outlines four key objectives: promoting "good moral character"; ensuring that students are "well-equipped with [a] basic education"; giving "precedence to the teaching of science" and strong vocational training programmes, and a "strong foundation" for continuing to tertiary education.[8] The government has outlined a series of national plans for education loosely based on the Basic Education Law, but these plans tend towards generalities and promote widely disparate priorities.[9]

The Thirty-Year National Action Plan on Education, which the previous government began in 2001, is still in effect. In March 2012, at the Direct Policy Options Conference, the Minister of Education, Dr Mya Aye reiterated that the government would continue the 2001–30 plan. The Thirty-Year Plan ensures universal education in phases across successive timed phases ending in 2030–31. However, the ten broad programme areas lack work plans. For example, one programme area is the "Emergence of an Education System for Modernization and Development", but the plan makes no mention of devolution, decentralization, or increasing sub-national decision-making authority. Dr Mya Aye also stated that the government was committed to reviewing the education sector.[10]

The 2008 Constitution is another piece of legislation which states priorities and standards in education. As contentious as the Constitution may be to some, both the domestic and international communities have widely accepted it as a guide for policy formulation. The Constitution states in section 28, "the Union shall provide free, compulsory primary education system". It also states that citizens have the "right to education" and "the right to conduct scientific research, work with creativity", and "the right to develop the arts".

A crucial aspect of the Constitution is that it divides legislative responsibilities into two "schedules". Despite the fact that the new constitution reinvigorates the state parliaments as part of a process of decentralization, regional *hluttaws* have no ability to enact legislation over areas that fall under Schedule 1, which includes health, security, and education. They are able to do so for areas under Schedule 2, which includes state-level budgets and state-level development. Crucially, education falls under Schedule 1.

In July 2014, the Parliament of Myanmar passed a new National Education Bill. Though approved by Parliament, President Thein Sein sent the document back without signing off with instructions to rework at least twenty-five key points in the Bill. As per Myanmar's constitution, the President can send legislation back to the Parliament within two weeks of passage. The National Network for Education Reform, a civil society collaboration comprised of academics, teachers and advocates opposes the strict control of the education system carried forward in the new draft law. It criticizes the law on multiple grounds. Firstly, they state that the creation of a National Education Commission is "unnecessary" and may contribute to ongoing control over education content and limited quality assurances from the central government. Additionally, they find provision for students with disabilities to be inadequate and discriminatory. Lastly, they argue that as opposed to central control over Basic Education, localities led by a local school board should manage schools in their area.[11]

Education in Historical Context

Under the British, who began colonizing the country in 1824 before completely taking it over in 1885, the state managed education. Previously, under the Burmese kings, monastic institutions provided education, which was largely a male domain. Under the British, a greater number of children — both boys and girls — began to attend 7,000 basic education schools, where instruction was in Burmese.[12] Other government schools used English as the medium of instruction, as this was useful for employment in government service, and so these schools were well funded.

Under colonial rule, schools — especially colleges and universities — became centres of social and political activism. By the 1920s, university students had begun to strike against the University Act Bill which established English as medium of instruction and set fees for instruction, placing higher learning out of reach for most Burmese.[13] A widespread perception is that this history of student activism, which has continued sporadically into the recent past, has led the Ministry of Education to become highly centralized.

After independence in 1948, the Burmese administration launched the "Simla Scheme", a policy that brought various types of schools under a single system under the central government. Education was made free, with the entry age set at age six. The Simla Scheme continues to influence basic education. When General Ne Win took over the country in 1962 in a military coup, a new University Act decreased the size of Rangoon and Mandalay Universities by having them focus on specialized courses of study. Since then, school matriculation examination results determine students' choices of course of study.[14] Myanmar Language and Literature is the lowest-ranking course of study. Over the decades, the government has enacted policies to restrict the ethnic make-up of certain courses of study, such as medicine, in which people of Chinese descent were considered over-represented.

In 1965, as part of a larger campaign, General Ne Win nationalized all schools, including mission schools and schools operated for the Chinese and Indian communities. Many of the buildings that housed missionary, Chinese, or Indian-run schools serve as public schools today, including some that we visited on our research trips.

Contemporary Provision of Education

Overall, the education system is characterized by poor quality, out-dated pedagogy and insufficient geographic coverage. Rural and border areas are poorly served.[15] According to the recent Human Development Index, the mean for years of schooling in Myanmar is just under four.[16] Roughly half of Myanmar's children do not complete primary school.[17] When viewed against the benchmark of "Education For All" (EFA),[18] to which Myanmar became signatory in 2001, the government system does not address the core needs of students or society. Enrolment levels are low; transition rates from primary to middle school are low at about one quarter, although with dramatic regional variation; and of those who do continue through the final year of high school, only 50 per cent pass the matriculation exam.

In addition to the government system, there are community-based schools, monastic schools, and in areas with non-state armed groups, ethnic education departments, such as in areas of Mon State that are under the control of the New Mon State Party. Throughout the country, local communities often bear the burden to provide education, which while in theory free, usually entails various costs because of the chronic state of underfunding. On top of paying for school uniforms, books and stationery, parents are often obliged to pay "fees" to school administrators for a seat in the classroom, school ceremonies and school equipment. Parents are also expected to send their children to "tuition", after-school tutoring usually by the local school teacher, who reviews class lessons.[19] Many teachers depend on this tuition as their primary source of income. Students who do not attend risk failing examinations.

Even in places served by government schools, many families send their children to monastic schools in order to escape the burdens of fees. These schools often operate through the support of donors and do not ask families to pay the basic costs of schooling. The curriculum in the monastic system is the same as in government schools, but falls under the purview of the Ministry of Religious Affairs.

Another final type of school are the so-called national schools. The set-up, funding and curricula of these schools varies widely depending on the particular non-state group that runs them. The Mon National Schools, for example, combine elements of the government schools and Buddhist monastic education: they follow the government curriculum with the addition of Mon history and language. Many are held in monastic compounds. The teachers in these non-government schools are not government-certified. It is not clear to what extent other so-called national education departments of non-state armed groups follow the government curriculum. For example, at least some Karen national schools teach only in a Karen language and English, thus preparing students for national life in no country.

Currently, there are eleven years of schooling in the education system: five years of primary, four of middle school, and two of high school. The system is designed for students to enter First Standard at age five and graduate from high school at age sixteen or seventeen. The central government, not local governments, hires and pays teachers in government schools. Teachers must complete a series of pre-service programmes at one of the country's twenty Teachers' Colleges. The Ministry of Education increased the number of teachers in 2013–14 and so has recruited 10,000 Assistant Junior Teachers. These new teachers will not have attended the two years of preparation courses that other teachers must complete in order to qualify as teachers in state schools.

Table 7.1 gives a sense of the magnitude of the task confronted by the Ministry of Education. The ministry sets the curriculum for all schools,

TABLE 7.1
School Enrollment Statistics, 2011–12

Government Schools	
Primary	28,968
Post-primary[a]	6,761
Middle	3,163
High	2,395
Total schools	41,287
Teachers	
Primary	184,170
Junior Teachers	67,398
Senior Teachers	26,612
Total teachers	276,180
Students	
Primary	5,195,952
Middle	2,332,249
High	672,394
Total students	8,200,595

Note: "Post-primary" refers to a type of school that the Ministry of Education and the Ministry for Progress in Border Areas and National Races and Development Affairs have created by adding middle-school levels to primary schools as a strategy to expand overall attendance rates.
Source: Myanmar, Ministry of Education, "Education for All: Access to and Quality of Education in Myanmar", Conference on Development Policy Options with Special Reference to Education and Health in Myanmar, Nepyidaw, 13–16 February 2012, p. 5.

whether government, monastic, or private. These schools mostly use the textbooks the ministry has prepared. There are five main subject areas taught at the primary level: Myanmar Language, Mathematics, English, Science, and General Studies. The latter includes life skills, social sciences, and civic education. Lessons are officially taught in the Myanmar language. Rote learning and group chanting are common.

Spending on Education

In Myanmar society, there is a widespread perception that the quality of education has declined in recent decades. Although funding has generally been exceedingly minimal for several decades, government financing for education has risen in recent years. In the 2000s, spending as a proportion of GDP fell from 0.4 per cent in 2002–03 to 0.1 per cent in 2007–08, before again rising significantly to 7 per cent by the end of the decade.[20] Spending, when calculated as a proportion of the total budget, has been quite low in recent years. According to EFA, Education Sector Development Plans under the Fast Track Initiative (FTI) Framework that the Myanmar government released in 2004, the recommended spending on education should be 6 per cent of GDP. In 2006, Myanmar's spending rate for education was five times lower than the regional average of 3.6 per cent.[21]

For the 2010–11 academic year, however, the Department of Educational Training and Planning reported a total expenditure, including capital costs, of approximately $231 million.[22] Based on the Department's figure of eight million enrolled students, annual spending per student from the first to final year of high school is roughly US$30.[23] In February 2012, the Minister of Finance reported the total expenditure on basic education for the 2012–13 academic year increased to approximately US$757 million, which is 4.9 per cent of the total government budget,[24] while about a year later, the Hluttaw announced a further increase to approximately US$1 billion, or about 5.8 per cent of the national budget.[25] This figure raises government spending to roughly US$94 per student, but given problems with the accuracy of government data, this figure may not be reliable.[26] Salary costs comprise around 80 per cent of the education budget (compared to 70–90 per cent in most developing countries)[27] and capital costs are about 5 per cent of the budget, leaving little for school supplies and maintenance. A further caution is that the education sector has begun to attract more foreign aid, so that as the amount being spent in education increase, it will become more difficult to untangle the total state input from that international assistance.

DECENTRALIZATION IN MYANMAR'S EDUCATION SECTOR

Models and Debates

Decentralization is generally understood as some form of devolution of power, responsibility, and decision making. It has risen to prominence across the world since the 1980s. In the midst of a reform or transitional process, powerful outside development agencies may recommend or require that recipient countries implement it as a condition to receiving aid. Stated and unstated goals of decentralization include economic development, increased management efficiency, increasing democratization and generally improving the quality of education. In some sectors, it has the potential to reduce ethnic conflict.[28]

Decentralization in education usually includes policy development, the creation or revision of curricula and student evaluation, rationalizing the allocation of funds and budgeting, generating revenue, and the management of resources.

Organizations such as the World Bank, who are active in Myanmar, have given recommendations on reform, of which decentralization is a central feature. In 2006 the World Bank released a study which set "improved learning outcomes" as the central objective of education reform. The study suggested that improving the management of education is crucial to this goal.[29] Administrators must have better abilities to make decisions and evaluate their system analytically. Other areas that governments must address include language policy (which in Myanmar is the question of mother tongue education), pedagogy, parent involvement, curriculum and curriculum reform, and education philosophy. This latter is an articulation of the kind of student, citizen, or person that the education system aims to create.

There is some debate about the purpose of decentralization, and the best outcomes of it. Policy advisors tend to see decentralization as a way to make administration and governance more responsive to the population, more effective, and more accountable. Advisors also see it as a way to save money. There have been cases where decentralization has been an excuse to under- or de-fund the education sector, with the central government "encouraging" lower levels of administration to find funds on their own. In Pakistan, for example, the government simply closed the national Ministry of Education. Each province was given responsibility for education.

On the other hand, not all forms of centralization are necessarily bad or connote inefficiency. In Anglo-American countries, such as the United States, which has allowed a high degree of local autonomy in education, there have been moves towards greater centralization and standardization. In Thailand, a centralized education system has been successful in increasing enrolment and retention rates, although centralization does not necessarily improve quality, especially in rural areas.[30]

The actual type of decentralization — the philosophy, implementation, and outcome — reflect the situation in which the process is undertaken. Overall, there are three major forms: *Deconcentration* is the redistribution of decision-making authority and financial management to various levels of the central government.[31] This form is the least radical and is the kind most often found in unitary states. As such, *deconcentration* merely shifts responsibilities from central government officials to those working in lower-level administrative units. *Delegation* is a more extensive form of decentralization through which central governments transfer responsibility for decision-making and the administration of public functions to semi-autonomous organizations not wholly controlled by the central government, but ultimately accountable to it. These organizations include public enterprises and corporations, which usually have decision-making power. In the case of education, this would include private educational institutions. *Devolution* usually transfers responsibilities for services to municipalities or other subnational levels that elect officials and raise revenue.

In the short term, *deconcentration* is the form that decentralization will take in the Ministry of Education, given that education falls under Schedule 1 of the Constitution as discussed above. Private and monastic schools operate outside of the purview of the Ministry of Education, and so represent an unexpected form of *delegation* of administrative, decision-making, and budgeting authority.

Decentralization in the Context of Myanmar's Education Reform

The Framework for Social and Economic Reform (FESR), released in December 2012, is a major component of the decentralization in education. This document lists the policy priorities of Thein Sein's government across several sectors, including the economy, environmental sustainability, poverty alleviation, and health and education reform. The FESR provides short-term recommendations as a bridge to the Comprehensive Development Plan, a twenty-year plan which the government has drafted. The FESR does not, however, offer a comprehensive vision of reform in the education sector, or a clear articulation of the expected outcomes of the reform process. Rather, it focuses on "quick wins", of which there are nine. One of these is changing the funding structure of basic education, as well as undertaking a Comprehensive Education Sector Review. The

FESR addresses the potential for cash to be transferred to lower levels: for school grants, and student stipends, or "conditional cash transfers," which we discuss in detail under Research Findings below.

> While [the Government of Myanmar] strengthens regulatory policies to streamline various private and community-run educational programs, it is also moving ahead with the decentralization of education management in line with the requirements of the Constitution by integrating locally-designed teaching curriculum as well as non-formal programs in basic education system. This reform policy and strategy will focus on the need to expand the system of basic education from eleven to twelve years, on child-centred teaching methodologies, upgrading teacher training and other curriculum reforms necessary to enhance the quality of basic education, on teacher remuneration and broader issues of education financing, on establishing a rigorous system for education quality assessment and performance, and on further reforms in the management of basic education including the importance of active engagement in the process by the parents themselves. In addition, [the Government of Myanmar] will also pay attention to other supportive measures that can address high drop-out rates and out-of pocket cost burdens on the families.
>
> "Framework for Social and Economic Reforms",
> December 2012, pp. 28–29

The FESR and the Thirty-Year National Action Plan on Education are not in harmony. The latter was created under the previous regime and does not address decentralization or devolution, nor the shifting of any administrative or decision-making power to lower levels. However, both of these government plans do provide a standard against which to understand the experiences of, and opinions expressed by, officials from the Ministry of Education that were interviewed.

As we discuss in greater detail below, decentralization in the education sector in Myanmar is a form of *deconcentration*. Some responsibilities have moved from higher to lower levels. When asked how they understood the term "decentralization" (in the Myanmar language, people use the English term), interviewees answered along the lines of, "The centre used to control everything, but now they won't." Most of the subsequent discussion had to do with *deconcentration* — the creation of new levels of administration and providing lower levels of administration with a discretionary budget. Throughout all government administration, perhaps reflecting bureaucratic culture, there is limited delegation. Rather, people in positions of power retain their privileges. Greater delegation and *deconcentration* will happen within that context. We also note that there is a certain amount of *de facto devolution* in education provision in ceasefire areas, which we discuss in greater detail below. Some of the ethnic national education systems follow government curriculum, but the extent to which the central government will recognize them and oversee them, remains to be seen.

Privatization is often part of decentralization and falls under *devolution* because private companies handle decision-making and other responsibilities. A recent change in law has allowed private schools to be registered more easily. There are now sixty-two private schools providing basic education nationwide.[32] Looking elsewhere in the region for possible outcomes of this development, India provides an example of decentralization which features the growth of private schools. In India, this system has exacerbated inequities in access and differences in quality.[33] In Myanmar, many private schools provide intensive English language instruction, as English skills help in gaining education and work abroad.

RESEARCH FINDINGS

Overview

The following are the main themes that emerged from our research: administrative, which focuses on distributing managerial responsibilities among different levels of government or administration; fiscal, or how expenditure responsibilities are assigned and corresponding resources provided; and political, which involves the transfer of decision-making and accountability to lower levels of administration.[34]

Administrative

- The government created a new level, the *khayaing* "district", in 2012. Some decision-making power has been moved up to the district from the township, although as of this writing, this is more theoretical than actual. Interviewees explained this development as bringing the Ministry of Education in line with all other ministries, which have this level. This move will shift some responsibilities up one level, and others down from higher levels. Data aggregation will be moved up to the district from the township, while the authority to move teachers from school to school within a district moves down to the district level from the state or region. These changes represent an attempt at *deconcentration*, reflecting a national decision to build up more administrative capacity at a lower level in the administrative structure.[35] In actual fact, this new level may simply represent a greater extension of ministry authority in a new fashion.

- There have been a few small changes related to appointments. According to the interviewees, in 2013, for the first time, region and state-level ministry officials were allowed to appoint one type of teacher, the Junior Assistant Teachers. All other teachers continued to be appointed at the Union Level, as is all education-sector leadership.
- Curriculum and assessment were still under central control of the Ministry of Education.

Fiscal

- For decisions related to infrastructure, school repairs and maintenance, the authority remained mixed. Some decisions were made at the Township, others at Departments of Basic Education. Township officers must seek approval from the Departments of Basic Education, apparently skipping the state and regional levels. More investigation is necessary, especially since these decisions involve potentially lucrative building contracts.
- According to interviewees, budget decisions continued to be made at the national level, with no authority delegated to lower levels. A limited, small exception was that starting in 2012, school principals have been given a limited discretionary budget, under which expenses have already been narrowly allocated by type of expense. Principals had no authority to diverge from a pre-set plan and must report up to the Township Education Officer.
- Policies on raising revenue at lower levels were unclear. No one below the central level could approach international donors. In practice, however, the School Welfare Committees or Parent-Teacher Associations of individual schools could raise revenues, as was the case, for example, for emergency repairs through School Welfare Committees or Parent-Teacher Associations. The principal must seek

approval from either Township or District Officers. Because local levels had no authority over curriculum or special programmes, they could not raise funds for such uses.

- According to interviewees, in 2012 the central government created a new programme under which schools must choose needy students to receive scholarships from the Ministry of Education. The schools must form a committee to evaluate and select the students, typically very low in number, such as four students per school. The schools could not ask for more funding for more students, nor could they move budget allocations from elsewhere to help those students.

Political

- Regional and state-level *hluttaws* had no authority over education. There appeared to be no formal connection between the Ministry of Education and the regional *hluttaws* and their members. In any case, education falls under Schedule 1 of the constitution and therefore it is not clear how these *hluttaws* could become involved in education. Several Ministry of Education officials interviewed for this study appeared to view the state legislatures as irrelevant to their work. As one official put it, "They do their own things."
- Below the Union Hluttaw, no elected officials play a role in education. All other officials were appointed. Similarly, the authority to appoint teachers and principals lay with the Union Department of Basic Education. No lower level organizations or committees have authority to make these appointments.
- A few "national education" systems associated with non-state ethnic groups who had reached cease-fire agreements with the central government had created what appear to be viable ethnic education systems, such as the Mon National Schools, which developed out of the New Mon State Party. These systems, however, are not legal and represent an ad hoc form of accommodation in what could be considered a form of "decentralization through devolution".

DISCUSSION

As of this writing, there are very limited signs of decentralization happening in the education sector. Much of what we observed and what interviewees described may be better understood as providing social welfare services, which have been decided at a central level of the Ministry of Education. The provision of these services represent a form of *deconcentration*: people at lower levels have more work and responsibilities, but no greater authority. Rather than decentralization, another interpretation of these new programs is simply an extension of central control.

An example of apparent change are two new programmes to provide student stipends and cash transfers, projects intended to increase the number of students who go to primary school.[36] The first programme gave parents 1,000 kyat for each child they enrol. Yet this programme created new work and responsibilities for school principals and teachers, but gave them no decision-making authority. Some argued that 1,000 kyat (about US$1) is not a significant incentive. In fact, school principals reported that some parents found that coming to pick up the money was not worth their time or transportation costs. One high-ranking official quoted a Myanmar proverb to describe the programme as "like throwing sesame seeds at an elephant".

The second programme provided a modest stipend to poor children for them to be able to attend school. While the goals of these programmes are admirable, some respondents criticized them. The student stipends created more work and responsibility for low-level administrators, also without carrying any discretionary powers or responsibilities. Township Education Officers were required to form a committee to create the criteria for selection. The committee, in turn, selected the students based on the criteria that they have agreed to. In Mon State, there was money for only four students. The Township Education Officer told us that they were required to use this money only for these four students. She could not, for example, divide up the money in order to help more students, nor could she apply the money in other ways, such as organizing transportation to allow students living far away to come to school. Additionally, this committee did not have the permission to raise outside funds to expand their ability to help more students. Many respondents said that they would like to have the authority to seek funds from local donors to undertake special programmes, trainings, and to help more poor students.

Authority to implement work tends to flow down from the Ministry of Education to the townships, with little information or feedback flowing back up. Several interviewees did state, however, that they were able to provide suggestions to, and make requests of, higher administrative levels.

One state-level official, when asked whether he had any influence over decisions made above him, replied, "They [i.e. higher levels of authority] listen to what I say. Not exactly, but they listen." In this interview and elsewhere, it was not possible to elicit any concrete examples of when suggestions from state, region, or lower level officials had had an influence on planning or operations.

Administrative practices varied between Yangon Region and Mon State. Interviewees' understandings of their authority also varied regionally. A school principal in Yangon Region, for example, said that she could approve a special programme for her high school but, as a matter of courtesy, she should inform higher level officials about her plan. She already had one such programme in place: students from an international school in Yangon had come to play with the children at her high school. In contrast, a principal in Mon State said that she wanted to start a sports programme but was not authorized to do so. These variations in local authority may reflect differences in administrative culture, personal connections, or power relations.

A final area of change was in the hiring of teachers. As discussed above, the government has worked to hire 10,000 new Assistant Junior Teachers, which appears to be the responsibility of the state and region-level officers, although this was not explicitly stated. One way to interpret this deconcentration is the central authority is giving lower level officials the power to hire only less qualified teachers. It is not clear whether the state-level officers will be able to fire these teachers. The hiring and firing of all other teachers remains centralized. We had assumed that questions about hiring and firing teachers might prompt school principals to speak about a desire for greater control over this process. This was not the case. When we asked them what they would do with a difficult teacher — someone who was not performing up to expectations — all the principals emphasized their close relationships with their teachers and described how they would encourage an erring individual to change. In the abstract case of a teacher having to be dismissed, the principal would submit a request to a higher level for further action.[37]

Another point to consider is the education system of the non-state armed groups. We examined the Mon system as a way to gauge the state of accommodation between the central government and these groups. The Mon national education system illustrates some examples of delegating educational authority, as the educational systems of such non-state armed groups have reached an accommodation with the official, national system. The Mon National Education Committee (MNEC) developed out of the New Mon State Party, and is operating largely — though not solely — in areas formerly under the control of the New Mon State Army. The MNEC provides education in a variety of formats, from schools they operate wholly themselves, to teaching Mon language and Mon perspectives on such topics as history in government-run schools, made possible through informal arrangements. The schools operated wholly by the MNEC and the Mon-specific programmes are funded through non-government sources. Important features of the Mon national school system are that it allows for instruction in a mother tongue other than the Myanmar language, but also allows the teaching of a local language and local content, while at the same time working as a bridge to the government system. Students who pass through the Mon national education system are then, in theory, allowed to transfer into the government system and take the government matriculation exams. Thus the system both satisfies demands for an "ethnic" education, while also promoting an integrated nation.

The MNEC and their system is not, strictly speaking, legal. Myanmar law does not allow any deviation from the standard curriculum, nor is instruction in a medium other than the Myanmar language allowed. Demands for mother tongue education are vigorous among many other ethnic groups, who are calling for the use of local languages during school hours, not simply the use of government school buildings for ethnic-language instruction outside of school hours, as the government has allowed on a limited scale. The system exists as part of a ceasefire agreement, and the extent to which local government-run schools will accommodate and allow Mon-content programmes is not standardized or systematized, but rather a matter of local, ad hoc, informal arrangements. Nevertheless, to the extent that the Mon national education system is functioning, popular, and has the support of local communities, it represents an opportunity for promoting greater levels of local autonomy and the devolution of decision-making authority to local communities, starting with ethnic minority groups. This system has already attained a high degree of autonomy, as for example in curriculum, fund-raising, and the hiring of teachers, yet it is not legally recognized by the government system.

A final point to keep in mind about the national schools is that they offer the possibility of government accommodation to local needs. In theory, then, local communities in ethnic-majority Burman-dominated areas may be able to make greater demands of the central government related to the provision of education.

Synthesis: Institutional Culture and Limits for Change

Having reviewed our findings, we now step back to view the larger context in which our findings make sense. We draw out aspects of the larger institutional culture of the Ministry of Education, in the sense of shared practices and understandings. The institutional culture or "ethos" of education provides some insight into the shared beliefs, values, goals, and priorities of people working in the Ministry of Education. We have drawn up this depiction based on our observations and discussions, and is meant to be illustrative rather than exhaustive or definitional. In the course of our interviews, views and beliefs common to many began to emerge.

Interviewees took their work and responsibilities seriously and were concerned with providing an education to as many children as possible. As alluded to above, government plans often include vague terms and slogans such as:

> Our Vision: "To create an education system that will generate a learning society capable of facing the challenges of the Knowledge Age."
>
> Our Motto: "Building a modern developed nation through education."[38]

Our interviewees' statements reflected such slogans, with people speaking of education as a way to advance and develop the nation and the people. There was a widespread concern with providing education to children of poor families. Many spoke in abstract terms about improving or modernizing the nation, but gave little concrete indication of what that would mean in terms of the school system, curricula, or teaching practices. As once principal put it:

> We're bringing up students so that they will try hard. However poor they are, they must be in school. They must try hard. They have to know that they are Burmese. They must not betray their country. They must love their country. That's how we are raising our students.

When asked about hopes for the future, responses tended towards concrete terms of hopes for filling specific gaps and needs and providing services, rather than articulations of a vision for their individual schools or area. When asked what decentralization could mean for his area, one district official replied that it could be a way to find money more easily for extracurricular activities. Another said that he would like control over school construction and the geographic distribution of teachers. He specifically stated that he saw no need for him to be able to make changes to curriculum, teaching, or learning outcomes.

Another aspect to the education ethos is how individuals view themselves, their institution, and the practice of administration. Respondents did not discuss the possibility of developing policy themselves to achieve specific outcomes. As we alluded to earlier, individuals in the Ministry of Education work in a hierarchical, top-down structure. This arrangement has an impact on how they view their abilities to make decisions, the authority they do and do not have, or can and cannot ask for, and the processes of accountability and responsiveness, both to higher and lower levels of administration. The system requires following precedent and guidelines; to do otherwise carries great risks. In this context, since teachers and administrators do not see themselves as responsible for defining or shaping education, but rather as implementers of the education process. Questions such as whether decentralization was desirable or possible fell outside of what most interviewees saw as concerning them. As one Education Officer put it, "Over time, decentralization will happen by itself." His reply indicates an understanding of decentralization as happening outside of the individual and their efforts, at an abstract level.

This institutional culture reflects a wider societal discourse on the importance of being educated, and the importance for children to become educated people. It is not clear, however, what "educated" means, and therefore, it is difficult to understand what the purpose of education is. Interviewees seemed to suggest that if education happened, then everything else would fall in place. Perhaps the most important goal of education is simply to have students participate in the school system. Following this understanding, it is enough for students to be participating in the system, but it is not the place of teachers and other administrators to define what that education is — its goals or desired outcomes.

Given the Ministry of Education's institutional culture, substantive decentralization seems unlikely without individuals reassessing their roles, together with a more general reassessment with the practices of administration. At least one interviewee recognized this for themselves, saying, "We need to change ourselves and our habit of obeying and fulfilling the instructions of those above us, who tell us what to do."[39] In the current system, there is no accountability to a local constituency, including the students themselves. The parent-teacher associations and school management committees that have been set up in recent years do not represent local constituencies. Instead, they carry out predetermined tasks and members are usually appointed, not elected. The institutional culture — no doubt both reflecting and shaping wider society — views students as recipients, rather than active participants, in the education process. Decentralization, however defined, includes such democratizing features as accountability to, and consultation with, local communities. The example of stipends for poor students could be an opportunity to build these practices, not only within the various levels of the Ministry of Education itself, but between the Ministry and the communities.

CONCLUSION

In the scholarship on decentralization, there appears to be an assumption that people lower down in an administration will welcome greater decision-making authority. A benefit of decentralization is that people lower down in administration have taken, and see the advantages of taking on, more responsibilities and of having greater authority and autonomy. Before the process of decentralization, they have responsibilities but only limited authority over budgeting, decision-making, or ability to influence the policies made higher up.

Interviewees spoke of decentralization in concrete, not abstract terms. No one spoke of fundamentally re-evaluating their roles or the administrative processes in the Ministry of Education. Rather, they spoke of wanting more discretionary power in relation to specific matters. Some made it clear they were not eager to take on more authority. For many people interviewed, to ask for certain kinds of authority would go beyond what they thought of as possible, or desirable, for providing an education. Many saw their role as something more akin to providing social welfare services, such as helping poor students. One kind of authority that many saw as desirable was for township-level officials and principals to be able to seek outside funding. Interviewees also tended to focus on what, in time, could become possible at lower levels of administration, rather than on what changes they would like to occur at higher levels in the Ministry of Education.

These views of our interviewees help us build a more complete understanding of the prospects for change in the education sector. In Myanmar, there is great concern with getting the right kind of legislation, funding, and advice to improve education. Unsurprisingly, the government itself and outside agencies have placed an emphasis on reorganizing and rationalizing administration and administrative practices. But as our findings reveal, the institutional culture is also central to processes of reform.

Notes

1. Zobrist has been working in education related to Burma/Myanmar for the past fourteen years, many of which she spent on the Thai-Burma border, and has been living in-country full-time for the past five years, working as a research and education consultant. McCormick has worked as a researcher and consultant for education, civil society, and livelihoods for the past seven years, and has lived in-country for the past nine. He has worked for the EFEO and the University of Zürich. The authors wish to thank the Asian Foundation, our many interviewees, and the government officials whose generous help made this research possible.

2. There are fourteen states and regions in Myanmar. In English usage, "states" refer to areas inhabited by the so-called ethnic minorities (Kachin State, Mon State, Chin State, Shan State, Karen State, Kayah State and Rakhaing State), in contrast to Bamar (Burman)-dominated areas, which are called "regions" (Yangon, Taninthayi, Magwe, Ayeyarwady, Mandalay, Sagaing and Bago). In addition, there are six self-administrated areas and several ceasefire areas, which are associated with the central administration in various ways. Here, terms such as "state-level" encompass both states and regions.

3. In Mon State, we interviewed high-level officials in the State Education Office, one District Education Officer, one Township Education Officer and four school principals. In Yangon Region, we interviewed the highest official in the Regional Education Office, one District Education Officer, one Township Education Officer and two school principals. All interviews were conducted in Burmese following a semi-structured format designed to draw out the procedures and protocols of the Ministry of Education. Discussions of hypothetical situations helped us gain an understanding of how these officials and officers dealt with specific situations and helped us gauge their understanding of decentralization. The interviews lasted between thirty and eighty minutes. While conversations tended to be open, there were instances where we had to produce official

permission in order to hold our conversations, despite the fact that upper-level officials had stated such permission was not necessary. Overall, however, interviewees gave us their opinions, at times quite outspokenly.

4. U Thein Sein gave a speech on 9 August 2013 in which he announced five key public administration reforms meant to clarify relationships between state and region departments and the state and regional *hluttaws*.

5. On earlier rounds of ceasefire negotiations, see Mary Callahan, *Making Enemies: War and State-Building in Burma* (Singapore: NUS Press 2004).

6. For a succinct description, see David Steinberg, *Burma/Myanmar: What Everyone Needs to Know* (Oxford: Oxford University Press, 2010).

7. According to the Basic Education Law of 1973, the Departments of Basic Education operate schools based on geographic region. Department 1 is "Upper Myanmar", Department 2 "Lower Myanmar", and Department 3 Yangon city.

8. Ministry of Education, Department of Higher Education (Lower Myanmar), *Education System in Myanmar: Self-Evaluation and Future Plans* <http:// www.myanmar-education.edu.mm/dhel/education-system-in-myanmar/ evaluation-of-current-implementation-situation/>.

9. See the "Ten Points Education Policy", which U Thein Sein released in March 2011 at the first session of the *Hluttaw*. This and other plans state that education should be free and compulsory. The emphasis of individual plans is often quite different. Some concern improving teachers' skills, others focus on non-formal education or developing life skills.

10. Mya Aye, presentation at the Conference on Direct Policy Options with Special Reference to Education and Health in Myanmar, Nepyidaw, 13–16 February 2012.

11. "The Statement Issued by NNER in Response to the National Education Law Approved by the Parliament", National Network for Education Reform, Myanmar, 19 August 2014.

12. Dr Thein Lwin, *Education in Burma (1945–2000)*, 2nd ed., September 2000.

13. There is again a move afoot to make English the medium of instruction in Burmese universities.

14. A "matriculation examination" is administered at the end of the tenth standard, and works as something of a university entrance examination.

15. "Presentation on the Concluding Observations on the Third and Fourth National Report on the Implementation of the Convention on the rights of the Child (The Republic of the Union of Myanmar)", Ministry of Foreign Affairs, November 2011.

16. UNDP, "Myanmar; HDI Values and Rank Changes in the 2013 Human Development Report", March 2013.

17. The recent Multiple Indicator Cluster Survey, based on households, puts the

net intake ration (NIR) at 74 per cent, and the Net Primary Completion Rate at 54 per cent. See Ministry of National Planning and Economic Development, Ministry of Health and UNICEF, *Myanmar: Monitoring the Situation of Women and Children, Multiple Indicator Cluster Survey, 2009–2010* (Nepyidaw: Ministry of National Planning and Economic Development and Ministry of Health, 2011). The data in this survey were collected from a representative sample of the population, and therefore may be more reliable than data collected on the basis of problematic measures and projections of population figures, such as the census.

18. Not to be confused with the above-mentioned Myanmar Government plan, "Education for All", which UNESCO developed and which 164 countries adopted in 2000 at Dakar, Senegal. It is comprised of six goals, including "Goal 2: Free and Compulsory Primary Education for All". Along with the Millennium Development Goals, the EFA is a key framework for economic development and poverty reduction through improving education.

19. Brooke Zobrist, *Mapping Teaching-Learning and Operational Experiences in Fifty Monastery Schools Across Myanmar* (Yangon: Pyoepin, 2010).

20. Statistics from the Annual Myanmar Laws, published by the Attorney General's Office.

21. 2010 EFA Global Monitoring Report.

22. US$1 = 1,000 kyat. The kyat has decreased in value against the dollar since the time of research.

23. Department of Education Planning and Training, "Brief Presentation on Basic Education", presented at the Educational Thematic Working Group Meeting, Yangon, 24 January 2011.

24. U Hla Tun, Minister of Finance and Revenue (January 2012).

25. Ministry of Education, quoted in "Back to School Insert", *The Myanmar Times*, May 2013.

26. The quality, reliability, and completeness of data in Myanmar is generally quite poor. Moreover, data is often aggregated, making it difficult to assess gaps and variation.

27. E.M. King, "The Global Economic Crisis, Education, and Development Partnerships", keynote presentation at the HDN-WBI Course on Innovations in Partnerships, Washington, D.C., 2009 <http://info.worldbank.org/etools/docs/library/252253/Keynote%20presentation%2C%20Elizabeth%20King.pdf>.

28. Political decentralization may help to curtail such conflict, but is not always successful. Ethnic conflict has been at the heart of the civil war that has been a constant since independence, and which in turn has had a deep impact on education, especially in areas that have been controlled by non-state actors. See Dawn Brancati, "Decentralization: Fueling the Fire or Dampening the Flames of

Ethnic Conflict and Secessionism", Institute for Quantitative Political Science, Harvard University, September 2005.

29. World Bank, *From Schooling Access to Learning Outcomes: An Unfinished Agenda — An Evaluation of World Bank Support to Primary Education* (Washington, D.C.: World Bank, 2006).

30. Alan Mounier and Phasina Tangchuang, eds., *Education and Knowledge in Thailand: The Quality Controversy* (Chiang Mai: Silkworm Books, 2010).

31. These definitions are based on those presented in Jennie Litvack and Jessica Seddon, eds., *Decentralization Briefing Notes* (Washington, D.C.: World Bank, 2000), p. 2.

32. *Union Daily*, 18 June 2013.

33. Gretchen Rhines Cheney, Betsy Brown Ruzzi and Kartikh Muralidharan, "A Profile of the Indian Education System: Prepared for New Commission on the Skills of the American Workforce", National Center on Education and the Economy, November 2005.

34. These definitions are a modification of those of Hamish Nixon et al., *State and Region Governments in Myanmar* (Yangon: The Asia Foundation and Myanmar Development Research Institute-CESD, 2013), p. 4.

35. Interviews with multiple education officials in Mon State.

36. Interviews with school principals and officials in Mon State and Yangon Region.

37. This process of firing is not necessarily lengthy. A recent report in the Irrawaddy describes how a teacher was fired after attending a commemoration of the events of 8 August 1988. Lewi Weng, "Sacking of Naypyidaw School teacher Draws Condemnation", *Irrawaddy*, 26 August 2013 <http://www.irrawaddy.org/reform/sacking-of-naypyidaw-schoolteacher-draws-condemnation.html>.

38. "Education for All: Access to and Quality of Education in Myanmar", Conference on Development Policy Options with Special Reference to Education and Health in Myanmar, Nepyidaw, 13–16 February 2012, p. 1. Here as elsewhere, terms such as "modern" and "developed" are not defined.

39. We learned later that this person retired the very next day after meeting us.

References

Brancati, Dawn. "Decentralization: Fueling the Fire or Dampening the Flames of Ethnic Conflict and Secessionism". Institute for Quantitative Political Science, Harvard University, September 2005.

Callahan, Mary. *Making Enemies: War and State-Building in Burma*. Singapore: NUS Press, 2004.

Cheney, Gretchen Rhines, Betsy Brown Ruzzi and Kartikh Muralidharan. "A Profile of the Indian Education System: Prepared for New Commission on the Skills of the American Workforce". National Center on Education and the Economy, November 2005.

King, E.M. "The Global Economic Crisis, Education, and Development Partnerships". Keynote presentation at the HDN-WBI Course on Innovations in Partnerships, Washington, D.C., 2009 <http://info.worldbank.org/etools/docs/library/252253/Keynote%20presentation%2C%20Elizabeth%20King.pdf>.

Lewi Weng. "Sacking of Naypyidaw School teacher Draws Condemnation". *Irrawaddy*, 26 August 2013 <http://www.irrawaddy.org/reform/sacking- of-naypyidaw-schoolteacher-draws-condemnation.html>.

Litvack, Jennie and Jessica Seddon, eds. *Decentralization Briefing Notes*. Washington, D.C.: World Bank, 2000.

Mounier, Alan and Phasina Tangchuang, eds. *Education and Knowledge in Thailand: The Quality Controversy*. Chiang Mai: Silkworm Books, 2000.

Mya Aye. "Opening Speech at the Conference on Direct Policy Options with Special Reference to Education and Health in Myanmar", Nepyidaw, 13–16 February 2012.

Myanmar, Attorney General's Office. Annual Myanmar Laws. Various years.

Ministry of Education, Myanmar. "Education for All: Access to and Quality of Education in Myanmar". Conference on Development Policy Options with Special Reference to Education and Health in Myanmar, Nepyidaw, 13–16 February 2012 <http://yangon.sites.unicnetwork.org/files/2013/05/Education-for-All-in-Myanmar-Final-2012-FEB-2.pdf>.

———, Department of Education Planning and Training. "Brief Presentation on Basic Education". Presented at the Educational Thematic Working Group Meeting, Yangon, 24 January. 2011.

———, Department of Higher Education (Lower Myanmar). "Education System in Myanmar: Self-Evaluation and Future Plans" <http://www.myanmar-education.edu.mm/dhel/education-system-in-myanmar/evaluation-of-current-implementation-situation>.

———, Department of Higher Education (Lower Myanmar). "Administrative Structure of Basic Education Sector" <http://www.myanmar-education.edu.mm/dhel/education-system-in-myanmar/education-structure>.

Myanmar, Ministry of Finance and Revenue. "Statement by U Hla Tun, Minister of Finance and Revenue". January 2012.

Myanmar, Ministry of Foreign Affairs. "Presentation on the Concluding Observations on the Third and Fourth National Report on the Implementation of the Convention on the Rights of the Child (The Republic of the Union of Myanmar)". November 2011.

Myanmar, Ministry of National Planning and Economic Development, Ministry of Health and UNICEF. *Myanmar: Monitoring the Situation of Women and Children,*

Multiple Indicator Cluster Survey, 2009–2010. Nepyidaw: Ministry of National Planning and Economic Development and Ministry of Health, 2011.

Myanmar Times. "Back to School Insert". Ministry of Education, May 2013.

National Network for Education Reform. "The Statement Issued by NNER in Response to the National Education Law Approved by the Parliament", Myanmar, 19 August 2014.

Nixon, Hamish et al. *State and Region Governments in Myanmar*. (Yangon: Asia Foundation and Myanmar Development Research Institute-CESD), 2013.

Steinberg, David. *Burma/Myanmar: What Everyone Needs to Know*. Oxford: Oxford University Press, 2010.

Thein Lwin. *Education in Burma (1945–2000)*. 2nd ed. September 2000 <http://www.ibiblio.org/obl/docs/Education_in_Burma_(1945-2000).htm>.

Thein Sein, U. "Ten Points Education Policy". Opening remarks at the first regular session of Pyidaungsu Hluttaw (Parliament), Nepyidaw, 18 March 2011.

The Union Daily, 18 June 2013.

United Nations Educational, Scientific and Cultural Organization. "Education for All (EFA): Meeting Our Collective Commitments". Adopted by the World Education Forum, Dakar, Senegal, 26–28 April 2000 <www.unesco.org/carneid/dakar.pdf>.

———. "EFA Global Monitoring Report 2010" <unesdoc.unesco.org/images/0018/001866/186606E.pdf>.

United Nations Development Programme. "Myanmar; HDI Values and Rank Changes in the 2013 Human Development Report". March 2013 <hdr.undp.org/sites/default/files/Country-Profiles/MMR.pdf>.

World Bank. *From Schooling Access to Learning Outcomes: An Unfinished Agenda — An Evaluation of World Bank Support to Primary Education*. Washington, D.C.: World Bank, 2006.

Zobrist, Brooke. *Mapping Teaching-Learning and Operational Experiences in Fifty Monastery Schools Across Myanmar*. Yangon: Pyoepin, 2010.

INDEX

Note: Page numbers followed by "n" denote endnotes.

www.ingramcontent.com/pod-product-compliance
Lightning Source LLC
Chambersburg PA
CBHW062026270326
41929CB00014B/2334